Unbecoming Subjects

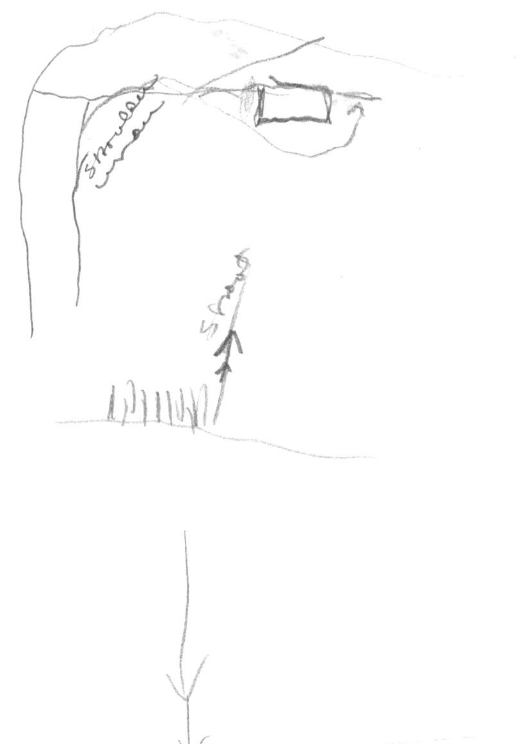

Unbecoming Subjects

Judith Butler, Moral Philosophy, and Critical Responsibility

Annika Thiem

FORDHAM UNIVERSITY PRESS
NEW YORK 2008

Copyright © 2008 Fordham University Press

All rights reserved. No part of this publication may be reproduced, stored in a retrieval system, or transmitted in any form or by any means—electronic, mechanical, photocopy, recording, or any other—except for brief quotations in printed reviews, without the prior permission of the publisher.

Library of Congress Cataloging-in-Publication Data

Thiem, Annika.
Unbecoming subjects : Judith Butler, moral philosophy, and critical responsibility / Annika Thiem. — 1st ed.
p. cm.
Includes bibliographical references and index.
ISBN 978-0-8232-2898-0 (cloth : alk. paper) —
ISBN 978-0-8232-2899-7 (pbk. : alk. paper)
1. Butler, Judith, 1956– 2. Ethics. 3. Responsibility.
4. Criticism. 5. Poststructuralism. I. Title.
BJ37.T45 2008
170.92—dc22 2008003064

Printed in the United States of America
10 09 08 5 4 3 2 1
First edition

CONTENTS

ACKNOWLEDGMENTS

This project has seen several instantiations and transformations; the most radical transformation was the last one, which separates this book from its sibling submitted as a dissertation at the University of Tübingen during the winter term of 2003–4. The overarching arguments of the two versions are quite different from each other. The dissertation centered on staging scenes of how subject formation happens through also being undone in order to open the responsiveness inherent in the unbecoming undoing toward thinking about responsibility. This book considers responsibility and critique as central quandaries and practices that bind and entangle subject formation and ethics with each other. One common feature that the various instantiations share is the title, *Unbecoming Subjects.* Although the unbecoming and the subjects have undergone several shifts and changes themselves, the title has remained and accompanied the development of the project. Several people also accompanied this project from the very beginning through its repeated becoming and being undone: Chris Adams, Hille Haker, Rebecca Kennison, and Ursula Konnertz.

Hille Haker advised me on this project at the beginning and saw to it that it would turn into a dissertation project. In particular, I am grateful for the innumerable discussions, her interest, and her continued support even after she left the University of Tübingen to take up a professorship at Harvard Divinity School in fall 2003. At that time, Dietmar Mieth took over the task of chairing my dissertation committee and oversaw a smooth completion of the process. I am very grateful for his support throughout my years as a student in Tübingen. I would also like to thank Magnus Striet for being on my dissertation committee and for stimulating conversations. During my stay at Harvard Divinity School, Francis Schüssler Fiorenza encouraged me to write on Butler and Ricoeur, and he and Elisabeth Schüssler

Fiorenza made it possible for me to pursue my scholarship through independent studies with them.

My gratitude extends as well to Libby Anker, Nima Bassiri, Wendy Brown, Scott Ferguson, Sara Kendall, Hagar Kotef, Katherine Lemons, Patricia Purtschert, Corinna Unger, Johannes Vorster, Yves Winter, and Benjamin Wurgaft for reading chapters, for discussing and working through ideas with me, and for their encouragement throughout the process. It might seem perfunctory to thank one's anonymous reviewers, but without their readings and comments the book would not have become what it is now. I am also grateful to Helen Tartar for her enduring support of this project and for providing the space and time in which it could undergo a transformation to become this book. Villanova University kindly provided support for the preparation of the index. Finally, I would like to thank Judith Butler for her work, which provided—obviously—the occasion for this project and for conversations that were always thoughtful and thought-provoking.

ABBREVIATIONS

BTM
Judith Butler. *Bodies That Matter: On the Discursive Limits of "Sex."* New York: Routledge, 1993.

CHU
Judith Butler, Ernesto Laclau, and Slavoj Žižek. *Contingency, Hegemony, Universality: Contemporary Dialogues on the Left*. London: Verso, 2000.

EN
Emmanuel Levinas. *Entre Nous: On Thinking-of-the-Other*. Translated by Michael B. Smith and Barbara Harshav. New York: Columbia University Press, 1998.

ES
Judith Butler. *Excitable Speech: A Politics of the Performative*. New York: Routledge, 1997.

FS
Michel Foucault. *Fearless Speech*. Edited by Joseph Pearson. Los Angeles: Semiotext(e), 2001.

GA
Judith Butler. *Giving an Account of Oneself*. New York: Fordham University Press, 2005.

GM
Friedrich Nietzsche. *On the Genealogy of Morals* and *Ecce Homo*. Translated by Walter Kaufmann and R. J. Hollingdale. Edited by Walter Kaufmann. New York: Vintage-Random House, 1967.

GT

Judith Butler. *Gender Trouble: Feminism and the Subversion of Identity*. Rev. ed. New York: Routledge, 1999.

HS

Michel Foucault. *The History of Sexuality: An Introduction*. Translated by Robert Hurley. New York: Vintage-Random House, 1978.

OTB

Emmanuel Levinas. *Otherwise Than Being, Or Beyond Essence*. Translated by Alphonso Lingis. Pittsburgh, Pa.: Duquesne University Press, 1998.

PL

Judith Butler. *Precarious Life: The Powers of Mourning and Violence*. London: Verso, 2004.

PLP

Judith Butler. *The Psychic Life of Power: Theories in Subjection*. Stanford, Calif.: Stanford University Press, 1997.

PMP

Theodor W. Adorno. *Problems of Moral Philosophy*. Edited by Thomas Schröder. Translated by Rodney Livingstone. Stanford, Calif.: Stanford University Press, 2000. German original referred to as *Probleme:* Theodor W. Adorno, *Probleme der Moralphilosophie*. Edited by Thomas Schröder. Frankfurt am Main: Suhrkamp, 1996.

PTT

Jean Laplanche. "Psychoanalysis, Time and Translation: A Lecture Given at the University of Kent, 30 April 1990." In *Seduction, Translation, Drives*, translated by Martin Stanton, edited by Martin Stanton and John Fletcher, 161–77. London: Institute of Contemporary Arts, 1992.

TPA

Jean Laplanche. "Transference: Its Provocation by the Analyst." In *Essays on Otherness*, translated by Luke Thurston, 214–33. London: Routledge, 1999.

UG

Judith Butler. *Undoing Gender*. New York: Routledge, 2004.

Introduction

While it is a commonplace to begin with the question of how to live well, it seems to me that we still run up against this question time and again—this question that Socrates posed as the central question for philosophy. Living with others as we do, this question also means how to live well given the social circumstances we find ourselves in. How to live well? How to know what to do? What resources can aid and guide us in our personal and social life? These questions, perhaps generally considered as questions of ethics and morality, have ambivalent histories. Moral and ethical codes as part of social codes of conduct do not always make life more livable; they can also be socially restrictive. In particular, it seems to me that Nietzsche's criticism of morality for relying on feelings of guilt and bad conscience continues to be an important caution. Moral conduct cannot be reduced to what we owe others, to duties and obligations, and also not to virtues, which can have equally restraining effects. When, for example, critical opposition is devalued in the name of humility, then humility silences and becomes a questionable virtue that restricts us rather than enabling us to undertake the difficult labor of learning to live together well. Living together is never conflict-free, and how to know what to do is also another name for how to learn to sustain and negotiate conflicts well, both personally and socially. We are thus constantly embroiled in moral quandaries as much as in political ones, and often the two are not easily separable.

These dilemmas of knowing how to respond and what to do are also difficult because of the complexity of the societies that we live in. In our globally interrelated world, environmental destruction, poverty, and violence are only three pervasive problematics that defy easy analysis or straightforward solutions, either on the global or on the local level, levels that in the age of the Internet can no longer be easily separated anyway. In the face of these challenges, hopes for moral certainty and for individual agency to change the world very quickly retreat into either defeatism or dogmatism. Against these alternatives, a wide variety of thinkers have responded to help us rethink contemporary ethical and political problematics and to renew the moral resources to address them. Among these philosophical responses have also been increasingly more poststructuralist ones, even though poststructuralism has been denounced, because of its trenchant criticisms of traditional moral philosophy and its centering on rational subjects and universal norms, as a philosophy of nihilism that has contributed to a perceived erosion of the "moral fabric" of society. These so-called "turns" to ethics have not settled, but rather have reinvigorated, philosophical debates over how to live well and how best to enable ethical life.

While theorists drawing on poststructuralism have been rediscovering ethics for several years now, the normative aspect of ethics seems to remain beyond what can be easily reappropriated.[1] Instead, what is ethical is often located in practices and commitments that are neither normatively arguable nor normatively enforceable. In return, moral philosophers have tended to view poststructuralism with great suspicion at best, and for the most part appear to have chosen to ignore it entirely. Until now, poststructuralism and moral philosophy seem to have remained two mutually exclusive endeavors. In this book, I am turning to the work of one particular poststructuralist theorist, Judith Butler, to articulate a rethinking of moral philosophy through the challenges posed to it by Butler's work, especially on subject formation. My main aim in this book is to articulate responsibility and critique as key concepts in moral philosophy.

Through this reformulation of moral philosophy as both responsibility and critique, this book also critically engages the poststructuralist embrace of ethics as an ethos of responsibility and ethical self-formation. The book aims to trouble and complicate the debate by insisting on the term "moral philosophy" and on the critical value of the problematics this term produces.[2] By approaching moral philosophy as an indicator for ethical problematics and by not assuming that moral philosophy already resolves the problematics it makes graspable, my argument in this book is aligned with poststructuralist and other lines of thought that find in moral philosophy the problem rather than the solution.

Nevertheless, I side with moral philosophy to the extent that it considers the problem of normativity as a crucial problem for questions of ethics that cannot be put to rest.[3] This is not to say that there is an insurmountable distinction between ethics and moral philosophy or between the moral and the ethical, and it seems to me even less helpful to advance definitions of moral philosophy and ethics that are based on constructing them as mutually exclusive fields and modes of inquiry. My aim is to retain the provocation regarding the problems of normativity and justice that "moral philosophy" still seems to evoke more distinctively than does "ethics," while at the same time foregrounding the more encompassing concern of responsiveness and responsibility for which the term "ethics" seems to allow. If the term "ethics" should turn out to be more suitable over the course of engaging justice as social justice, politics, and power as problematics, then in the future moral philosophy could well give way to ethics. However, for the time being, it seems to me that the problems that "moral philosophy" as a philosophical endeavor raises are useful reminders of the problem of normativity, of how power and social norms as well as the horizon of justice are necessary perspectives for critical inquiries into social life and moral conduct.

Regarding how to enable the practical inquiry into moral conduct, the concept of responsibility has a role equally if not even more prominent in much of moral philosophy as does justice. When responsibility is invoked, it can mean someone taking, accepting, or assuming responsibility for actions or situations. Responsibility in that sense is a question of one's actions for which one is held accountable according to a set of norms by which we evaluate these actions and their consequences. The key aspects of responsibility in these terms are the attribution of actions to individuals or groups and the evaluation of past actions, insofar as they can be attributed to a particular agent. If we begin thinking from this perspective about what it means to be responsible and how to act responsibly, then the anticipatory stance of deliberation within the horizon of responsibility arises as a question of anticipating what one owes to others and what one ought to do to avoid being held accountable. With such an approach, responsibility is established as a moral-philosophical category through the context of judgment and justification of particular actions for which one is deemed "responsible."[4]

Although I will argue that this approach to responsibility is problematic, it nevertheless highlights how responsibility singles out subjects by making them answerable to a demand. This responsiveness is key to understanding ethical subjectivity and agency; however, the critical question for moral philosophy is how we relate to and negotiate these demands. I will argue that we might consider this responsiveness not primarily as a matter of justifying and evaluating actions but as a matter of being addressed by others and of having to respond and—more specifically—of having to respond well. Responsibility framed as accountability turns responsibility into a narcissistic endeavor that centers on the subject and the subject's moral status. By instead foregrounding the dimension of responding to an address by an other, the agent's justifiability, moral guilt, or glory take second seat to the concrete address and actions that need to be determined. Considering the justification of past actions as key to responsibility covers up the problem of this futurity in moral deliberation which asks what ought to be done when the present situation has come into question and now demands a response.

Furthermore, by casting responsibility in terms of accountability, the problem of future actions is leveled, because what one ought to do is deliberated through imagining and evaluating future actions as past, so that one can know what one's responsibilities are because one will be held accountable for fulfilling or failing them. Yet this calculability of the future through imagining it as past resolves too quickly the problematic at the core of moral conduct, namely, its particular relation to the future. The question "what ought I do?"—which I take to be key to moral conduct and moral philosophy—poses a question about the future. It puts forward a particular problem because it is a question not only about what will or might happen in the future but also about what should happen. While certain plausible predictions can be ventured about what *might* happen in the future by turning to what is and what has been, the question of what *should* happen presents as problematic what sources we can and should rely on for deliberating about what should be done. Settling on understanding responsibility through the framework of accountability levels the temporal problematic of moral conduct that lies in the question of how to draw on the resources available to us to forge a future.

It seems to me that this problematic of this future dimension is fundamental to moral conduct and to moral philosophy in general, not only to a notion of responsibility. Instead of generalizing responsibility into that which comprises every form of moral inquiry and is characterized only by the question of what one should do, in this book I will treat responsibility more concretely as being a demand for a response that arises through our relationality and being addressed by an other. This address necessarily comes from a human other. While we can be responsible for the environment not directly, but only mediatedly, to respond well to addresses from fellow human beings also demands that the environment, as our shared condition for our life, be preserved. Although it seems to me that we can very well find ourselves addressed by nonhuman others, insofar as there is an address through which a demand arrives, it seems that the structure of the address implies and constitutes an other as a "one" whose presence makes demands to which a response becomes necessary. So even if the structure of address need not be anthropomorphic, it nonetheless seems to mobilize a certain rendition of subjectivity that renders the other into a being in such a way that the encounter with this other issues demands that cannot be simply ignored; but that poses the question of how to respond well as an ethical as well as a moral question. As a matter of an ethical response, the other's demands impose themselves on us, insofar as these demands seem to carry a force in themselves that exceeds the socially expected or strategically useful. I would therefore like to keep responsibility as a question of responding well as a question that arises out of our relations to others. In this way we can also critically examine the ways in which other entities become such addressing others, such as states, social institutions, and economic structures. Against the background of the different others that might be addressing us and the question of the way in which ethical beholdenness might in particular be a question of the life of an other, it is key to keep in mind and keep open the ambivalences that condition the demand to respond well, insofar as no address occurs outside social and historical conditions.

Responsibility as responding to others carries in itself ambivalences, insofar as being beholden to others and having to respond well to them is not a pure experience of ethical demands that occurs independently or even fully separably from social and cultural norms and demands. As I argue here, we can retrieve neither a pure ethical desire to extend ourselves and respond well to others nor a pure ethical demand that others make. Nonetheless, even if desires as well as demands are always socially mediated and conditioned, neither the responsiveness nor the demands, insofar as they carry ethical valence, are reducible to their social conditions. In other words, I argue that responsibility and the ethical claims of responding well to others are not simply reducible to internalized and moralized social demands in relation to which one becomes accountable and has to justify one's actions but that there is an ethical dimension that we can rethink at an angle to social normalization by approaching responsibility as a question of responding to others and of being in relations with others.

In this book I argue against grounding responsibility primarily within a framework that holds agents answerable for their actions and thus conceives of responsibility and ethical deliberation in the first place through what is owed and through which potential guilt can be incurred. To argue against taking what is owed as a starting point for responsibility does not mean that there will be no room left for accountability. Instead, I hope to demonstrate that a different understanding of responsibility as well as of accountability becomes possible when we begin by understanding relationality and responding to others as constitutive of what it means to become responsible.

Since, however, responsibility as responding to others never happens outside the framework of social relations that go beyond the concrete others to whom one responds, the focus on a critical relation to social practices and institutions cannot be fully subsumed under the concept of responsibility. This critical examination of the social conditions for responsibility is the task of critique. The disjuncture between critique and responsibility remains, insofar as we become critical when we ask how social norms and constellations of power determine through discourses and social practices where and how situations can appear as situations that demand our attention and reaction. In particular, this book advances the view that as critical moral philosophy, critique must interrogate the limits of moral and political knowledge and probe methods of social criticism to uncover and oppose injustices.

In considering responsibility and critique in the light of Butler's work, I am addressing the poststructuralist return to ethics, especially as it approaches the recovery of ethics through Levinas. In particular, Levinas's philosophical work on alterity has made an important contribution to the timely recovery of the ethical project. Against understanding the subject and reason as stable realities that then only belatedly come into contact with otherness and the demands of others, Levinas articulates reason as well as the subject as formed only in response to being addressed by the other and in the ethical demands this address delivers in the form of the commandment "Thou shalt not kill." Being beholden to the other and to the vulnerability of the other and being responsible for the other all condition the emergence of the subject as thinking and acting. The demand of the other eludes all settlement, is absolute and inescapable, arrives through every other, and cannot be transformed into a principle of action or a legal right or duty. Consequently, the argument Levinas offers is one that is neither ontological nor moral-philosophical; it is a preontological argument that insists on the incommensurability of the ethical demand with any actual reality as well as with possible normative principles, even though this demand traverses and structures all experiences. Owing to this insistence on the incommensurability of this responsibility with the empirical reality, we can read Levinas not only as articulating a primary ethicality that inheres and exceeds all our actions; his insistence on the incommensurability of the ethical demand that brings about the subject and empirical reality also allows us to take Levinas's work as an occasion to caution against using the demand from the other to ground accounts of ethical action. The demand and the responsiveness to it emerge as what exceeds and undoes grounds and principles and hence do not lead simply into an account either of virtue ethics or of normative ethics.

In this book I draw on Levinas's work insofar as it challenges us to dislodge the starting point of moral-philosophical thinking that grounds itself in rational choice, intentional action, duties, rights, obligations, and norms as much as in sympathy, compassion, and love. I argue also that Levinas's work is not an unambivalent starting point for ethical thought, because the priority of this demand from the other is inescapable, nonnegotiable, and absolute. If ethics is anchored in the demands of an alterity beyond argument, reason, and empirical reality and experience, this understanding of ethics also elaborates on a transcendent relation to the other. The question for ethics as a philosophical endeavor is, then, how it attends to this theological dimension through which it proceeds with its reflections. If this relation to the other, as in Levinas, defies reflecting on the normative consequences of this relation, then taking this encounter with the other as a starting point for ethics can provide an occasion to foreground the ethical valence and value of vigilance in the infinite attempt to respond to what cannot ever be responded to adequately. It seems to me, however, that this inroad into ethics also raises at least two problematics for further consideration in the context of elaborating an ethical theory. First, with a focus on the nonnormative and modes of ethical subject formation in relation to the other or to others, one has to be careful that considering ethics as a matter of responsiveness does not come at the expense of critiques of power and institutional practices. Second, if the preconditions of becoming a subject and agent are assumed to be endowed with ethical demands that stem from a source that can no longer be argued, then such arguments or elaborations run the risk of foreclosing a critical examination of how these conditions and their demands attain and sustain their particular ethical value and force.

In order to think ethics critically, Butler's work on subject formation is enormously productive in its incisive analytics of social and psychic forms of power. To my knowledge, to this point there has been no book-length study that reads Butler explicitly within the discourse of moral philosophy,[5] and it might seem as though this context would undo precisely what makes for the explosive and critical force of Butler's work. However, in my opinion, it is this conjunction of and confrontation between Butler and moral philosophy that allow for a critical opening in two directions, both with respect to moral philosophy and with respect to poststructuralist theories. While Butler might be best known for her work on gender, sex, and sexuality, her contribution to practical philosophy cannot be reduced to this aspect of her work, important as it is. There is an ethics that is performed through her mode of inquiry, which is committed to beginning from the margins and the marginalized to query the social norms and structures that condition, enable, and animate forms of marginalization. With this approach to an ethics of critical inquiry, the ethical dimension in Butler's work is thoroughly linked to the inquiry into contemporary political and social questions.[6]

Although this ethical dimension, I would argue, has characterized her work all along, her most explicit theoretical forays into the domain of ethics have been in her more recent work, that of several essays in the volumes *Precarious Life* (2004)[7] and *Undoing Gender* (2004)[8] and perhaps most prominently in *Giving an Account of Oneself* (2005).[9] Here in this book, however, I am not just concerned with elaborating this ethical dimension that emerges through Butler's particular mode of critical thinking, but I will take up the challenges that her work poses to moral philosophy in particular through her critiques of the subject. The question of the subject and its formation is, as Butler's work demonstrates, not a matter of ontological preconditions that precede ethical and political questions. Instead, Butler's work intervenes in ontological questions and makes them legible as political and social problematics by interrogating how there is no facticity of bodies and subjects that does not already rely on socially produced and administered ontologies.

These ontologies through which we become subjects, as she demonstrates, are conditioned by histories of power embodied in social and cultural institutions. In other words, her work does not attempt to establish ontologies in order to deduce ethical demands from the ontological preconditions. Rather, Butler's work examines how political and social conditions produce certain ontologies in such ways that particular effects—such as, for example, that bodies are either male or female—achieve the status of a fact. So far from being an unquestioned factual presupposition for ethics or a basis from which to elaborate ethics, the subject and the modes of its formation become in turn a subject for critical inquiry. As I argue in this book, this critical inquiry becomes ethical insofar as it interrogates the modes of subject formation with respect to asking what understandings of the good life and justice are presupposed, how they work in making lives less rather than more possible, and what justice, thought otherwise, might mean and require. Such considerations become possible insofar as accounts of subject formation and moral philosophy are not rendered into a continuum and when their relation is questioned rather than assumed unquestioned as one in which the results of the former simply yield ethical criteria.

Attempts to deduce rules for moral conduct from inquiries into subject formation are interrupted by Butler's work on normalization and on how social norms regulate and produce subjects. Her inquiries into how power constitutes our social, bodily, and psychic realities confront moral philosophy on two counts: first, on moral philosophy's reliance on an ontology of the subject as a knowing and acting individual; and second, on its blindness toward the productive, subject-formative effects of social power. In the tradition of Nietzsche and Foucault, Butler radically calls into question the subject as a philosophical and practical presupposition by making the subject into a political and historical problem and, further, into an ethical problem for moral philosophy.

Taking up the challenges of Butler's work, the contribution of this book to rethinking moral philosophy is its formulation of responsibility and critique as modes of theorizing ethics in relation to how we, as agents, are always implicated in the lives of others, in social practices and institutions, and in politics. This book takes as its starting point the philosophical predicament that poststructuralist critiques of the subject have produced by undoing the subject as the unifying principle of action, experience, and knowledge. Poststructuralist critiques have demonstrated that we can no longer retrieve an individual, a person, or a self in a way that could ground theory and practice across history and cultures, because this ground is itself a product of a particular culture and history. The ensuing difficulty for practical philosophy cannot simply be overcome by recovering the subject as always developing in relations to others, because such a recovery would not take seriously how radical the critique of the subject as a nodal episteme and epistemological anchor is. Even with a relational subject, we still ground our inquiries in a framework that presupposes the existence of distinct subjects who experience, act, and know, even if their experiencing, acting, and knowing happens only in relation to others.

The critique of the subject is radical in the sense that it not only calls into question the presupposition of a particular kind of subject—such as the autonomous, self-sufficient, and arelational individual. Instead, poststructuralist critiques call into question—radically—the subject of any kind as an entity that can be presupposed as the one who thinks and does. Against the epistemological comfort of the subject, poststructuralism argues that this presupposition of the subject is a metaphysical remnant and that if subjected to the rigorous critique of all grounds of experience and knowledge, it is no longer possible to retain a subject of whatever kind as a stable structure prior to contingent realities. The challenge, in other words, is to undo the certainty that where there are experience, action, and knowledge, there must be also subjects who precede these acts, cause them to happen, and undergo them. Poststructuralism, however, does not do away with the subject; experience, action, and knowledge are not without subjects. Instead, the subject emerges as a belated effect of discerning experiences, actions, and knowledges.

The challenges to our bodies and desires as realities outside social norms are related to each other in several ways, particularly insofar as they crucially arise because there is no longer a subject outside of subject *formation* to which moral philosophy could have recourse. The accounts that Butler offers are not developmental accounts of the subject in the sense of outlining a series of events that we all undergo and from which in the end we emerge maturely, finally, as subjects. Instead, the subject emerges as a question and problem for moral philosophy insofar as it does not have a secure status or position. "The subject," therefore, is better rendered as an ongoing process, an ongoing formation in relation to norms as well as in relation to others. In *The Psychic Life of Power*,[10] this process of subject formation is termed *assujetissement* (subjectivation) to describe this emergence of the subject through subjection. The process of becoming a subject is for Butler a process of becoming subordinated by norms through which power relations work, and to exist socially as well as self-consciously requires not only relating to norms but also to become subjected to them.

In *Giving an Account of Oneself*, Butler explains that we do not encounter norms and power on their own, but they become knowable through encounters with others. Often these encounters are quite personal encounters, but even the very personal encounters still are not presocial or outside the scope of social norms and power relations (see *GA* 30). Through Butler's work on subject formation, we can grasp how far-reaching the consequences of poststructuralist critiques of the subject are for practical philosophy. If we attend to the modes of subject formation in its social, bodily, and psychic dimensions, then traditional accounts of agency and criteria for moral conduct are thoroughly called into question. Neither the needs of our bodies nor our desires and even less so our conscience can be easily accessed as a resource for ethical action and ethical critiques of the status quo.

The ensuing question for a critical ethics is then twofold. On the one hand, it is a question of resources for critical inquiries into social conditions, and on the other hand, it is a question of changing those conditions so that they sustain lives and lessen rather than intensify violence. The question of social change is not exclusively a question of moral philosophy, but social change is also a question of moral philosophy insofar as moral philosophy poses the question of what ought to be done and how currently existing conditions ought to be transformed. At stake are not merely philosophical concepts but articulations of justice and responsible ethical and political action.

One problematic with respect to these questions is the possibility of distinguishing among competing visions of social and political change. Butler's work makes it possible to articulate this problematic critically by considering the double dimension of norms and normativity both as evaluative and deliberative with respect to what ought to be and as social norms and working in a normalizing manner. In her essay "The Question of Social Transformation" in *Undoing Gender*, Butler sums up this difficulty: "[W]e need norms in order to live, and to live well, and to know in what direction to transform our social world, we are also constrained by norms in ways that sometimes do violence to us and which, for reasons of social justice, we must oppose" (*UG* 206). Norms are necessary, Butler insists, but they are not necessarily good or conducive to the good life in whose name they might even be promoted. Even with an appeal to social justice, the question that reemerges is how to discern between different understandings of social justice and how to reinvigorate critical reflection as well as ethical and political action.

With this focus of critique on social criticism and the critical interrogation of norms, I would like to hold this understanding of critique at an angle to responsibility as a question of responding well to others. Certainly critique as a practice implies and becomes discernible as a particular mode of ethical conduct and a particular practice of responding to the social and political conditions in which and through which we live. Nonetheless, in this book I would like to insist that the ethical dignity of critique is not reducible to the practice of calling normative frameworks into question. In conversation with Butler's Foucauldian commitments, my argument is that critique becomes a key concept for moral philosophy insofar as critique raises both questions of normativity and questions of social justice and social change. In my considerations of critique, it will not be my aim to argue for the practice of critique as a value or norm of moral conduct—even though at the back of critique there is always an ethos emerging and an ethical subject formed. Rather, I will argue that in critique, the question at stake is how to examine norms and values in how they normalize subjects as well as in how they can possibly orient moral conduct.

More specifically, critique in the context of moral philosophy will be framed as the question of how to interrogate power in relation to justice. Justice in this context will be at issue not as a transcendental or quasi-transcendental category but as a question of social justice. If we take seriously that questions of moral conduct and moral norms never arise outside the context of social relations, then the justice at issue needs to be framed in terms of social justice. This social and political dimension of justice will have to attend to the difficulties that characterize human life in community, which arise in questions of human individuality, sociality, plurality, and vulnerability. The horizon for the emergence of critique is, then, one could say, distinctly social and political, and within that, critique has the double dimension of raising questions that are both epistemological and moral. In other words, critique becomes a question for moral philosophy not only because acting responsibly as an individual, as an ethical agent, is at stake but also because the understanding of subjects formed in subjection raises issues of power and justice.

Through this perspective we can also reassess the relation between ethics and politics and formulate an account of how through the horizon of justice—which cannot be separated from questions of power—morality and moral deliberations become political. They become political insofar as justice is at stake in particular as a question of social justice, which asks that we deliberate and negotiate how we ought to arrange the collective conditions of our lives. Not all questions of moral conduct are political in the same strong sense; for ethics to be political, the larger social scale of arranging shared conditions of how we live together must be at stake. In return, these conditions become a matter of political ethics, insofar as the political stakes and perspective of the inquiry have to pose the question of justice, the question of a more just arrangement of our conditions of life.

The consideration of justice, however, is not reducible to matters of equal distribution or a collectivism that forsakes the individual, insofar as the claims of responsibility have to return here in our considerations. The challenge of the other's singularity that lies at the core of responsibility remains at odds with collective visions of justice that would abolish the claims of the particularity and singularity of the other. How to act responsibly cannot be severed from demands for justice, which require that one must compare and adjudicate between the singular claims of each one by asking what collective sharing and equality among all could mean such that we could live well together. Insofar as we retain responsibility as a question of responding to others and the concreteness of every individual other, the move to justice remains equally tied to and bounded, or unbounded, by the more prior relationality to the other. Insofar as these concerns are formulated as ethical quandaries, the ethical dimension emerges as the horizon of the good life, and justice for all, as well as for each, circumscribes the question of how to respond well, animating it rather than putting it to rest. The question of how to respond well and what to do emerges as a political question when we pose it as a question of how to organize and govern our communal life and when we present it with respect to power and with the aspiration to power.[11] Insofar as power and structures and practices of governance are at stake, ethical ideals and normative aspirations are already constituted politically and not as aspects of truth prior to or beyond political life.

Over the course of this book, I hope it will become clear that bringing poststructuralism and moral philosophy together allows us to reassess, reformulate, and revitalize the critical potentials of moral philosophy and its theoretical contribution to addressing the problematics both of living well with others and of justice. Both critical reflection and responsibility as responding begin with and take as their precondition the question of what to do and how to respond. In other words, as I argue over the course of the second and third part of this book, not-knowing—rather than knowing and certainty—is at the core of ethical deliberation. A second important thread running through the book, therefore, is an elaboration of the various ways in which practical philosophy is structured and driven by the aporetic situation of responsibility and critique. On the one hand, there is the epistemological impossibility of finding and securing critical vantage points beyond relations of power, and on the other, there is the ethical impossibility of giving up the need for critical vantage points that cannot be reduced to their historical and cultural formation through particular constellations of power. As a consequence, critical moral philosophy has to be theorized at the crossroads of ethics and politics as continuously working against nihilism and moralism. With these considerations in mind, this book explores our implication in relations to others and social justice as two crucial horizons and tasks of moral philosophy and ethical life.

A Brief Overview

The first part of this book lays out the challenges that Butler's work poses to the subject of moral philosophy. In the first chapter I engage Butler's theorizing of subject formation as a productive mode of subjection. The ensuing challenge to moral philosophy is that the body, bodily materiality, and desire are undone as perspectives within which to seek recourse in order to elaborate normative perspectives on what constitutes violence and to criticize the way social norms, practices, and institutions operate.

The second chapter takes up the challenges that Butler's accounts of subject formation pose to ethical deliberation, conscience, and agency. In returning to Nietzsche, this chapter also, more explicitly than does Butler, addresses the formation of conscience as the development of our particular and peculiar susceptibility to moral norms. The validity of moral norms is taken and experienced as distinct from social demands precisely through the formation of conscience and bad conscience. Hence the experience of moral demands is neither reducible to social normalization nor radically different from it. As a consequence, conscience becomes problematic as a backdrop for moral deliberation. This chapter turns to the debates over Butler's account of agency and performativity, first, in order to grasp the challenge to ethical deliberation and criteria for such deliberations, and second, to allow us to clarify the stakes for moral philosophy in a seemingly ontological account of agency as a capacity of subjects. The question of how one accounts for agency is shown to be not just an ontological debate, but it conditions what understanding of moral conduct moral-philosophical inquiries will produce.

Against the background of these challenges, the second part of the book rearticulates responsibility as reducible neither to a mode of subject formation nor to a purely moral-philosophical concept that considers the question of subject formation settled in a different realm prior to the question of moral conduct. The third chapter, which opens this section on responsibility, presents a critical engagement with Emmanuel Levinas with and through Butler's most recent work. This chapter takes up Levinas's approach to responsibility through the notion of response and as matter of our relations to others rather than as holding one accountable. Additionally, this chapter develops a critical perspective on Levinas on two counts. First,

I argue for the importance of the gap between responsibility as a generalized and inescapable demand from alterity that awakens the subject and responsibility in the concrete sense of deciding what to do. Second, drawing on Butler's work on social norms and these norms as frameworks of intelligibility allows us to examine critically how social and political conditions determine who becomes legible as an other delivering an ethical demand.

In the fourth chapter I turn to the work of Jean Laplanche in psychoanalytic theory to aid moral philosophy in theorizing the ambivalences in responsibility as a response with respect to desire. In this context, Butler's work is very helpful in its sustained attention to desire and in its theoretical exploration of the relation between psychoanalysis and philosophy. I draw especially on Butler's most recent work, in which she takes up Laplanche's considerations in order to theorize the opacity of the self in relation to others, to itself, and to social norms as foundational insight for critical ethical theory. This chapter elaborates on the conjunction of our not being able ever to fully know ourselves or others and on the ambivalence of desire not only as problematic but also as an occasion that compels and guides a critical reflection on how to theorize responsibility as responding to others while taking into account the limitations of responsibility. In particular, taking up psychoanalytical theory allows moral philosophy to form a complex understanding of how desires disorient and propel our relations and how one cannot retrieve "ethical passions" out of an account of our desires in relation to others because of the complications that the unconscious life of desire introduces. Moreover, I draw on Laplanche's psychoanalytical considerations of how this dimension of desire is complicated by a temporal aspect, insofar as the present never fully overcomes the past as it moves into the future. This understanding of temporality and how the conscious subject is never fully constituted in the present allows, as I argue, a way into rethinking accountability as a process of translation and as a process of reworking of the past without abandoning it. Responsibility without accountability forsakes its critical relation to the past. But, as I argue in this chapter, accountability must open rather than foreclose the possibility of a future.

Turning to critique in the third part of the book, the fifth chapter lays out the aporia of normativity that ensues because critique as a critical inquiry into knowledge is itself contingently conditioned and because critique in undoing normative commitments cannot but also implicitly articulate and perform normative commitments. I argue in this chapter not for theorizing critique primarily as a kind of responsibility and a practice or ethos of responding and ethical self-formation; rather, I argue for foregrounding the normative problematic that critique addresses, both in the social and institutional aspect of power as well as in the normative aspirations of social criticism. This chapter demonstrates how the Foucault-Habermas and the Benhabib-Butler debates cannot be resolved nor turned into a question that demands deciding on which side one eventually stands. Through these debates it becomes possible to grasp the epistemological side of the aporia of normativity that moral philosophy cannot put to rest. Finally, this chapter elaborates how this aporia puts critique as an endeavor of moral philosophy at the crossroads of ethics and politics.

In the final chapter I take up the epistemological aporia again, but focus on the side of critique that is aligned with social and political criticism and the question of categories that can guide inquiries without effacing the aporia. This chapter argues that it is too thin an account of ethics and politics to conceive of them as eventually coming down to wrestling with making decisions about the undecidable. In particular, I am less concerned with justice as a condition of possibility and impossibility in Jacques Derrida's sense; instead, I argue that justice, and especially social justice, as a question must be the perspective for critical ethical inquiries into the present. The question of justice as social justice is precisely what opens moral philosophy to a critical political ethics. Justice is neither a purely political question nor a question adjudicated in a realm of ethics prior to politics and then only implanted and realized by means of politics. Rather, the question of justice implicates ethical reflections in political contestation over the conditions of sustainable life, while the question of justice as a horizon and a subject of political contestation implicates political debates in ethical reflections. To open the lines of inquiry into political ethics and social justice for more substantial elaborations, I return in the final pages of this book to Butler's critiques of social norms as they become formulated as questions of recognition and of universality in cultural specificity. With this rethinking of justice as a question on which critique insists, this final chapter signifies the limits of this project but also opens the possibility for further inquiries into social justice with respect to sustainable conditions of life beyond distributive justice.

PART ONE

Challenges to the Subject

ONE

Subjects in Subjection: Bodies, Desires, and the Psychic Life of Norms

That our bodies, our desires, and even our psychic lives are not separable from the way that norms and social power act on us is not just an uncomfortable thought or a theory that adequately seems to sum up experiences that we might have had. If we think about it a bit longer, then this concept puts our commitments to the test about how we think about our capacity to decide and act independently from these norms. The subject of moral philosophy is often cast as that of an agent who breaks with the power of these norms in rational deliberation. Yet this capacity of rationality and its scope are called into question when we consider precisely how this subject of rationality is continuously formed and sustained through its subjection to social norms.

When we deliberate ethically, this deliberation is traversed by the social and psychic life that norms and our past take on. We are never completely reflectively aware of our own desires and of how we were formed through traditions, interactions with others, and our cultural contexts. So in terms of the subject of moral deliberation and conduct, the problematic is that rational reflection on desires and inclinations cannot be taken to establish the subject's ability to deliberate what to do at a distance from social norms. If bodies and desires as well as our capacity to consciously reflect on them are formed through normalization, then neither the facticity and materiality of bodies and desires nor the nonspecified assertion of their existence can be critical vantage points from which to evaluate the effects of social norms. The desire for the good life as a traditional resource for ethical thought becomes problematic if one takes seriously how this desire and the kind of good life that one can desire are socially formed and how the norms that determine what can be desired as good can make lives and bodies less rather than more possible.

By examining how the subject is continuously formed in subjection to social norms and hence through social normalization, Judith Butler's work takes the subject as a presupposition and vantage point of moral philosophy critically into view. Subjects and bodies, so Butler argues, are far from being settled entities whose nature we could ascertain ontologically, anthropologically, or biologically in distinction from being formed through social and cultural practices. As Butler contends, we have no access to what subjects or bodies are outside frameworks of social norms and the consequent plight of subjects and bodies as material effects of normalization, although subjects and bodies are not reducible to these processes of normalization. Equally, desires and passionate attachments are not retrievable outside or beyond normalization, while at the same time not being therefore fully reducible to social norms.

The first challenge—Butler's account of the subject as emerging through subjection to norms—delimits a predicament of interest to moral philosophy insofar as this subjection is more specifically understood to constitute the subject as a bodily subject. So the body, knowledge that we might gather about bodies, or the "factum" of bodily experience cannot simply be claimed as a backdrop for critiques of social norms and practices. The second challenge that ensues from Butler's argument is that the subject not only emerges through subjection and the formation of the unconscious but that the subject is also passionately attached to this subjection. For moral philosophy this account implies the quandary that passionate attachments and desires surreptitiously and unconsciously bind us to social norms and others in ways that we can never become fully aware of, so that the desire to live and to live well do not simply stand apart from prevailing social norms and the demands that others make on us. For some approaches to moral philosophy, in particular approaches of virtue ethics, this means that the desire to live and the desire to live well can no longer unquestionably serve to ground ethical theory and reflection. Further, with the unconscious and its social formation and continued insolent existence, Butler introduces us to a constitutive unknowability of the subject, a constitutive opacity that none of us can ever escape because the scenes of one's becoming can never be fully recovered through reflection. Moreover, any attempt to grasp and account for the conditions of formation implies an unraveling of the subject itself. This unknowability is not only the impossibility of fully recollecting one's infancy, in psychoanalytic terms, but also the impossibility of comprehensively knowing the ways in which social and cultural norms "make" and traverse us. This unknowability complicates the possibilities for delineating critiques of social norms and poses a challenge to the notion of accountability as grounded in self-knowledge.

In engaging these challenges, it seems important and even decisive that the aim be not to "refute" or "accommodate" them within existing approaches to moral philosophy but to use them as occasions to facilitate a critique of the possibility of moral philosophy without recapitulating the same problems of moral philosophy to which these challenges alert us. Such a critique means that while attempting to outline key aspects of how moral philosophy might still be possible, we will need to open considerations to the ways in which these challenges seriously pose the question of whether moral philosophy is still possible at all. The task is to grasp these challenges, to examine how they traverse and transform the horizon of the possibility of moral philosophy, and finally to offer considerations of how it might be possible to continue to pose the question of moral philosophy under the changed and changing conditions.

Subjection to Norms: Normalization's Material Effects

In line with Michel Foucault, Butler argues that subjection to norms offers a way of understanding social and moral norms not simply as repressing subjects but, rather, as producing subjects. When *Gender Trouble* came out in 1990, Butler's position gave rise to wide discussions because she insisted that the subject as well as consciousness is produced through subjection. Moreover, Butler argued that this subjection is a material process outside of which we have no access to bodies.[1] Thus "the body" cannot function as backdrop against "normalized" consciousness or as a reality that we can be certain of independent of social norms. In other words, Butler refutes a strand of phenomenologically informed arguments that seek to establish the facticity of the body's materiality as independent from social constructions. These positions hold that even though we cannot have any positive, substantive knowledge about the materiality of the body outside of discursive constructs and social understandings, we can nevertheless know *that* there is a material existence of the body; this existence, then, is a kind of pure or presocial "facticity" of bodily materiality.[2] Butler argues that even the understanding of the body as material is neither prediscursive nor presocial, but the possibility of a bodily referent is always bound to the efficacy of social norms and the ways in which social norms regulate and construct bodies.

To argue that individuals and their bodies are discursively constituted through the workings of norms does not mean that there are no real bodies, pains, pleasures, and desires. The reality of these bodies, pains, pleasures, and desires as discursively constituted is, however, understood as dependent on their becoming intelligible and being experienced as such. Both the intelligibility and the experience of bodies, in a self-reflexive way as well as in relation to others, depend upon interpretational frameworks that make these bodies and experiences available as experiences. Certain bodies, pains, pleasures, and desires, however, remain unlivable as human bodies, pains, pleasures, and desires precisely because of a foreclosure that renders them unavailable as objects for interpretation as human experiences. The difference between speaking about intelligibility and speaking about experience is that intelligibility pertains to the question of being recognizable in general from the perspective of the subject as well as from that of others. One's experiences, however, are not prior to the frameworks of intelligibility that are in place, and in that sense there is no perspective of authenticity that can be recovered beyond social norms and taken-for-granted frameworks. These frameworks are in play in how experiences attain recognition in the sense of affirmation and negative recognition in repression or in attempts to undo, repress, get rid of certain meanings of experiences that remain perhaps even unrecognizable, precluded, or displaced from the start.

There is usually not merely one single framework that renders experiences intelligible; instead, there are various frameworks that compete with and among each other. Some are culturally prevalent and dominant; others are relegated to the margins. Yet such frameworks, as ways of making sense of the world, others, and oneself, are not unchangeably closed, fully consistent worldviews in themselves within which one is immersed and to which one is unalterably confined. Consequently, experiences of pain or pleasure can bring the prevailing modes and frameworks of intelligibility into crisis and open them up for critical questioning and reworking. One runs in many ways up against and thus in a way experiences the limits of one's hermeneutic framework which is one's epistemological field. Since one operates from within that field, however, one is not in a position to look upon the field as a whole and so have reflective access to the field's topography. The limits are experienced, but they resist total sublation into reflective knowledge. This resistance depends on the fact that every paradigm works according to a certain foreclosure that occasions the preservation and return of that which cannot be signified within the given order of being. Experience as interpretation is thus a practice that depends on codes and norms of intelligibility. Codes and rules cannot function if they are not in use, and using codes is always a matter of these codes being embodied and thus repeated and cited.

This repetition by inhabiting and embodying these codes and norms establishes discursively the intelligibility of bodies. Bodies in their materiality become fully material as they become intelligible in this process of materialization. The citation and repetition of these codes and norms that have material effects do not, then, operate like a divine performative. Bringing Foucauldian and Derridian scholarship to bear on each other, Butler explains that it is not as if discourses (somehow becoming unified agents of their own) speak and designate a subject and suddenly bodies appear out of nothing. So the exclamation "let there be a perfect American-citizen subject!" does not unilaterally produce such a subject, as if once this is spoken, suddenly a person fitting the description would appear ex nihilo. Rather, discourses produce bodies by seeking out, targeting, regulating, defining, delimiting, shaping, and working over the entirety of our existences from before our births until after our deaths.

Butler emphasizes that to claim that the body is available only in and through language does not mean that it is fully reducible to language: "For my purposes, I think, it must be possible to claim that the body is not known or identifiable apart from the linguistic coordinates that establish the boundaries of the body *without* thereby claiming that the body is nothing other than the language by which it is known."[3] Bodies and materiality cannot be utterly reduced to a linguistic effect, which would mean to propose some kind of monistic linguistic idealism that proffers the unilateral production of matter through an immaterial principle. With regard to the body-psyche distinction, Butler cautions in *Bodies That Matter* against such an idealistic monism: "[T]he materiality of the body ought not to be conceptualized as a unilateral or causal *effect* of the psyche in any sense that would reduce that materiality to the psyche or make of the psyche the monistic stuff out of which that materiality is produced and/or derived" (*BTM* 66).[4] Understanding materiality as reducible to language as its origin and cause would, in fact, only mean to reverse the problem, insofar as instead of understanding matter and language as originally or ontologically radically distinct, matter and language would then be understood as originally and ontologically absolutely indistinguishable. By reducing matter completely to immateriality, linguistic idealism relies as well on the purity of the opposition between materiality and immateriality, because in the end there is only immateriality as sufficient cause and principle of matter.

While language and matter are often figured as opposites or as eventually indistinguishable from each other, Butler attempts to rethink the relation between language and matter by asking us to think of them as both irreducible to each other and at the same time as not absolutely ontologically distinct from each other. Drawing on Derrida, this relation can be understood as a kind of radical contamination of both language and matter.[5] The distinction between language and matter, then, no longer holds as a solid ontological distinction; consequently, we have to reconsider the way in which the assumed ontological difference of language and matter is taken to relegate words to the side of the immaterial that then takes material realities as the referents of words. If reconsidered, this assumed ontological difference between signifier and signified cannot be taken to precede its intelligibility; our being able to know and communicate this difference between signifier and signified and the process of signification become itself as much a material process as it is linguistic. But—and this is the difficulty—this does not mean that all language is simply matter or that all matter is nothing but language, because such a reduction to one ultimate principle and origin would again be an ontological claim, attempting to establish a secured domain of being that can be known of independent of our ways of knowing it affecting the positive knowledge that we can have of that domain.

Signification works through establishing relations of difference; this differentiation is the horizon and condition of the possibility of intelligibility. Even as I am trying to think this relation, this differentiation and nondifferentiation, and the unintelligible, the unknowable, or that which might be prior to and irreducible to that which we can know, I am caught insofar as I am trying to understand and *know* and speak *intelligibly* about that which escapes knowing and intelligibility. In return, this knowing is not an immaterial process, since bodies and matter are already implicated in this process of forming and articulating knowledge, and language does not exist apart from matter. Butler explains that "every effort to refer to materiality takes place through a signifying process which, in its phenomenality, is always already material" (*BTM* 68). Language, concepts, and categories by which we refer to bodies are not fully reducible to their referents, but they are equally not ontologically different in an absolute way. This "signifying process" does not take place apart from material conditions that make it possible, repeat it, and produce it, such as words written on matter, brain matter, neurons, vocal cords, mouths, ears, eyes, faces, and bodies producing the effects that make up knowledge and language—even if the matter through which language works is not tied to any particular individual. As much as bodies do not precede language and frameworks of intelligibility and are not knowable outside of categories and concepts by which we refer to these bodies, language, categories, so concepts as frameworks that render bodies intelligible and knowable equally do not precede or exist apart from bodies and material reality.

The distinction that establishes materiality as different from immateriality is made by acts of signification. Signification works through differentiation, which allows signs and referents to become intelligible, insofar as relations between them are established. Strictly speaking, this means that the relation precedes that to which it relates. As bodies as referents come to be intelligible in the relation to particular signs, the differentiation also means that the materiality of the sign is instantiated as distinctly different from the materiality of the bodily referent. This difference becomes for Butler "the site where the materiality of language and that of the world which it seeks to signify are perpetually negotiated" (*BTM* 69). The materiality of the world is not fully incommensurable with language and knowledge—since, if that were the case, it would be impossible to have any kind of knowledge about it. Nor is this materiality that which precedes our knowledge about it, but the negotiation of knowledge about our world and its materiality is constitutive of this world. Therefore the world, matter, and bodies as such cannot be taken as fixed existences against which one could in any easy way evaluate and judge one's knowledge about them. But neither is the relation between knowledge and matter one of free invention, because there is a relative fixity through histories of meaning, practices, and relations of difference. Butler speaks therefore about a perpetual "negotiation of materiality" that neither is a linguistic monism nor would assume that we could gain any kind of access to material reality other than through language and discourse, which in themselves are material practices.[6]

In *Gender Trouble*[7] and subsequent works, Butler takes up the Derridian understanding of materiality as not radically other than language but constituted through signification, and she brings this understanding of materiality to bear on Michel Foucault's analytics of power and discourse. Drawing on Foucault allows Butler to inquire into the formation of the subject as bodily through subjection to societal mechanisms shaping that body through norms and discourses. Drawing on Derrida makes it possible for her to radicalize this social and discursive formation of bodies by arguing that there is no body as materiality that preexists or exists apart from this social formation. But as we have seen, this social and discursive formation of the subject and of the body does not mean that bodies are "caused" by discourse or even fully "determined" by it. Rather, Butler explains in *The Psychic Life of Power*, pointing to the Foucauldian prisoner in *Discipline and Punish*, "subjection is neither simply the domination of a subject nor its production, but designates a certain kind of restriction *in* production, a restriction without which the production of the subject cannot take place, a restriction through which that production takes place" (*PLP* 84).[8] Repeated here, as in many instances in Butler's work, is the claim that there is no individual subject that precedes its formation through subjection. But even though there is no existence apart from discourse and power, this does not mean that norms and discourses arbitrarily and randomly give birth to subjects. Rather, it is precisely the restriction and subjection that achieve the definition and formation, the norm that shapes, coerces, and seduces to life.

This kind of Foucauldian *assujetissement* is not merely a subjection in the sense of domination; it is not merely an exertion of power on a preexisting body that shapes the substance that has existence outside and prior to the workings of power and social norms. There is no "raw" body or materiality prior to and outside of power; power itself, in return, is for Foucault not an immaterial form but exists and works in the form of political and social practices and institutions. *Assujetissement* thus is a bringing of the bodily subject into existence, since "there is no body outside of power, for the materiality of the body—indeed, materiality itself—is produced by and in direct relation to the investment of power" (*PLP* 91). Materiality has no existence aside from power relations, even if this does not by necessity mean the positive recognition and affirmation of this material reality.

By arguing for understanding materialization as an effect of power, Butler problematizes theoretical approaches that attempt to find a dimension of the body, namely, its material reality, as the primary and presocial reality of subjectivity that is not yet determined or occasioned by power relations. It seems to me that Butler's arguments and the ways in which they challenge theorizing the bodily subject in moral philosophy are important to consider because the stakes in her arguments are not purely epistemological. The critical force of her argument stems rather from the way in which she brings the approaches of Foucault and Derrida to bear on each other. Not only does she demonstrate that the epistemological problematic of thinking materiality has political and ethical consequences. Rather, this epistemological problematic arises as such and becomes urgent as a thematic for theoretical inquiry because to start with, there is the political and ethical problematic of bodies that are rendered unlivable because they fall outside the scope of bodies that are recognized as legitimate and livable bodies. Drawing on Foucault's work allows Butler to theorize the question of power in the context of Derrida's reflections on the ways in which language and matter are never fully ontologically distinct but are instead implicated in each other. Bringing Derrida to Foucault's work on how power and discourse form bodies and lives allows Butler to examine rigorously the epistemological difficulties of understanding bodies thoroughly as effects of power relations and discourses without reducing either power and discourse to immaterial forces or bodily materiality to being indistinguishable from power and discourse. Butler's arguments call into question attempts to seek recourse to the body and its materiality as a critical vantage point for moral philosophical reflections because her arguments demonstrate how the possibility of social and political critique is at stake and enabled by refusing to discover or posit a primary materiality.

The issue of social and political critique arises insofar as Butler argues against understanding materiality as independent from power or as a substance prior to investment with power. In rejecting theorizing power as a secondary effect, Butler offers a critique of taking the body as a materiality that has fundamental and original characteristics and that is only subsequently shaped and marked by the history of subjections that form it over time.[9] Materialization happens to the extent that bodies exist in and through power relations, or, as Butler explains, "Insofar as power operates successfully by constituting an object domain, a field of intelligibility, as a taken-for-granted ontology, its material effects are taken as material data or primary givens" (*BTM* 34–35). In the process that installs matter as material, this materiality is also established and discursively posited as a sort of positive fact that exists apart from discourse, hence *discursively* offering this materiality *as if* it were a nondiscursive positivity that precedes its being known. If we now take this insight and use it to understand how the bodily subject emerges, we can turn with Butler to Foucault and interrogate how this formation happens through a linkage between knowledge and mastery. Knowledge about bodies is a discursive as well as material practice that constitutes bodies in power relations, insofar as the production of knowledge gives rise to practices of mastery, shaping how bodies are treated and perceived and how subjects comport themselves. Knowledge about the body has practical, bodily effects to the extent that this knowledge informs social and institutional practices.

Among the most well-known examples that Foucault investigated in his works are the practices that form bodies in the penal system, in clinical institutions, and more widely in society through the administration of populations by means of death and birth statistics. This means that in the production of "ontological knowledge" about the body, similar today in the life sciences and public health discourses, the body does not precede this knowledge but the living bodies as subjects and objects of this knowledge are constituted through these discourses. The problematic emerges when the "facts" about these bodies and their lives are invoked as a recourse and ground from which to derive concrete visions of how these bodies ought to

be treated and how to become meaningfully a human person. In other words, insofar as our knowledge of features that characterize bodily "reality" is always also a product of the concrete social practices and institutions that determine which kinds of bodily realities become important, relevant, and intelligible, these features of bodily reality as truths about our bodies cannot be simply claimed as being endowed with moral worth.

In *Discipline and Punish* Foucault suggests about this production of bodies and bodily facts through the production of knowledge that subjection happens not exactly through ideology and violence but through the production of knowledge that yields practical consequences. He argues that "there may be a 'knowledge' of the body that is not exactly the science of its functioning, and a mastery of its forces that is more than the ability to conquer them: this knowledge and this mastery constitute what might be called the political technology of the body" (26). It is the conjunction of this knowledge and this mastery that makes up the political technology of the body that Foucault distinguishes from ideology and violence. He seems to suggest that somehow this knowledge is different from ideology and this mastery is different from violence. Knowledge would be ideological—in the sense of an abstract, disembodied ideality of concepts—if it were understood as purely "the science of [the body's] functioning" (26). Furthermore, this mastery is not precisely violence, because this mastery is not simply a question of subjugating the body. Both knowledge and mastery are distinct from ideology and violence in their conjunction, insofar as knowledge turns out to be a kind of mastery and mastery turns out to be a kind of knowledge.

This knowledge is bound up with power—and not only because it can be applied usefully to control bodies and their functions. The intertwinement of knowledge and power also operates insofar as this mastery implies complicity by those who are worked over by this power-knowledge nexus. It is a mastery that somehow is no longer simply external subjugation and coercion, because there is an individual created through this act of being worked over. As Foucault explains with regard to the panopticon, the panopticon works not because there is someone who is indeed always watching but because there always could be. In fact, it is even crucial that "the inmate must never know whether he is being looked at any one moment; but he must be sure that he may always be so" (201). It is precisely not the actual gaze which controls the prisoner's behavior, but rather the operation of subjection works through ensuring the *knowledge* of the *possibility* of the omnipresence and omniscience of this gaze. The coercive effect of this knowledge has primarily the inmate himself as its source, rather than the guard who might be watching and thus know what the inmate does:

> The efficiency of power, its constraining force have, in a sense, passed over to the other side—to the side of its surface of application. He who is subjected to a field of visibility, and who knows it, assumes responsibility for the constraints of power; he makes them play spontaneously upon himself; he inscribes in himself the power relation in which he simultaneously plays both roles; he becomes the principle of his own subjection. (*Discipline* 202–203)

Subjection here is revealed to work because the gaze is reduplicated, in a sense; as the prisoners begin to watch and monitor themselves, they become self-reflexive, establishing a sense of themselves through self-surveillance. This means that a certain knowledge is created, but it is not a knowledge about biological functions per se; rather, it is a knowledge of the subject with regard to certain norms and rules as well as a knowledge emerging through becoming self-reflexive. The subject as a bodily subject emerges in this particular form through inhabiting and reduplicating the norms to which it is subjected through knowing itself as bodily in relation to rules and norms by knowing how to comport this body accordingly.

For the account of subject formation that Butler offers, particularly in *The Psychic Life of Power*, it is important that this knowledge is produced by the subject turning on itself and taking itself as an object of its knowledge. In this knowledge production, the subject emerges as a principle of its own subjection, but also, by virtue of this operation, a certain interiority and individuality are created. The bodily subject emerges as a conscientious and conscious subject; the formation of the body through social norms and practices goes along with the formation of a self-consciousness. Butler points out that in Foucault's essay "Nietzsche, Genealogy, History," he characterizes the body as an "inscribed surface of events (traced by language and dissolved by ideas), the locus of a dissociated self (adopting the illusion of a substantial unity), and a volume in perpetual disintegration" (*PLP* 83).[10] The body becomes the materialization of events over time and the material effect of their dissolution into experience by ideas that then institute the "self" as the unifying principle of this bodily formation. The emergence of the self—which is constitutively a dissociated one—occasions and is itself caused by the displacement of the body and its dissolution to some extent, which leads Butler to suggest that thus we might read "the self . . . as the body's ghostly form" (*PLP* 92).

Not only does this way of thinking about the self as bodily have resonances with Freud's dictum that the ego is a bodily ego, but Butler offers an approach to reflecting on how the formation of a self-understanding occurs in relation to the body and implies a peculiar disintegration in relation to this body. This disintegration and formation of the body in subjection give rise to a reflective relation to this body and create an interiority around this body that Butler and Foucault suggest align with the dimension of the self. Considering the self as "the body's ghostly form" and considering how the self and a self-reflective interiority are formed in subjection and self-subjection to social norms and institutions dislocates the self as a source for authenticity and authority for a critical reflection on different modes of subjection and subject formation.

Understanding the self as produced around the body in relation to social norms and becoming the principle of the body's subjection challenges moral philosophy to reconsider the notions of the self or self-concept. Instead of seeking in the self a narrative, an integrated truth of a person, it becomes possible to draw on the notion of the self to understand how stories and histories produce the self through and in relation to the formation of the body.[11] The self reconsidered as an effect of the bodily effects of subjection to social norms is not, then, a repository of a person's authenticity or an authentic self-expression of one's body. Rather, the self comes to join social norms in bringing about the body as a certain kind of body, and the self becomes the very mediation and agent of normalization. This does not mean that narratives are inherently oppressive or nothing but perfidious instruments of social regulation, yet they are also not radically other than social norms and cannot offer an authenticity of the self as recourse to oppose social norms.

The notion of the self nonetheless continues to be helpful in understanding how the bodily subject emerges and is shaped in subjection over time and through history by the production of a memory around the body. This subject as self that is bodily is not produced in a single instant but repeatedly over time. Yet this continuous emergence of the subject does not mean that it is a fully new creation time and again; rather, a renewal within and against the restrictions performed and produced by the history of social relations and regulations orchestrates the subject's emergence. Butler emphasizes the historicity and sedimentation of norms and regulations, which imply both their changeability as well as their relative fixity. In addition to this relative stability as well as changeability of norms, I would like to take up Butler's considerations to reflect on how one's becoming a self-conscious, bodily subject is enabled and restricted by the history that one comes to consider as one's own. Individuality and the self are not reducible to the ways in which norms and social regulative practices work, but Butler's work on subject formation as a bodily, material process and as a process of forming attachments in relation to social norms and others allows us to formulate the self and individuality as a kind of memory that is both bodily and social. This kind of memory is not only a conscious and accessible memory but also a host of memories, relations to past events, unconscious as well as conscious. The body as a site of inscription, the unconscious as storage in excess, as well as conscious recollections and attachments, implicate the subject in a history of itself that it is constantly only becoming. One cannot *have* one's own history; rather, a personal history becomes the history that a given individual as an "I" understands and designates as "my" history. This history is one by which this "I" is constantly dispossessed, as it does not simply come upon this "I" strangely as someone's history, but the "I" relates to it in some sense as "*mine*."

This "memory," this "history," is never only one's story as one might explicitly or merely somehow as a belated effect of one's actions come to tell it to oneself; in fact, insofar as we eventually become able to speak of "my" memory, "my" story, and "my" self, these stories and memories have from the beginning been implicated in the lives and stories of others. Moreover, the stories and the languages in which we become able to access these stories and memories have come upon us only through others. Through these encounters with others and their ideas and stories about "me," the "I" comes to be, though never reducible to these ideas, concepts, roles, and stories. No individual is ever reducible to her story or her self-understanding and self-concept, and equally, there is nothing such as "the irreducible individual" or "the individuality of the individual" that we could claim and secure as prior to and untethered by discourse and relations of power. I am not reducible to a conglomerate of descriptions of me, social roles, and stories, and yet I am who I am always to a certain extent only through them. These descriptions, roles, and stories as well as this "I" as linguistic position and as a particular individual, are in certain ways always beyond the control of any individual. The "I" comes belatedly and uneasily to this person who has come to be "me."

Moreover, insofar as the "I" is not only a linguistic position but for an individual comes to be more than a position, namely, a body with a set of histories, these histories are, more often than not, the identity patterns, social roles, stories, and memories that are most resilient, as they are written on the body and writing the body. What one could call the ascription of a story is a process of social inscription and is not at all an immaterial process. Norms do not simply work upon the body, but for norms to be effective, and thus *active*, they need to be embodied, both embodied and thus *activated* by that very body upon which they are said to work.[12] With this question of appropriation and embodiment of the norms that become the occasion for subjection and subject formation, we can now articulate a relation among self, body, and normative frameworks and practice that can become the basis for a critical inquiry into different occasions and modes of subject formation. On the one hand, considering the aspect of the self and self-concept allowed us to understand how our formation as bodily and self-conscious subjects is not reducible to the social and moral norms, roles, practices, institutions, and relations that condition our formation. On the other hand, we developed at the same time a critical perspective on this self and self-concept as effects of one's formation in relation to social norms. We considered not only how subject formation is a bodily formation that is a subjection to the normative and regulative frameworks that compel subjection to them, but how the self and self-concept become the principles of active appropriation and self-formation in relation to these norms.

To understand subject formation as a process of materialization and bodily formation in subjection to social norms does not necessarily mean to propose a mechanical relation of subjection to norms and a deterministically ensuing production of subjects. Instead, Butler's work offers this process of subject formation as one in which the subjects as well as the normative frameworks are sustained as well as possibly altered. The challenge that this understanding poses to thinking about the bodily subject in moral philosophy is that neither the fact of the body nor the bodily self can serve as unambivalent grounds for normative arguments. Nonetheless, the critical potential that this challenge offers is that it allows for a more detailed inquiry into how this appropriation of regulative norms and practices works and how and why changes can take place, because this subject formation in subjection makes change both possible as well as difficult to achieve. To understand the difficulty of attaining change, I would like to suggest that we turn to Butler's considerations of desire and psychic life to inquire into the ways motivations and attachments are both consciously and unconsciously formed in relation to normalizing and normative practices.

To understand the ways in which we appropriate and inhabit norms, Butler argues in *Contingency, Hegemony, Universality*, we need an analytic of psychic life and the life of fantasy that animates subjects as well as norms:

> The analysis of psychic life becomes crucial here, because the social norms that work on the subject to produce its desires and restrict its operation do not operate unilaterally. They are not simply imposed and internalized in a given form. Indeed, no norm can operate on a subject without the activation of fantasy and, more specifically, the phantasmatic attachment to ideals that are at once social and psychic. (*CHU* 151)[13]

The dimension of psychic life is crucial for Butler in understanding subject formation through subjection to social norms, because norms depend in their efficacy not on repressive power that dictates behavior. Rather, social norms and their normalizing effects are brought about through psychic investments and, more particularly, through the specific ways in which fantasy and desire work to animate social norms. Although—or importantly, precisely because—fantasies and psychic investments live not only in the sphere of the conscious but also in the unconscious, the dimension of the psychic life of subjects and norms becomes crucial for thinking about subjects, moral conduct, and ethical and political deliberation.

I return to the psychic and the attachments through which subject formation in relation to social norms is sustained and animated in the next section of this chapter, but to conclude this section I would like to mention that one intricacy of Butler's account of subject formation lies in its critique of accounts that attempt to secure a prediscursive reality for the bodily subject. Butler's critique brings together Derrida's arguments on signification and materiality and Foucault's analytics of power relations and discourses. This juxtaposition allows her to offer an account of the political and social relevance of thinking materiality as not independent of signification. Matter comes to matter not prior to social norms and relations of power but as social practices and institutions render matter intelligible. Drawing on Foucault's analytics of power, Butler offers these "social conditions" as mechanisms of normalization. The challenge that her accounts pose regarding the bodily subject is that bodies, bodily reality, or "facticity" cannot be invoked as providing some sort of more original freedom, a point of departure prior to social norms to launch a critique of social normalization.

Violent Turns, Passionate Attachments, Psychoanalytic Challenges

While Foucault rejected psychoanalysis and the notion of the unconscious, Butler draws on psychoanalysis for her critiques. She insists that understanding the formation of the unconscious and of passionate attachments to subjection plays an important role in offering an analysis of social life. She has argued in various forms in her works that there is no self-consciousness without the formation of the unconscious and that the unconscious and its formation are not prior to the social or a locus outside and apart from social relations, practices, and institutions. Rather, the unconscious is formed in relation to social rules and norms through the regulation of desires and their objects. In her arguments Butler sides with formulations, such as the ones offered by Spinoza, Hegel, Nietzsche, and psychoanalysis, that understand the human being as a fundamentally desiring being.[14]

Butler similarly theorizes desire and passionate attachments as fundamental but at the same time as not preceding sociality. Desires and attachments are not created ex nihilo—just as bodies are not created ex nihilo by social norms—but just like bodily materiality, our desires and attachments are not outside the horizon of the social. Social regulation not only is a curbing of desire but orients and fuels desires. In fueling and forming desires, social regulation becomes the very site for desire and brings forth a passionate attachment to that regulation, insofar as this regulation becomes as well the condition that sustains the possibility of this desire. In other words, insofar as desires are not easily given up or willed away, social regulation becomes what makes the survival of this desire possible, albeit in an ambivalent, regulated, or even repressed and reoriented form.

To theorize the way in which these passionate attachments are nothing to which the subject could easily have access in conscious reflection, Butler holds to the notion of the unconscious. These attachments work in ways that remain unconscious, making up a part of the subject's psychic life. These unconscious attachments are neither simply the internalized version of the social norms in relation to which the attachments are formed nor are these unconscious attachments simply possible psychic resistances equivalent to deliberate opposition against normalization. Crucial to Butler's understanding of how our desires and passionate attachments are formed and reinforced is a combination of the notion of the unconscious, the formation of desires through regulations and prohibitions of certain desires, and the impossibility of fully rendering these psychic mechanisms conscious.

The challenges to moral philosophy ensuing from this account of psychic life and subject formation in subjection are that if our desires are not prior to social and psychic regulation, then the "desire for the good life" cannot provide grounds or criteria for the critical evaluation of social norms. Such calling into question the role of desire does not mean that moral philosophy has to give up an inquiry into desires. Rather, precisely because of this formative history, desire remains an important topic for moral philosophy, but does so as a problematic and a question for inquiring into how moral subjects develop. The critical import of Butler's readings of psychoanalysis lies in their contribution to formulating a critical theory of subject formation, which in return offers an analytic for examining how psychic and social lives delimit and complicate the "desire for the good life" and conceptions of the good life.

Although Butler differs in this regard from Foucault, who rejects psychoanalysis precisely because of its own promise of the good life, Butler nonetheless does not reverse Foucault's critical assessment of psychoanalysis. Foucault criticizes the way in which psychoanalysis functions as a discourse invested with and proliferating hopes for redeeming the modern subject by liberating it from social taboos. Butler agrees with this criticism, but still continues to draw on psychoanalytic theories insofar as they allow for a symptomatic reading of subject formation and hence offer an analytic for examining subjects and their desires as effects of the conditions of their formation. Butler's considerations thus pose a challenge to moral philosophy, because subjects and desires emerge as symptoms of the very conditions that moral philosophy wants to assess not only in how they *do* work but in how they *should* work. In other words, Butler's critical perspective on

desires as being socially formed implies at the same time a critical inquiry into the possibility of criteria for evaluating normative aspirations and perspectives of social criticism.

For the moment I would like to defer this latter aspect of moral normativity and would like to focus on the particular critique of normative aspirations and criteria as well as of nonnormative elaborations of the good life that become possible by drawing on psychoanalysis. I would like to point out here three aspects that we can grasp through Butler's drawing on psychoanalysis to theorize the formation of subjects and desires. First, Butler's critical approach to psychoanalysis provides a way to inquire into how idealizations undergo a surreptitious naturalization by which these ideals attain a normative or teleological status that lies beyond their contingent formation. In particular, with Butler and Foucault we are offered a refusal of attempts to substitute normality and health as normative criteria instead of transcendent arguments about the state of nature or human destiny. Second, putting the insights of psychoanalytical theories to work aids in examining how desires and attachments are formed in relation to social norms and regulation, even if these norms and regulations are not consciously perceived. Desires are understood as symptomatic and not radically different from the demands of norms that condition the ways in which desires are formed. Third, Butler's arguments drawing on psychoanalysis caution against framing moral philosophy and ethical discourse as therapeutic discourses that aim for a social or individual therapeutic.[15] Psychoanalysis in Butler's works functions not as prescriptive or therapeutic discourse but as a critical and analytical perspective, calling into question the opposition between individual desires and social regulations as well as the possibility of attaining full self-reflective knowledge about one's desires.

In order to elaborate in the following pages on the psychoanalytical challenges to the subject of moral philosophy, I briefly discuss Foucault's resistance to psychoanalysis before turning to Butler's analytics of the passionate attachments to subjection and the life of the unconscious through repression and foreclosure in relation to social norms. In particular, I would like to attend to the implications of Butler's argument that social norms are not simply a regulating of desires and a subsequent internalization by the subject, but that the very distinction between interiority and exteriority is produced only by way of subjection. This subjection brings about the distinction between interiority and exteriority, insofar as self-consciousness and interiority are formed by the subject's "turning on itself," as Butler argues in *The Psychic Life of Power*. If we understand the subject and its desires as formed in and depending on subjection, then to "liberate" subjects and desires from subjection would mean to abolish them. In other words, there are no desires or an unfortunate subjected subject in need of liberation for a life beyond social norms, because "liberation" means undoing the subject as well as its desires.

Finally, Butler's argument that the subject emerges passionately attached to subjection raises questions for how moral philosophy theorizes responsibility and accountability. To argue that there is an investment in and attachment to subjection might seem objectionable because it might raise the question of whether this attachment then implies some kind of responsibility for this subjection. However, if one holds that the attachment does not already in and of itself imply responsibility, then this claim becomes an occasion for reconsidering how will and desire are theorized as connected to intention and responsibility and how responsibility becomes quickly limited to the sense of accountability. Accountability, as I will argue at greater length in Chapters 3 and 4, is a limited and specific sense of responsibility, because of its focus on past actions and in particular on past wrongdoings for which an agent is to be found who can be held accountable for the present condition. If, then, this focus on the past is dislodged, responsibility as accountability becomes a consideration of responsibility through the lens of potentially being held accountable for certain actions. In this way, accountability shares tight ties with an inquiry into potential or actual forms of guilt and into what punishment might become necessary. It seems to me that in this approach to responsibility as accountability, a crucial difficulty characterizing responsibility is effaced, namely, the question of how to respond to and deliberate over what is best to do in a given situation in order to respond well to a situation and the demands of others. Moral philosophy's focus on accountability for thinking responsibility becomes in particular problematic when we attend to the ways in which will and intention are never fully knowable to the agent but constituted by the opacity of our desires and unconscious attachments. So one part of the challenge presented is that passionate attachments and the workings of the unconscious make patterns of subjection more intricate to understand, undo, and rework. The other part of the challenge pertains to questions of will, intention, and accountability.

In the first volume of his *History of Sexuality*,[16] Foucault criticizes psychoanalysis for its blindness to the fact that rather than emerging as a liberator of the repressed, especially of sexually repressed individuals, and setting sex free, it continues to produce these individuals and their sexuality as repressed in order to be liberatory. In other words, as Foucault explains, the problem with psychoanalysis is that as a technique it relies on the inscription of its own theoretical premises as truthful discourse: psychoanalysis is "a theory of the essential interrelatedness of the law and desire, and a technique for relieving the effects of the taboo where its rigor makes it pathogenic" (*HS* 129). The ruse Foucault is explicating here is a double movement of psychoanalytic discourse that first essentializes the effect of the taboo, namely, the sex-desire, and then institutes psychoanalytic discourse as an effect of the workings of that taboo, thereby concealing the taboo's constitutive reliance on being exerted. According to Foucault, psychoanalysis is therefore first unable to understand sexuality as an effect of the interdiction; rather, it has to institute sexuality as preceding the interdiction and then cast the interdiction as arriving later on the scene and repressing sexuality. Second, psychoanalytic discourse cannot understand the workings of this interdiction and thus the production of sexuality as an effect of its own discourse; rather, psychoanalysis has to understand itself as being in opposition to the taboo and the repression of sexuality. So psychoanalysis—understood by Foucault as resistance against the norms and prohibitions regulating sexuality—is unable truly to break with and undo that which it opposes, because it receives its own power entirely from the power of that which it attempts to resist. In the process of resisting and allegedly liberating the repressed sexuality, it reinstantiates sexuality as repressed.

Foucault emphasizes that it is impossible to ask simply for a liberation and emancipation in the sense of transgression of and revolt against that which restricts and constricts. For her part, Butler underscores this position in her argument that in any political struggle one becomes entangled with that which one strives to oppose. On the one hand, transgression reinvests and reinstitutes that which is being transgressed, and on the other hand, that which is supposed to be liberated cannot exist independently from that which regulates it. But this does not mean that resistance is impossible. Foucault states in *The History of Sexuality* that "there is no single locus of great Refusal, no soul of revolt, source of all rebellions, or pure law of the revolutionary" (*HS* 96). For him, there is no unified position from which to disrupt, because there is no "outside" to power from which to attack it, since power itself produces that which it seeks to control. Yet it is precisely this productive aspect of power that invests every one of its effects with power that exceeds the control by that exercise of power that conditions the emergence of the particular effect. In other words, power continuously and irresistibly generates possibilities for disruption, and there is necessarily "a plurality of resistances, each of them a special case" (*HS* 96). The question that then arises is this: How can there be change and what kind of change does this proliferation of possibilities of resistances effect? While Butler continues in her work to engage with Foucault and his thinking about subject formation and resistance, unlike him, she takes up psychoanalysis to address these very issues. Psychoanalysis allows Butler an approach to inquiring into exclusion and foreclosure as constitutive and as producing a remainder and investments that cannot be fully recovered, that are unconscious but nevertheless not at all static or inactive.

Butler does not read psychoanalysis as a technique for redeeming the modern subject but she does deploy psychoanalysis as a critical tool, namely, as a methodology of reading symptomatically. Taking this approach, psychoanalysis for Butler functions as a framework through which it becomes possible to reread relations that present themselves as a direct cause and effect in a way that asks what has to be excluded, disavowed, rendered unconscious in order for this particular constellation to appear.

This approach to psychoanalysis as a methodological, critical tool rather than solely as an ontological theory and clinical discourse allows Butler to oppose Foucault's rejection of psychoanalysis without disregarding his criticism of it. By putting psychoanalysis and Foucault in conversation, Butler offers an explanation of how the subject emerges as passionately attached to the scenes of its subjection only through a necessary disavowal of these attachments and how passionate attachments thus never work independently of frameworks of social norms and cultural horizons but also never work deterministically in accordance with them. The relation between social norms and subject formation with regard to desire is traversed and made possible through the emergence of the unconscious. Norms are not first external to preexisting subjects and then subsequently encountered by those subjects and possibly internalized. Rather, the differentiation between the "I" and the others and the world, the differentiation between internal and external, is formed in relation to these norms: "[The] process of internalization *fabricates the distinction between interior and exterior life*, offering us a distinction between the psychic and the social that differs significantly from an account of the psychic internalization of norms" (*PLP* 19, emphasis in the original).

The social and the psychic are implicated within each other because the differentiation between the perspective of the "I" and the world outside which is "not me" happens only through internalization of norms. Social regulations and norms are not simply pressing on a subject that has its own wills and desires until at some point this subject integrates these norms into its ego-ideal and reworks its desires accordingly; the subject having its "own" desires is formed through the differentiation and organization of passionate attachments and objects of desire. This process works through internalization of and identification with norms and their ideals, because the landscape of available objects is structured by social norms to begin with. In other words, emerging as a subject who is capable of taking up the perspective of the "I" in relation to others and the world happens not without the internalization of norms and not without the formation of ego-ideal and unconscious. Butler's point is that if this internalization brings about the distinction between interior and exterior, between a sense of the "I" as distinct from others and the world surrounding it, then we cannot simply identify the internalization of norms as that which oppresses subjects and has to be overcome.

This does not at all mean that all forms of internalization are the same and all normative ideals are rendered indistinguishable, but we need to understand precisely what this situation means when the internalization of norms cannot simply be denounced and when there is no recourse to desire prior to or even in pure opposition to social regulations curbing it. In order to elucidate these situations, Butler draws on different psychoanalytical positions. Until her most recent work, she drew mainly on Jacques Lacan and Sigmund Freud before turning to Jean Laplanche in *Giving an Account of Oneself*. While these accounts differ from each other and are interrogated carefully by Butler in distinction from each other, here—at the risk of not doing justice to the differences among these approaches—I would like to concentrate on the point that for all these psychoanalysts and for Butler, desires are formed insofar as they cannot simply take any object; rather, object choices take place only in relation to norms.

The key notions that Butler puts into play, particularly in her earlier work, are foreclosure and repression. The analytic of repression explains how regulation itself becomes the site for satisfaction and proliferation of the very desire that is being regulated and thus produces an attachment to the regulation itself. Foreclosure can be understood in a certain way as more prior than repression, insofar as through foreclosure the field of possible attachments and objects is constituted at all. "Foreclosure," Butler explains in *Contingency, Hegemony, Universality*, "is a way in which variable social prohibitions work. They do not merely prohibit objects once they appear, but they constrain in advance the kinds of objects that can and do appear within the horizon of desire" (*CHU* 149). While repression seeks out and then regulates attachments that may already exist, foreclosure works as a mechanism providing and forming the conditions of possibilities for attachments. The difference, Butler clarifies, is that "a repressed desire might once have lived apart from its prohibition, but that foreclosed desire is rigorously barred, constituting the subject through a certain kind of preemptive loss" (*PLP* 23). While repression seems to suggest that the prohibition could be lifted in order to recuperate the repressed desires, foreclosure implies that there is an inevitable and irrecoverable loss accompanying the emergence of the subject. The constitution of the subject occurs through the formation of the unconscious, which means the closing off of the unconscious as the locus of an irrecoverable loss in the infant in response to already finding a world infused with rules about the possible love-objects before it and establishment of attachments in response.

If we accept that foreclosure and thus a kind of loss and dissociation are indeed necessarily part of what it means to become a subject, then stipulations or even therapeutic ideals aimed at recovering a "full" version of the subject that restitutes the lost are, to say the least, problematic. At the same time, claiming that subject formation entails an inevitable loss does not imply that the particular forms of this loss and the acceptance thereof are to be valorized and thus maintained as a condition of our existence. One strength of Butler's theorizing lies to my mind in her insistence on not foreclosing on ambivalences that lie at the core of our existence. It must be possible to affirm that there is a kind of loss through which we emerge, a continued "tarrying with negativity" that haunts the trajectories of our subsequent passionate attachments. But this negativity must not necessarily compel acceptance. The contrary is the case precisely because by insisting on the social and thus historically contingent conditions of this negativity, the particularity of the loss becomes the very occasion and site of critique and resistance. Despite being inevitable, the loss occasioned by foreclosure is never prior to the social but occurs through the horizon of and in relation to social norms. These can and must be interrogated, criticized, and possibly reworked and changed.

The notion of foreclosure explains how a certain "preemptive loss," as Butler argues, makes the subject possible in the first place. But subject formation is not conclusively achieved as a result of foreclosure undergone. Subject formation is instead a continuous process of formation, and as such, our desires and attachments are subject to and the subject of ongoing renegotiation in response to the social norms of the cultural horizon within which we find ourselves. This ongoing negotiation of desires and attachments works through the ego-ideal. The ego-ideal controls the desires of the ego, demands the repression of certain desires, and becomes the agency of producing and preserving precisely the desires it seeks to regulate. The economy of desire and its repression, or libido and its repression, as Butler argues it, is always a libidinally invested effort itself: "[T]he desire is *never* renounced, but becomes preserved and reasserted in the very structure of renunciation" (*PLP* 81). The effort to get rid of certain desires through repression must fail because "the libido is not absolutely negated through repression, but rather becomes the instrument of its own subjection" (*PLP* 55). We can see here a crucial feature of Butler's understanding of the productivity of the turning on oneself that makes and drives subjection: the relation between desire and repression shows how the norms that are regulating and subjecting are not external to the desires of the subject that they seek to regulate. The opposite is the case: repression is part of the dynamic that sustains the libidinal economy. Libido or desire thus not only reemerges in the form of the repressed but is also present in the form of stock taken in the repressing activity.

Desire does not simply disappear in repression but is displaced and transformed. This displacement of desire means that now the act of turning against itself is libidinally invested. Regulation becomes the site of satisfaction, the very act of repressing becomes an experience of satisfaction, and "[b]ecause this displaced satisfaction is experienced through the application of the law, that application is reinvigorated and intensified with the emergence of every prohibited desire" (*PLP* 56). The internalization of norms implies not only that social norms regulating desires and attachments are taken up by the subject itself but that self-regulation in accordance with these norms allows the preservation of the very desire that is regulated by repression. So turning against oneself, turning against one's "own" desires by repressing them, becomes a site of satisfaction. Consequently, not only is it impossible to transcend social regulation, but now it also becomes possible to see the difficulties in reworking patterns of social regulation.

In this way, the desires one comes to call one's "own" are traversed and constituted through social norms: one did not make the conditions of one's desires, one did not even choose them, one cannot ever give a coherent explanation of why one came to desire this way. One's desires are contingent upon social norms and ideals. While it is possible to realize and acclaim *that* they are socially and historically contingent and not an upsurge of authenticity, it remains impossible for anyone fully to grasp precisely *how* one's desires are orchestrated through and bound up with social norms because of the unconscious. This does not mean that the psyche is an unbroken continuation of social norms, now enforced by the subject itself on itself in self-subjection. Here again the unconscious, as Butler presents it, complicates matters, because the mechanisms of foreclosure and repression enable the subject only by concomitantly producing remainders that resist normalization. This unconscious resistance is not already a kind of ethical or political agency, but nonetheless these resistances of the unconscious remainders are relevant for Butler's account of agency. I return to this aspect of these necessary discontinuities and remainders and Butler's account of agency more generally in Chapter 2, but for now I would like to focus on articulating the challenge to ethical critiques based in "the desire for a good life" offered by Butler's account of the bind of desire and subjection.

This challenge is, as we have seen, that it is not possible to seek recourse to discovering more original versions of desire that might precede social regulation. Further, matters become complicated with regard to attempts to rework patterns of social regulation. Critique cannot mean simply to impart knowledge and give reasons about what is repressive, as if this means that we could then simply get rid of these conditions. Instead, critique comes to be bound to an archaeology of passionate attachments, and such an archaeology means an unbecoming practice of undoing the very subject and its passionate investments in that which it is opposed. Such an archaeology will constantly run into its own limits, because these attachments are not transparent and hence readily avowable.

So one difficulty for ethical critiques is posed by the impossibility of gaining full knowledge of the ways in which our desires and attachments are formed, and another difficulty lies in that in these critiques the subject offering them is risking its self. But a further problematic is circumscribed in relation to the argument that there is a passionate attachment to subjection, namely, the question of whether this implies that one is "responsible" for one's own subjection. Butler explains:

> The salience of psychoanalysis comes into view when we consider how it is that those who are oppressed by certain operations of power also come to be invested in that oppression, and how, in fact, their very self-definition becomes bound up with the terms by which they are regulated, marginalized, or erased from the sphere of cultural life. It is always tricky territory to suggest that one might actually identify with the position of the figure that one opposes because the fear, justifiably, is that the person who seeks to understand the psychic investment in one's own oppression will conclude that oppression is generated in the minds of the oppressed, or that the psyche trumps all other conditions as the cause of one's own oppression. (*CHU* 149)

Despite or precisely because of the questions that might be raised because of this approach, Butler insists on the analytic importance of psychoanalysis in order to understand passionate attachments. The problematic encountered, however, is not limited to an epistemic difficulty. It is not only a question of how to attain knowledge about passionate attachments constituted and traversed by operations of foreclosure and repression. It is not even only the difficulty that a certain kind of self-knowledge also means an undoing and unraveling of this self itself. Beyond these problematics, all relevant to theorizing ethics, we encounter a further problematic as these critiques enter into a wider discourse in which certain connections and conclusions seem implied that might thwart the critical potential of these analyses. The problem is, we could say, that the performative effects turn the analysis against itself when understanding psychic investments means that psychic conditions come to champion and silence criticism of economic, physical, and structural institutional oppression. The other conclusion that Butler reaches is that oppression comes to be disparaged as a delusion of the oppressed. In the following pages, I would like to take this conclusion into a related but different direction, namely, more pointedly toward the discussion of moral philosophy, especially as the reaction of "pathologizing" the oppressed as delusional, psychotic, paranoid, and so on has its nonpathologizing counterpart in the assumption that psychic investment in the oppression implies a responsibility for this oppression.

While the argument that subject formation brings about passionate attachments to the social norms that regulate us often does not in itself raise this question of responsibility, this question is raised very quickly in response to the claim that there may be psychic investments, indeed even passionate attachments, to forms of oppression, and I believe that it is justified and even important to be concerned about the conditions and horizons of wider public debates and discourse within which analyses of such psychic investments come to be heard only as rendering the oppressed responsible for their state of oppression. But rather than demonstrating that psychic investment does not incur responsibility, I would like to ask what the underlying assumptions are that make this link between psychic attachment and responsibility possible. Further, I would like to suggest that we inquire in what ways these assumptions might be more generally at work in theories of ethics and thus are challenged by Butler's theorizing subject formation as bound up with the formation of passionate attachments to forms of subjection and self-subjection.

When we ask: If one is passionately attached to one's subjection, is one responsible for it? a perhaps more pointed reformulation of this question is: If you wanted it, is it your fault? The notion of responsibility is here narrowly defined as the question of accountability. While Butler emphasizes that accountability does remain an important notion to moral philosophy, her arguments in *Giving an Account of Oneself* focus on an extended inquiry into the limits of accountability and offer a way of articulating the problems that arise if we restrict responsibility to considerations of accountability or approach responsibility primarily through questions of accountability. In *Giving an Account of Oneself* as well as at various points in *Precarious Life*, Butler offers productive inroads into reconsidering the notion of accountability, albeit without fully elaborating them.

Taking up her critiques and engaging Levinas and Laplanche at greater length, I argue in Chapters 3 and 4 for conceiving of responsibility as a response other than an account. In Chapter 4, I consider Butler and Laplanche together in order to develop an understanding of accountability as a kind of reworking in relation to responsibility. The problem that lies in the question: If you wanted it, was it your fault that it happened? is the problem of understanding responsibility exclusively as accountability, and even for the question of accountability it is not yet clear what the relation is between causing something to happen and desiring something to happen. If passionate attachments and desires are thought of as something one is to be held accountable for, this implies that desires and attachments are presumed to be something of which one is in control and which one could choose to change. Insofar as the criterion for accountability is whether or not one has willed something, then holding someone accountable on the basis of desires implies an equivocation of desire with free will.

With the introduction of the will as a notion in relation to desire, we are touching on what I would like to offer as a third challenge that Butler's thought poses to moral philosophy. This challenge is that it is problematic to posit a self-conscious free will and conscience fully separate from desires and thus able to ground moral deliberation and accountability, as Kantian moral philosophy does. With Nietzsche and Freud, Butler argues that "[T]he very notion of reflexivity, as an emergent structure of the subject, is the consequence of a 'turning back on itself,' a repeated self-beratement which comes to form the misnomer of 'conscience'" (*PLP* 67). The phenomenon of a will determined by reflection and conscience is called into question by Butler's insistence on Nietzsche's critique of the formation of the free will, also described as conscience, through bad conscience.

In the following chapter I discuss this challenge, which is framed by rendering the will and conscience as a problem in the formation of the moral agent. Before turning to the discussion of subject formation more particularly in terms of the formation of the moral agent, I would like to recapitulate the predicaments that become possible to grasp as we understand subject formation as forming the trajectories of our desires through patterns of subjection and regulation as well as bringing forth passionate attachments to these very patterns. Desire, even when conceived of as a "desire for the good life," cannot provide an adequate ground for opposition to social norms since desires are formed and maintained through social norms and through regulation by foreclosure and repression. This does not mean that all desires ought to be allowed and "liberated" from regulation, as, first, the belief in such a "great beyond" to all norms is problematic and, second, the existence of regulation through foreclosure and repression does not in itself warrant that all forms thereof are necessarily objectionable. Desires *by virtue of being desires* cannot serve as a backdrop for conclusions about what "ought" to be. Further, desires cannot provide an adequate ground for accountability as they are not consciously and "freely" willed while also not being radically other than what we will. The resulting antinomy that moral philosophy is to grasp and grapple with is, then, how a consideration of the limits of accountability proffers an opportunity to rethink accountability rather than concluding that all accountability is rendered impossible.

TWO

Moral Subjects and Agencies of Morality

The subject as an autonomous knowing and acting subject in control of him- or herself has come into question not only because of the theoretical interventions from various intellectual camps, such as psychoanalysis, poststructuralism, feminism, and postcolonial studies. Much more mundanely, our daily experiences often make us—sometimes painfully—aware of the limits of our knowledge of and control over ourselves, others, and the situations in which we have to act. How to best respond to the overwhelmed friend, the talkative person on the bus, the nagging child, or the heartbroken neighbor? When we read the newspaper or follow the daily news and wonder how things can be as they are and what we can and should do about what we read and hear, our powers and knowledge, as well as those of others, seem extremely, if not often overwhelmingly, limited. The individual who can know herself and has the capacity to know the good and just from the bad and unjust, this individual—in collective or individualized form—can no longer function as a backdrop to ethics and politics, if she ever really could.

Even so, the subject being at the heart of ethics and politics has been called radically into question both theoretically and practically. From a practical perspective, beyond our daily experiences, the historical events of the past century and of the first years of this century do not inspire great faith in the possibility and power of a moral individual. Any philosophical recourse that ethical and political theories might seek in the rational and moral agent continues to be denounced by the human rights abuses that have taken place in the past and that continue to take place on a scale that does not seem to shrink, for all the public discourse on human rights and the condemnation of such abuses. In her essay "Some Questions of Moral Philosophy," Hannah Arendt writes that after the events of the first half of the twentieth century, any self-evidence of moral conscience and for an innate understanding of the morally right thing to do can no longer be taken for granted.[1] She goes on in the same essay to maintain that nonetheless conscience remains crucial to moral philosophy, and she seems not quite ready fully to cede the existence and potential of conscience. Even so, she makes very clear that it would be a grave mistake to believe that moral conscience could provide, as was once assumed, the unquestioned foundation for moral philosophy and that it could ensure moral conduct.

If indeed moral conduct begins negatively—with not knowing what to do and needing to ask what one ought to do—then the question of how one can know is not merely an epistemological quandary over the conditions of possibility for certain modes of knowledge. Even if certainty and absolute knowledge are neither possible nor necessary for moral conduct, the complexity of the world (and of what we can know about it) seems to radicalize rather than mitigate the importance of the question of agency and of the meaning of moral and ethical agency in particular.

These complexities extend well beyond the individual, both onto the global scale as well as into the nano-universe, regarding intricate economic structures, the flow of global virtual and factual capital; the international entanglements of political and social entities, groups, and movements; scientific discoveries and medical breakthroughs; and international networks of media and communication that spread and create information and realities at an unprecedented scale and speed. One would be ill-advised to find in these complexities cause for nostalgic reminiscences about the days when the world was smaller and more controllable, since the world at any given time might never really have been more controllable or even seemed more controllable for those living in it; it was simply more unknown and unknowable. Nonetheless, the unknowability and uncontrollability of our present time seems to mock our fictions of individual or collective autonomy and agency. Agency in particular seems a rapidly vanishing fiction when we attempt to ask philosophically or practically how best to act as political and moral agents in relation to our experienced realities. These realities, which are constituted by transnational capital, technologies, and layers of political and social institutions, radically exceed our ability to develop sufficient insights about them in ways that would allow us to determine with a fair amount of certainty what courses of action we should follow.

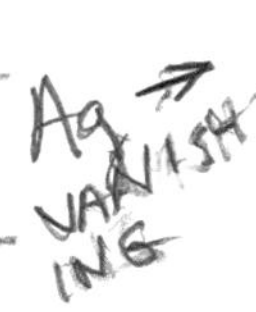

Agency, understood as moral knowledge that is locatable in and possible for the individual, has also been rendered more than problematic by Friedrich Nietzsche's critiques of morality itself as a repressive social institution.[2] One could perhaps think that Nietzsche and his critiques of morality are by now almost outdated because they are so widely accepted. We have taken due note of his scathing criticism of the roots of the "moral high ground" in moralism and of the ways in which the moral subject owes its good conscience to a disavowed genealogy of pain and punishment. We might generally accept that codes of morality are not as absolute and untainted by historical and cultural bias as they might have seemed at one time. We understand that social taboos shape not only our everyday perceptions of ethics but also our theoretical accounts and reflections. But does this mean that Nietzsche's critiques have become obsolete? It seems to me that even if we have already accepted that ethics—in practice and theory—is historically conditioned, Nietzsche still has critical purchase and his critiques remain provocative for reconsidering the claim that moral norms and deliberations are precisely not reducible to how social norms work.

With Nietzsche, Butler's critique of the subject questions the ways in which conscience and self-reflective willing are entangled in a history of bad conscience and a sense of guilt that are brought about through the internalization of punishment and the endowment of pain with moral value. The consequence for moral philosophy in these terms is damning: If the formation of conscience is bound up in such histories, then conscience—even in a localized, restricted, nonabsolutizing form—irrecoverably loses its status as an unquestionable resource for determining what is morally demanded. Conscience, as the resource for knowing what is morally good and what one should consequently will to do, becomes problematic if goodness and the faculty to know moral goodness are conditioned by a history of self-domination and by induced feelings of guilt. With Nietzsche's critiques, conscience and the self-consciously willing subject that actively wills what is good can no longer unambivalently ground the theorizing of ethics. Butler in turn radicalizes Nietzsche's critiques by arguing that the subject and its formation are temporally interminable processes, so that the long history that Nietzsche finds to have produced the self-conscious subject of moral conscience is for Butler an ongoing process that cannot be overcome or put to rest. In this chapter, I draw on Nietzsche to argue against retrieving even an encumbered notion of conscience in order to recover some ethical footing in an ever-expanding world. Given Nietzsche's and Butler's accounts, ethical self-reflection and finding ourselves beholden to demands and ideals that we come to experience as ethical are not retrievable without first attending to the ambivalences in their formation.

In addition to addressing the loss of conscience and the problem of moral deliberation in its reliance on our understandings of good and bad, I turn to the question of agency and the challenges Butler's work poses to agency beyond the issues of conscience and moral knowledge. With her famous (or, for some, infamous) arguments on performativity and resignification, Butler's work calls into question the subject as a site at a distance from and in control of actions and intentions. Against the fears that such critiques of the subject and of agency will render ethics impossible, I argue that in fact these very critiques afford a reorientation and reinvigoration of moral philosophy. It is crucial, however, to understand the extent and impact of these challenges to see that they cannot simply be accommodated within and assimilated into moral philosophy or philosophical ethics as it is usually conceived, when it retains the subject, rational agency, personal identity, or ethical desires as the ultimate criterion for understanding oneself as a moral being. As much as these challenges allow us to rethink moral philosophy, they also demand such a rethinking to tackle the grounds and tectonics of moral philosophy. In order to break with the usual focus on the rational, individual agent, I would like to suggest that Butler's work provides several inroads into theorizing responsibility and critique as key concepts of moral philosophy. As a consequence, these considerations will allow us to mobilize the critical potential of moral philosophy that lies in its insistent questioning of the status quo with respect to the horizon of what ought to be and of justice in particular.

Troubled Consciences: Butler, Nietzsche, and Moral Subjects under Siege

In the previous chapter I consider subject formation through subjection as a bodily and psychic process that works in particular through subjection to and in relation to social norms. This consideration renders both the body as well as desire problematic as notions for seeking recourse in which to ground critiques. I argue that neither the demands, needs, nor desires of bodies nor the psyches as such can provide us with criteria for assessing social norms and developing ethical visions for transforming these social conditions. In this section I would like to build on these ideas to draw out more clearly the challenge that Butler's account of subject formation poses to moral philosophy specifically insofar as she returns us to Nietzsche's critique of the will. The continued importance of this critique becomes most distinct when we approach it with regard to the claim that moral norms are different from social norms. This distinction seems to imply that while considering the role of social norms in subject formation is important and timely, these considerations do not in and of themselves quite reach the level of normative ethics or address the question of moral norms. This claim—that moral norms are not the same as social norms—is made with reference to the differences in the claims to validity.

Butler touches on the difference between social and moral norms in her essay "The Question of Social Transformation" in *Undoing Gender*, but never quite pursues this distinction. This distinction rests on the differences in how norms exert their normative force. While moral norms also perform as social norms, they do not simply claim normative force on the basis of delimiting and implementing what counts as socially normal and acceptable. To put forth that something ought to be considered as morally normative is based in claims referring to arguments about collective conceptions of what is good or what is right; validity—so is the position of normative ethics—is brought about not in reference to social normality but instead in reference to goodness, dignity, and justice. Further, according to the argument for a difference between social and moral norms, just because something is a custom or is generally practiced does not suffice as a reason to

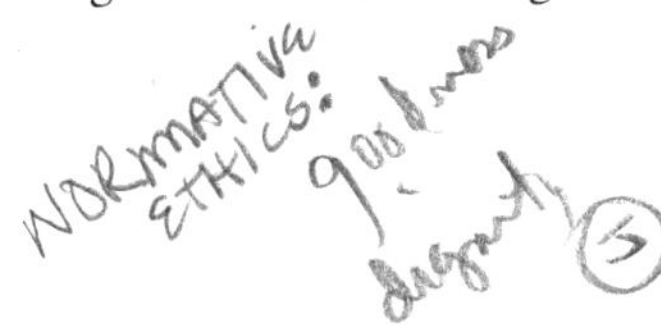

support moral norms. Thus the question at hand seems to be whether normative ethics does not operate very differently from social normativity.

While I believe that it is important to acknowledge that moral normativity is not reducible to social normativity, I believe that it is equally important to keep in mind that moral normativity never operates outside the horizon of the social. Nonetheless, I would not like to delimit differences and similarities between social and moral normativity; rather, I would like to shift the problematic and inquire instead into our susceptibility to and appropriation of morality as it occurs when one deliberates about what ought to be and determines one's will accordingly. Butler's keeping Nietzsche's critique present is particularly productive in this discussion because, as I hope to demonstrate, Nietzsche's critique does not ask the question of what kinds of appeals render claims valid and justifiable, but it presents us with an interrogation of subject formation, namely, the emergence of the moral agent as susceptible to and capable of making normative, moral claims.

This susceptibility to moral claims and the capacity to feel bound by them is the function of conscience. Conscience, in other words, is the site and faculty of appropriating and negotiating questions and claims of what one ought to do and what one ought not to do. Agency and moral action are thus not simply matters of consciousness, subject to questions of legitimate epistemic knowledge, but also crucial to an understanding of how subjects come to appropriate and negotiate questions of what one ought to do and feel compelled to agree with certain demands. Butler offers, with Nietzsche, a critique of understanding moral claims as persuasive solely on the grounds of their rationality and suggests a critique of understanding conscience as an unambivalent motivation and source for moral agency. Conscience and the susceptibility to moral claims are brought about, as Nietzsche and Butler insist, only through a long process in which debt and pain have been endowed with moral valence. The challenge to moral philosophy in these terms, then, is that conscience as consciousness of one's own actions is implicated in a history of internalized violence.

In what follows I first briefly address moral normativity as not reducible to social norms' stipulating and effecting mechanisms of normalization and lay out what we might come to understand as the "problem of the 'ought'" in moral philosophy. Then I would like to turn to the question of moral agency that is implied in the problem of the "ought" and discuss Nietzsche's critique of the will in order to clarify the two main dimensions to this challenge to moral philosophy: the valorization of pain and punishment and the problem of willed, deliberate, and indeed moral opposition to violence implied in forms of subject formation.

In *The Psychic Life of Power*, Butler draws on Nietzsche to ask how the trope of turning on or against oneself can be understood as creating the interiority that becomes the "precipitating condition" of the subject's emergence. In Nietzsche, this turning of "the will" back on itself is occasioned by becoming able deliberately to defer action instead of immediately and instinctually responding to a stimulus. The possibility of such a deferral means that the moment of willing and the moment of actualizing this will in action can occur at different points in time. Nietzsche argues that to achieve this capacity intentionally to defer one's action or reaction, a prohibition on immediate action or expression of the will must intervene. This inhibition of the will then creates the internal sphere that is necessary for a notion of self-reflexivity. This self-reflexivity in turn is that which enables deliberation and the determination of one's own will. Butler takes up from Nietzsche her notion of turning on oneself to theorize how the self-conscious subject is formed, especially who can refer to itself as "I" and determine its will in self-reflection. If we now take Butler's account to reflect on the question of moral agency, then one part of these reflections has to inquire into how intentionality and deliberation are delimited by the ways in which self-reflexivity and self-consciousness are brought about. Beyond what Butler explicitly does, these considerations also have to examine what it means that when moral agency is in question, intentionality and deliberation are in particular guided by the question "what *ought* I do?"

This particularity that characterizes moral philosophy focuses on the question of this "ought." There are different approaches that have been taken to this "ought," such as, for example, ethnographic approaches dedicated to inquiring into the topographies of a different ethos that, as ethical convictions and practices, frames the horizon within which these questions of what ought to be done can appear at all. While the question "what ought I do?" does not arise outside of social practices, what makes moral philosophy different from an ethnographic inquiry into ethics is a specific approach to this "ought." The validity of claims to morality, discourses that produce that validity, and inquiries into what comes to count as valid demands is shared between descriptive, "archeological" accounts and moral philosophy, and these different approaches benefit greatly from encountering each other. Among these approaches, moral philosophy—perhaps not to its advantage—is perhaps the least humble in dealing with this "ought," as its endeavor is not only descriptive and archeological but also prescriptive. The endeavors of moral philosophy are prescriptive in the sense of the desire to reorient how we approach the questions of "what ought I do?" This does not mean that moral philosophy is by necessity an endeavor to sever these deliberations from social horizons, but with moral philosophy's desire for an orientation that reflects on conceptual implications, we touch on a core problem of this approach. Moral philosophy focuses on examining what is, but it is also fundamentally oriented toward what is not and so toward what ought to be. Expressed in terms of implied temporality, moral philosophy deals with the question of how to forge futures. In this respect, even if moral philosophy is committed to the critique of moral norms, it remains nonetheless caught up in the predicament of opening itself toward what is not.

With this predicament of temporality, the problematics that the aspect of the "ought" brings about cannot be reduced to the question of the subject. With respect to my aim to articulate the consequences for moral philosophy of Butler's critical theory of subject formation, I would like to suggest that regarding the subject of ethical action, the following two crucial questions arise around this problematic of the "ought." There is first the epistemological question "How can one know what ought to be done?" and second the psychological question "How is one motivated to will this that ought to be done?" In his Second Critique, Kant struggled with precisely these questions and introduced respect for the moral law as "*vernunftgewirktes Gefühl*," a feeling brought about by reason, utilized to avoid the threat of heteronomy while at the same time to affirm that emotion, not reason alone, moves us to act.[3] Kant believed that we could not know enough about the effects of actions ahead of their occurrence to determine what one ought to do and thus held that only the good will can be called good in itself, without qualifications or restrictions.[4] Knowing what this good will would will and forming one's will accordingly are crucial to Kantian ethics—and not only to Kantian ethics, insofar as the will remains an important aspect and problem of ethics and ethical self-formation even in current thinking. In particular, as sources of moral knowledge come into crisis, this question of knowing what to do and to will haunts moral philosophy.

This problem of the will is not a necessary problem that is valid across all cultures and in all eras, but to the extent that the horizon for these considerations in this book is not outside the effects that the Enlightenment and various projects of modernity have had on philosophy, the will remains for our discussion as a problem in theorizing "moral agency." There are certainly other approaches to theorizing moral agency, centering around "meaning-making" in relation to norms, customs, and traditions by questioning how norms, customs, and traditions are inhabited and appropriated. In *The Politics of Piety*, Saba Mahmood makes the compelling case that considering agency too narrowly with regard to the possibilities of resistance and subversion returns theoretical approaches firmly into the hands of a certain Western liberal ideal of autonomy as self-determination in negative self-distinction from norms, customs, and traditions.[5] It seems to me that we can no longer theorize ethics as Kant could and that Kant's moral philosophy is not reducible to the "self-sufficient individual" and the "autonomous will" that serve as the bedrocks and "fighting concepts" of liberalism. My aim in this book is not to restitute the will or a truth of the moral self, but by taking up Butler's considerations on the will and agency, I begin by considering how the will remains a problem for moral philosophy.

In his 1963 lecture course "Problems of Moral Philosophy," Theodor Adorno suggests that a fracture of an accepted ethic is the precondition for the question of morality—"What ought I do?"—to arise at all, and in negotiating this question, deliberation and the will remain relevant.[6] I would like to use this inquiry into Nietzsche as an occasion to frame the question of the will as a predicament for moral philosophy. It is precisely that—a predicament—that is rendered rigorously problematic by Nietzsche's critique and by Butler's reformulations of his challenges.

When we consider the formation of the subject as a moral agent, moral agency is tied to the ability to will, and this will is in at least some way bound to the notion of self-consciousness, which implies the capability for self-inspection and self-evaluation. Even if this will need not be capable of full self-translucence, for one to speak meaningfully of moral agency, a certain self-consciousness, deliberation, and determination of one's will seem to be required. Taking oneself as an object in reflecting on oneself means that there must be an "I" that can to a certain extent distance itself from itself but also, in turning back on itself, identify with itself, insofar as it reflects on itself *as itself*. The enunciation of the "I," then, is, in Butler's words, constituted through "this capacity for reflective self-relation or reflexivity" (*PLP* 22). Butler argues that Nietzsche considers this self-reflexivity not as a given cognitive ability but as a self-relation brought about by an attachment that this "I" forms to itself through conscience.

Nietzsche's question is not how self-consciousness comes to be transformed into or give rise to the function of conscience. Rather, he calls into question precisely this notion of self-consciousness as being more primary than conscience.[7] The experience of having a conscience means that the "I" takes an interest in itself, measuring and evaluating itself. The "I" through its conscience not only takes itself as an object for reflection but also stylizes itself as a consciously willing and desiring subject in relation to a set of ideals and norms. The emergence of the subject as a moral agent implies, as Nietzsche insists, that one develops a consciousness of one's will and the ability to determinate that will with regard to future action. The epitome of this relation between consciously deliberating in the present and determining one's will with regard to future action is the ability to promise. Conscience, in these terms, is precisely this consciousness that allows this ability willfully to forge a future. The serious blow Nietzsche gives to moral philosophy is that conscience is but the product, the "late fruit," of bad conscience and punishment. Conscience and consciousness emerge through a long process that depends on the formation and transformation of bad conscience, which, according to Nietzsche's account, is itself brought about only by the painful curbing of instincts and internalizing what is socially acceptable. Conscience is neither the voice of God in man nor the moral law in us; our sense of what is good and right has no metaphysical grounding in truth, only a physiological and psychological grounding in the pain of past punishments.

By asking how conscience itself came into existence, Nietzsche demonstrates that a genealogical inquiry into conscience becomes possible once we suspend the assumptions and concepts we have come to accept regarding conscience's existence and operations. Genealogy is different from a psychological account, because Nietzsche's genealogical approach does not begin with the assumption that conscience is a fact of human development.[8] Genealogy is not an attempt to give an account of developmental psychology that would explain how conscience is formed in a growing child. While developmental psychology is able to help us understand that conscience is not present in the individual from the beginning but is formed over time as the child develops, it does not ask how it came to be that this development occurred, how it came that conscience itself became part of human development. In contrast, Nietzsche's genealogical critique conceives of the emergence of this kind of development as culturally and historically contingent and raises the question of how this particular aspect of human development became instituted itself. With regard to conscience, he argues that the individual conscience is not a constitutive dimension of the human being as a rational being, because conscience is acquired and formed through internalization. Beyond this historical process that pertains to the history of the individual, Nietzsche's genealogical critique is at its heart *Kulturkritik*, a critique of culture, which asks how the *notion* of conscience became instituted as necessary to the understanding of the development of the human subject.

More specifically, Nietzsche's genealogical critique calls into question the conscience that moral philosophy of the Enlightenment had offered in various forms as the possibility of the moral agent's freedom in relation to external forces. He attacks the proud assertion of morality's achieved emancipation and independence from religion as instead having its continued roots in the Judeo-Christian tradition and, more precisely, in a valorization of pain and suffering.[9] There are in *On the Genealogy of Morals* several instances in which Nietzsche attacks this religious tradition. One is the discussion in the first essay in which he explains the fabrication of values that he attributes particularly to the Jewish religion. Another criticism of religion as moral culture is found in the third essay, in which he discusses the institution of the ideal of asceticism, which he attributes especially to the Christian priests.[10]

In my discussion here I will concentrate on the second essay in *Of the Genealogy of Morals* and in particular on Nietzsche's concept of the formation of bad conscience as the process of forming a very specific susceptibility to self-evaluation. One way of renewing Nietzsche's critiques is to ask in what ways values stemming from religious traditions might be incorporated—without questioning and without acknowledgment—into a moral discourse that itself claims to stand apart from the dictates of religion. Such a critique of disavowed traditionalistic and religious sources of morality is a critique of liberal rational morality, which assumes to have done away with the authority of religion. This critique is not by the same token applicable to argumentations that openly assert the necessity of religion as authoritative source for morality. The critique that still applies to arguments drawing openly on religion is nonetheless whether pain and suffering in and of themselves are and can be unambivalently put forth as endowed with moral value. Even if pain and suffering cannot be abolished for once and for all but are part of the painful limits that go along with human finitude, this does not mean that pain and suffering and their endurance are therefore ethical values as such.

Pain and suffering in part testify to human vulnerability and finitude, and certainly how we comport ourselves with respect to our own limits and the limits of others does have ethical valence. In *Giving an Account of Oneself*, Butler emphasizes that through attending to our constitutive limits, "self-acceptance (a humility about one's constitutive limitations)" and "generosity (a disposition toward the limits of others)" might become possible as ethical attitudes (*GA* 80). The strength of Butler's argument is that at the same time as she insists on the ethical valence of attending to our limitations as human beings, she refuses to remove the ambivalence that arises from our relating to these limitations. An unambivalent institution of a morality or an ethic of enduring human finitude is, as Nietzsche asserted, a betrayal of the humanity of human beings, a *Verrat am Menschen.*[11]

In the following pages of this section I first briefly consider Nietzsche's critique of how debt and pain become linked to moral value, giving rise to the concepts of guilt, consciousness of guilt, and justice. I then suggest that this critique allows us to see the formation of a susceptibility to moral imperatives and the capability of regulating one's will as "good will"—the works of conscience—in a different light from as a unilateral internalization of social norms. This difference lies in the circumstance that the normativity of morality works through valuation and the persuasive force of notions of "good" and "right," while social normativity operates through normalizing practices and thus in relation to the normativity of "normality." In other words, my aim is to understand the formation of this peculiar susceptibility to moral norms and values in relation to but not as reducible to the internalization of social norms.

The first problematic that Nietzsche's genealogical inquiry poses to moral philosophy is that the ability of the subject to attribute deeds to itself and the ability of "feeling guilty" or having a bad conscience are of no help in grounding the ability to deliberate, distinguish, and decide on right versus wrong actions. Bad conscience is a self-indictment in an awareness of guilt, which means not only that the consciousness of guilt has to arise but that the consciousness of guilt has to become the consciousness of *one's own* guilt, whatever this guilt may be and whatever one may come to find oneself guilty of. Nietzsche, however, contends that at first there is no person who is aware of his or her guilt and who is then punished. On the contrary, the relation is exactly reversed: punishment is used as a means to "awaken the *feeling of guilt* in the guilty person" (*GM* 81/318; emphasis in original: "*das Gefühl der Schuld* im Schuldigen aufzuwecken"). Nietzsche's suggestion here is that the one who is to be punished is found guilty by someone else first. However, this feeling of guilt seems not to be purely a process of internalizing external judgments; rather, there seems to be a latent potential for feeling guilty that is slumbering. Punishment then awakens and actualizes this potential, which is a potential for the *feeling* of guilt.

The actuality of guilt is not necessarily a matter of some sort of objective guilt, but the guilt merely needs to be effective guilt and to be perceived as such. Nietzsche lucidly explains this circumstance with regard to the witch trials: "That someone *feels* 'guilty' or 'sinful' is no proof that he is right. . . . Recall the famous witch trials: the most acute and humane judges were in no doubt as to the guilt of the accused; the 'witches' *themselves did not doubt it*—and yet there was no guilt" (*GM* 129/376; emphasis in original). Both feeling guilty and the ability to feel guilty, and even being certain about one's own guilt—as Nietzsche indicates in the case of the witches—come into question regarding precisely what the voice of conscience is able to tell one in these circumstances. The usefulness of this capacity to feel guilty becomes doubtful if to feel guilty by no means offers any reliable indication of right and wrong actions.

It might seem that Nietzsche's proposal would challenge the role of conscience in moral philosophy if indeed his claims are seen to be true and the voice of conscience and the felt certainty about one's guilt were indeed externally stimulated and instigated. However, what Nietzsche is doing is not so much disproving moral philosophy as instilling doubt in it. The authority of conscience relies on its ability to produce convictions of right and wrong that rise above those of doubt and uncertainty. Insofar as Nietzsche renders the claims and formation of conscience potentially dubious in that feelings of guilt are brought about in the first place by punishment, his critique challenges the possibility of relying on conscience as a moral compass for moral conduct.

Nietzsche's critique thus renders the link between guilt and knowing about right and wrong contingent rather than necessary. More specifically, his critique casts doubt on a "morality" in which the capacity to feel guilty is fabricated through the experience of being punished and where this punishment is belatedly endowed with moral worth when the subject with the newly awakened bad conscience considers the punishment justified by his own guilt. The possibility for conceiving of punishment as justified and just is at the center of the genealogical account that Nietzsche offers through the scene of the creditor and debtor, a story in which guilt in its relation to justice as a moral concept comes into question (see especially *GM* 62–71/297–307). The question posed here is not only what kind of justice this is that is assessed in terms of punishment; Nietzsche asks how it happened that punishment ended up being understood as consequence and execution of justice. Rather than conceiving justice as the source of punishment, Nietzsche's genealogical provocation turns this relation around and offers an account of how the notion of justice was instituted as the justification and rationale that endow inflicting pain and the pleasure of vengeance with moral worth.

Nietzsche begins this account of how guilt as a moral concept emerged by suggesting that guilt in the first place was a debt, *Schulden*, in the material sense, and only later did this material debt become invested with moral value and became guilt, *Schuld*. The idea of justified punishment springs from the relation between debt and guilt, rendering guilt calculable and thus something one could pay for in the currency of punishment (see *GM* 62–63/297–298). By offering the scene of an exchange between a creditor and a debtor as an origin story of justice, Nietzsche poses the question of the ways in which morality might be not more than a calculus and justification of retribution in the name of this "justice." This creditor-debtor scene that Nietzsche offers as one scene of morality's and justice's birth is peculiar in the way that it stages a series of shifts between registers of debt, guilt, compensation, and justification. These shifts, which are performed with great facility, deliver an insult to justice and to the moral agent's sense of justice as a higher moral principle by offering the origins of this "justice" as base and material. Moreover, in the performance of these shifts and transformations as the origin story of "justice," justice itself is revealed as a logic of equivocations, producing equivalences while at the same time eradicating the traces of these exchanges, substitutions, and transformations. In the first equivocation, the debt of the debtor becomes his guilt as he fails to pay back his debt to the creditor. This guilt then leads to and justifies the punishment by the creditor, such that the inflicting of pain and punishment takes the place of the material compensation. In return, as the physical punishment by the creditor is justified as appropriate compensation for the debt, this debt has become an injury and pain the debtor caused to the creditor. In the story that Nietzsche tells here, justice thus emerges as a commutative justice that creates an equality among distinct and unequal orders of worth by rendering them interchangeable.

The crucial change that allows justice as this logic of equivalences to be instituted is the shift from a material, monetary "injury" to a still material but now physical "injury," when the creditor's suffering of a monetary loss is turned into a pain the creditor suffers at the hands of the debtor, such that the infliction of pain in return can be justified. What is strange about this transformation is that the original material loss should be compensated by the pain that the creditor now gets to make the debtor suffer. But with this shift from the externally material to the bodily physical, the external materiality is displaced and transfigured and the suffering at the hands of the creditor becomes justified and just. As Butler notes on this latter aspect, "the response takes on a meaning that exceeds the explicit purpose of achieving compensation" (*PLP* 74). The creditor's motivation is not merely justice in having the debt repaid in some fashion but also in the pleasure arising from a punishment that originates in the desire for reparation, through which "the infliction of injury is construed as a seduction to life" (*PLP* 74; see *GM* 66–67/301–303). This "genuine seduction *to* life" (*GM* 67/303; emphasis in original: "*einen eigentlichen Verführungs-Köder* zum *Leben*") is cast as a process in which the debtor becomes aware of his or her guilt and thus becomes redeemable through suffering punishment.

The rationalization that occurs as debt and punishment become linked is twofold. One part is that the punishment is conceived of as the justice of retribution, and the other is that the awakening of a sense of guilt allows a rationalization of the experience of suffering. Not only does punishment become justified and explicable by a logic of guilt that incurs pain; even beyond that, suffering turns out to be a "seduction to life" as it emerges as the site of expiation. So the formation of bad conscience as the awareness of one's guilt allows one to conceive of the pain as rendering moral worth. With that genealogy of "bad conscience," the moral subject's ability and susceptibility to bad conscience can no longer without problem ground a moral sense of right and wrong. Rather, the development of a sense of right and wrong is offered to us by Nietzsche as the effect of punishment and pain that become rationalized and endowed with moral valence.

The possibility of redemption by means of suffering is an all-too-familiar trope of Christian morality that Nietzsche criticizes throughout *On the Genealogy of Morals.* The insult Nietzsche delivers to these notions of justice and redemption lies in this account, which offers this redemptive quality of suffering as having its roots in the materialistic, monetary-exchange logic of a creditor-debtor relationship. Such a genealogy sits uncomfortably with aspirations of moral discourse that invoke justice as a motivation fully severed from and morally superior to motives of payback and vengeance. If the superiority of this commutative justice might, as Nietzsche suggests, indeed be tied to the sublimation of these motivations and logics of payback and vengeance, then this justice and the moral subject's susceptibility to claims about this justice remain implicated in the history of how the persuasive power of this justice has been formed through these logics of exchange and revenge.

We have now established a way in which to read how Nietzsche calls into question in particular conscience and justice as bedrocks of moral philosophy. Butler's renewal of Nietzsche's critiques has a slightly different focus that I would like not to lose sight of here, namely, the social formation of subjects. Butler offers a reformulation of Nietzsche by drawing on Foucauldian and Derridian insights. Bringing to bear a Foucauldian perspective on the productivity of social norms, she elaborates an analytic for grasping how moral norms operate in the same way as social norms to produce certain kinds of subjects as moral subjects. Taking up the temporization that Derrida's notion of iterability provides, Butler articulates the subject as the process of its formation, which is an ongoing process of acting on and being acted upon. In this process, the subject is never in full control of its formation and the conditions under which it is being formed, but these conditions are equally neither fully determining the subject nor unchangeable.

In the context of the challenges Butler's theorizing of subject formation poses to moral philosophy, a revisiting of Nietzsche allows us to articulate more explicitly than Butler does a critical perspective on the ways in which moral norms work not as social norms because they do not appeal to validity on the basis of normality or social acceptability. A critical perspective on this difference in the persuasiveness of moral claims becomes possible by taking up Nietzsche's genealogical accounts concerning the way this susceptibility to moral claims came about through a history of violence. Not only do conscience and justice become dubious as moral philosophical principles for deliberating and determining how to evaluate and respond to past actions; Nietzsche's critiques also call into question the ways in which deliberations of future actions are made possible. The possibility of determining one's will and holding to one's promises, as Nietzsche sets out to show, is based on the effectiveness of a bad conscience that has turned into a preemptive kind of bad conscience that makes us keep our word. In the second essay of *On the Genealogy of Morals*, Nietzsche introduces this perspective by offering that bad conscience is not only a product in response to suffering punishment for a debt in the past but also what brings about fear of punishment in the future.

Bad conscience as an internalized fear of punishment is what leads to conscience and the ability to keep one's promises. Nietzsche's critique of the moral agent's will presents a challenge to moral philosophy by demonstrating how the ability to make promises relies on bad conscience. Butler renews Nietzsche's critique when she remains reluctant with regard to attempts that "resituate Nietzsche within the ethical domain" (*PLP* 65) in order to argue for an ethics beyond morality. She proposes to "continue to pose the ethical as a question, one which cannot be freed of its complicity with what it most strongly opposes" (*PLP* 65). Butler suggests conceiving of ethics as a question in relation to violence as "what it most strongly opposes" and as a question about its own relation to and complicity with violence—and I would add that this understanding coincides with a possible way of delimiting moral philosophy, namely as a theoretical reflection on ethics. In response to the violent genealogy and practices of bad conscience that Nietzsche put forth, then, one should expect that ethics and moral philosophy would also be bound to object to and oppose the violence that is implied in a bad conscience. In *The Psychic Life of Power*, Butler continues to engage Nietzsche's critique in order to draw out a "political insight" (*PLP* 66) about how morality works in favor of social regulation. For the purposes of my argument here, I would like to focus, however, on the specific challenge that this critique poses to moral philosophy regarding the *moral* subject as agent.

Nietzsche's critique allows us to articulate how moral agency comes into question in two ways: more narrowly with respect to determining and willing what is good, and more generally with respect to the self-determination of one's will. First, the free will that can determine itself as "good will" becomes a problem for moral philosophy, if, as Nietzsche puts forth, internalizing the violence makes the self-evaluation of one's actions possible in the first place. Second, the very possibility of determining one's will becomes a problem for its complicity with the internalized punishment. This means that the possibility of moral evaluation is rendered problematic not only with regard to past actions but also with regard to future actions. Even more so, not only does the evaluation of future actions become problematic, but the very act of willing future actions is referred back to its ambivalent origins by Nietzsche's critique of the emergence and fabrication of the willing, conscious, and conscientious subject. In this critique, the promise comes to figure as a crucial problematic, because to be able to promise requires a constancy or memory of the will. This self-constancy of the willing subject is constituted through a reflexivity of the will that occasions the proliferation of the will. The will is capable of taking itself as an object, thus forming a certain kind of reflexivity in which the will binds itself to itself. Through this self-bondage over time, and regardless of the circumstances, the will thus constitutes its self-identity in the form of self-constancy through reflexivity.

This self-bondage is performed in the promise through which the utterance in which one gives one's word is renewed regardless of change, regardless of what one might want at a later point in time, until one finally acts upon one's word. This self-binding is an active counterforce to forgetfulness, namely, a *Gedächtnis*, a memory, as Nietzsche argues in the second essay of *On the Genealogy of Morals*, entitled "'Guilt,' 'Bad Conscience,' and the Like."[12] In the case of making a promise, forgetfulness, which Nietzsche characterizes as "a form of robust health" (*GM* 58/292: "*eine Form der starken Gesundheit*"), has to be suspended; otherwise, the promise could not be kept. This suspension of forgetfulness "involves no mere passive inability to rid oneself of an impression . . . but an active *desire* not to rid oneself, a desire for the continuance of something desired once, a real *memory of the will*" (*GM* 58/292; emphasis in original).[13] This memory, however, is not a natural trait of human beings; it is an active capacity and is created through a continually painful injury: "If something is to stay in the memory, it must be burned in; only that which never ceases to *hurt* stays in the memory" (*GM* 61/295; emphasis in original).

Memory is created and sustained by an ongoing painful impression, and thus Nietzsche speaks about the "severity, cruelty, and pain" that accompany promises. This severity, cruelty, and pain comprise the sting of bad conscience that has to have been there from the first to enable the possibility of promising and fulfilling the promise. So the passion with which promises are kept against all odds and despite changing circumstances relies on bad conscience, which is the internalized anticipation of punishment for breaking the promise. The shackles of bad conscience are the condition of the emergence of the self-reflexive and self-reflective subject; bad conscience not only turns the subject on itself but also makes self-constancy possible. Bad conscience is the function of a memory of the will sustaining the "long chain of will" (*GM* 58/292: "*die lange Kette des Willens*"), which implies that the agency of the subject who can deliberate, decide, promise, and act in the future in accordance with the earlier decision is a product of the pains and shackles of bad conscience. The challenge to moral philosophy, in other words, is to ask what mode of subject formation it presupposes and engenders and in what ways bad conscience and its efficacy become the disavowed sustaining principle of moral philosophy and the moral subject.

This task of inquiring what kind of subject moral philosophy stipulates poses the question of how pain and suffering are valorized as just and good. The inquiry goes further by allowing us to think about how we become susceptible to moral norms in ways that acknowledge those norms as not quite reducible to social norms. Nietzsche aids us in considering how moral norms are not purely social norms that are then internalized, but his critiques offer a way to theorize this susceptibility to moral norms more specifically with respect to how conscience as a faculty of evaluation, of a "feeling" for moral claims of right and wrong, is created. This shift from encountering social and external demands to encountering and responding to demands of what is good and valid is not just a matter of falling prey to manipulation and of becoming a puppet of external demands. Rather, conscience and the ensuing pride in responsibility in the form of keeping one's word dissimulate the origins of conscience in bad conscience. Conscience, in the light of Nietzsche's critiques, is less the capacity for morality than an explanation for a subjectively different susceptibility to moral claims.

From the perspective of the moral subject, the shackles of bad conscience on which conscience depends in its formation and continued efficacy are not explicitly acknowledged as belatedly endowed with worth, but the effects of bad conscience are also not taken as shackles and cruelty. As Nietzsche explains, for "the 'free' man, the possessor of a protractible and unbreakable will" (*GM* 60/294), the accompanying "cruelty" is not perceivable as cruelty or pain because he is proudly conscious of his privilege of being able to promise and of the awareness of his strength that has become his "dominating instinct." This instinct is what "this sovereign man calls . . . his *conscience*" (*GM* 60/294; emphasis in original), and thus the creation of the memory of the will through the infliction of pain is disavowed in the name of the freedom and strength of the "sovereign man." In the sovereign man, a transformation seems to have happened: the bad conscience that painfully coerces the will to extend over time and hold firm has become conscience and is now apparently endowed with positive value. In other words, "bad conscience" becomes seemingly "other" than conscience in its characterization as a "consciousness of guilt," and conscience becomes the consciousness of responsibility.

Conscience is, as Nietzsche tells us, the knowledge of the sovereign individual about his or her strength of will that allows him or her to make promises; it is "the proud awareness of the extraordinary privilege of *responsibility*, the consciousness of . . . this power over oneself" (*GM* 60/294; emphasis in original). This awareness has become so integrated in the strong individual's being that it has become a habitus, a sedimented bodily knowledge, or, in Nietzsche's wording, a "dominating instinct," and as such is called "conscience." Conscience, then, has—as "late fruit"—become in the first place a site of awareness of a responsibility for actions that one comes to acknowledge as one's own, as neither good nor bad.[14] However, the price of the privilege of this responsibility is that the violence of the punishments, the turns that initiated this responsibility, has to have been dissimulated and disavowed.

Nietzsche's genealogical account of conscience confronts moral philosophy with the question of what kind of subject and what forms of subject formation moral philosophy presumes and perhaps even renders necessary. Butler frames the problematic that emerges for ethical deliberations as well as for moral philosophy more generally as that of how to oppose the violence that the emergence as a moral subject implies. This violence would not seem a necessary aspect of becoming a moral subject with a conscience as long as bad conscience is assumed to be truly different and independent from conscience. If one were to disregard Nietzsche, one might indeed assume conscience to be entirely separate from bad conscience, insofar as only in bad conscience is the subject turning back on itself with violence and in a self-castigating manner. In this stark separation of bad conscience and conscience, conscience is recast as an innate or otherwise ontologically and genealogically distinct and independent capacity of the subject to become self-reflexive and evaluate its own intentions and desires according to standards of good and bad. If, however, the subject as a reflexive being is formed and cultivated in concert with the formation of bad conscience, then the self-formation of the conscious subject of moral agency is bound up with a violent and aggressive bending against oneself.

This violence of this turning on oneself, if it is necessarily violent, as Butler argues it to be, "cannot simply be opposed in the name of nonviolence, for when and where it is opposed, it is opposed from a position that presupposes this very violence" (*PLP* 64). This position, which depends on and presupposes this violent turn against oneself, is that of the subject who is aware of this violence and who is, therefore, able to object to this violence. The claim that becoming capable of ethical deliberating and acting presupposes a certain kind of internalized violence poses a great challenge to moral philosophy—one that seems to shake moral philosophy to its very foundations, especially if it understands itself as dedicated to and aiming for a critique of violence.

While Butler returns to Nietzsche more hesitantly in *Giving an Account of Oneself*[15] than in the earlier *The Psychic Life of Power*, she nonetheless holds his genealogy of bad conscience present as a challenge not to be too quickly believed to be settled by appeals to ethical self-formation: "[T]he formative and fabricating dimension of psychic life, which travels under the name of the 'will,' . . . proves central to refashioning the normative shackles that no subject can do without, but which no subject is condemned to repeat in exactly the same way" (*PLP* 64–65). This emergent will is crucial to the reworking and refashioning of the conditions of its emergence; it is never quite bound by these conditions, but neither can it can get fully beyond their restrictive function, because it is precisely this "shackling" that orchestrates the formation of this will. The will as well as its problematic formation therefore continues to be an important question for subject formation as well as for moral philosophy. One problematic is framed by the violence in the formation of bad conscience, of conscience, and even of consciousness and by the valorization of punishment, pain, and suffering. The challenge emerging from this constellation is that conscientious conscious deliberation and determination of the will cannot unproblematically ground responsible moral action. At the same time, the will remains bound up with the question of agency and the possibility for subjects to rework the conditions of subject formation. This reworking, in return, implies a reworking of the subject itself, which is possible only if the subject is not determined by the conditions of its emergence.

In the following section I would like to address some of these questions by returning to the question of agency and Butler's alleged elimination of this possibility. To that end, I would like to consider her different accounts of resistances and resignification as conditions for the possibility of change and lay out the predicament of the recurring problematic of accounting for, undoing, and deciding upon one's performatively emerging normative commitments.

Unruly Subjects, Resistances, and Contested Agency

One of the much-contested points regarding Butler's account of subject formation is whether there is a viable account of agency or whether in the end it is no longer possible for her to give a substantive theoretical account of political and ethical agency.[16] This question arose in particular because Butler has argued not only that there is no outside where one can situate oneself in relationship to power and social norms, but also that if we want to think adequately about agency, it is crucial to give up any vantage point beyond power and social norms. In *Precarious Life* Butler seems to allude to this discussion when she asks:

> If you saw me on such a protest line [in support of the rights of indigenous women to health care, reproductive technology, decent wages, physical protection, cultural rights, freedom of assembly], would you wonder how a postmodernist was able to muster the necessary "agency" to get there today? I doubt it. You would assume that I had walked or taken the subway! (*PL* 48)

Pointing to how we might reconsider the role of this debate over differing accounts of agency, she continues, "By the same token, various routes lead us into politics, various stories bring us onto the street, various kinds of reasoning and belief. We do not need to ground ourselves in a single model of communication, a single model of reason, a single notion of the subject before we are able to act" (*PL* 48). Not even a grounding in an agreed-upon understanding of agency is necessary in order to act. A closer look at Butler's work shows that the possibility of agency and acting is frequently asserted, inscribed, and performed as she recounts and reflects on instances in which individuals and groups very clearly take action, such as the activists of Queer Nation or the civil rights movement or against the actions of the Bush administration. Even so, these references have not quelled the debate about agency and the concern that Butler's account would no longer leave room for agential individuals.

For those with a bit of distance from these discussions, this concern and the great investment of time and effort spent in articulating, debating, and refuting this concern that a theoretical argument does not permit for thinking agency might seem bewildering. The level of the concern voiced seems to imply that one expects this argument would cause a paralysis in the world in general by philosophically denying the possibility of agency. Put this way, such a suggestion might sound absurd at first because it attributes a power and persuasiveness to a philosophical argument that is hard to imagine. How would such paralyzing power exude from the pages of a few books and articles? However, this perspective shifts a bit if we consider this question in the context of contemporary philosophical and theoretical discussions about how physiology, genetic makeup, culture, and perhaps other factors determine thought, will, and desire. These discussions actually do play an active role in shaping our conceptions of moral and legal accountability and policies on education, crime prevention, and general health, to name but a few. The ways in which we understand the preconditions and possibilities of how we come to make choices and act with or without conscious deliberation and intention—in short, our conceptions of agency—influence how we think about moral conduct and political and social institutions and practices.

At issue in the argument over "agency," then, is not whether and how we come up with definitions of what agency is and what counts as proper manifestations of such agency. Rather, the question of agency and the challenge that Butler's arguments pose are relevant to moral philosophy because what concepts of agency we operate with will influence how we think about responsibility, ethical and political values, and social change. The question of agency is, as I would like to argue in the remainder of this chapter, a site for examining the conditions and limits of the ways and situations in which we act, deliberate and make decisions, or comport ourselves more or less in ways that have become habitual.

It would be problematic to take the capacity to act and the ways in which we understand agency solely as preconditions of morality and moral conduct and as ontological questions that precede the field of moral philosophy. If agency were merely a precondition of morality, questions about agency would become relevant for moral-philosophical reflections only insofar as we discern whether or not an action was intentional and, if it was, then precisely what the intention was and how an action and its effects are connected. It would be problematic to presume agency without reflecting on the genealogy of this concept. As a consequence, moral philosophy would then only inquire into the effects and manifestations of what we have come to understand through the framework of "agency." Instead, moral philosophy, like all other philosophical approaches, has to reflect on how its concept or concepts of agency are not neutral but are already imposing a set of requirements that prevent events and actions from being read in other ways and responsibility and action being thought otherwise.

One of the key achievements of Butler's theoretical interventions is that they take what might be assumed to be ontological questions and make them legible as ethical, political, and social problematics, because, as she demonstrates, ontologies are conditioned by histories of power embodied in social and cultural institutions. With this insight in mind, I would like to take up the debate over the issue of agency that Butler's work has elicited to examine the challenges that it poses. I begin from the premise that the crucial question is not really whether Butler's understanding of subject formation produces subjects who are capable of deliberate action and forming intentions. Rather, I argue that the hinge and *scandalon* of reconsidering agency within Butler's thinking lie in the question of how to reflect theoretically on how we can know what to do and on the ways in which we cannot ever fully know—neither ourselves, nor our intentions, nor the consequences of our actions.

Philosophical attempts to respond to these questions of how to know what to do by forming some general principles that will offer guidance are called into question by Butler's work because it demonstrates how we cannot know ahead of time what any of those principles might mean in any given circumstance. Moreover, clinging to elaborating general principles might be detrimental not only for moral and political action but for moral philosophical reflections as well, because this clinging to the generality of the principle becomes what turns us away from the specificity of the situation at hand. By turning away from the specificity of particular situations within their historical, cultural, political, and social formations, an aspiration to the principle tends to foreclose on an examination of the ways in which these situations might importantly not fit the ways we understand and know to negotiate our encounters with others and the world around us.

Nonetheless, this book itself is a theoretical inquiry and, as such, not an ethnographic, anthropological, or historical study; instead it works with theories and in a conceptual register that is at a distance from concrete social phenomena, situations, and fields. As I would hope to demonstrate, however, not all moral philosophical reflection has to be an attempt to find and ground normative principles, even if it engages the question of normativity. The aim of this chapter, and of this book more generally, is to make room for a critical inquiry that is theoretical and philosophical and that understands itself as operating within the field of moral philosophy but that is also not primarily aspiring to elaborate and argumentatively ground a normative framework. In this context, then, a critical inquiry into how agency as a capacity and as a concept of moral philosophy is formed is key, because how we understand agency delimits how we conceive of the possibilities and limits of social change and collective and individual responsibility.

Critical moral philosophy cannot replace the work of other fields, and in order continuously to become critical, it is reliant on seriously entering into conversations with other fields of inquiry. Butler's work is an important interlocutor for quite diverse fields of study, in part precisely because her own work is not easily categorizable and spans several disciplines and in part because it elicits such strong reactions. My sense is that Butler's arguments are received as disconcerting because she offers trenchant critiques of how common understandings of liberal, enlightened, cosmopolitan subjectivity are less than liberal in their reliance on excluding and defending themselves against various kinds of otherness that loom as threats. Butler is arguably most famous for her work on gender, sex, and sexuality, which is in part so productive and innovative because it made speakable desires, lives, and bodies that had either remained unspoken or, if they were discussed, carried the stigma of the abnormal, aberrant, and pathological. Moreover, her work importantly offers a language and conceptual framework for lucidly demonstrating how this exclusion of the abnormal is part of what guarantees the normal its status. Butler demonstrates how the stabilities of gendered and sexed identities are attained through repressing what calls them into question and what attests to the ambivalence of gender and sex, of bodies and desires and their potentials and vulnerability. These arguments attain their force in part by virtue of the political potential that they are able to open up by not only demonstrating these instabilities but also mobilizing them in critical ways.

With these aspects of Butler's work in mind, I would like to return now to the question of agency and the specific challenge of Butler's arguments. Her arguments in *Gender Trouble* and *Bodies That Matter* in particular have produced two concerns that seem to be located at opposite ends—one worries that the potential for effecting change has been eradicated, and the other worries that change has become all too easy. The first concern suspects that there are only uncontrollable, powerful forces mostly driven by desires and unconscious drives. If there is still agency, then it is only within an array of events and only discernible retroactively through its effects, so that actively effecting change by concerted action seems to have become impossible. The other concern suspects that the hard labor of social change has been turned into an all-too-playful resignification of norms, practices, and institutions through reappropriation. These concerns pick up on aspects in Butler's account of agency that seemed to wreck havoc with agency as a kind of rational mastery and intentional exercise of capacities. This kind of mastery in the strong sense, one that implies a sovereign, self-sufficient, individualist subject, is indeed no longer recoverable if we take seriously Butler's challenges alongside many other feminist, postcolonial, and poststructuralist critiques.

While Butler does not do away with intention and reason, the productivity and provocation of her work lie in her arguing that the possibility of acting and effecting change relies precisely on this constitutive unknowability and uncontrollability of the conditions that act on us and to which we respond in return. This unknowability and uncontrollability implies a crucial theoretical undecidability in the sense that Derrida argued for in matters of ethics and politics, especially in his later work.[17] Yet, differently from in Derrida, in Butler the predicament of having to respond to this undecidability is not the key framework for approaching agency and the ensuing political and ethical problematics. Instead, the key to the issue of agency is power in the Foucauldian sense. While this impasse of having to know and act in the face of the impossibility of knowing and controlling one's actions is without any doubt crucial to Butler's critiques, the epistemological dimension is only one aspect of her engagements with contemporary political and social conundrums. It seems to me that especially her drawing on Foucault makes a difference in her analyses of these situations. The starting point for Butler's critiques is not so much the epistemological impasse from which political and ethical consequences then ensue, but concerns over the problems of violence, political action, social change, which then also lead us to consider epistemological quandaries. Even more specifically, one could perhaps characterize recognition and power as crucial threads that run throughout Butler's works.

The impasse of agency and our dispossession by the specificity of the situations in which we come to act, as a theoretical impasse of this undecidability, however, do remain important to consider. This impasse does not indicate a lack of rigorous theoretical reflection but owes itself to the loss of epistemological certainty that ensues if we accept that there is no neutral objective, no transcendent, transcendental, or ideal knowledge that we could attain beyond relations of power and cultural and historical specificity. Perhaps most prominently in *Gender Trouble*, *Bodies That Matter*, and her contributions in *Feminist Contentions*, Butler has criticized ways of theorizing "agency" that reinscribe "agency" as a transcendental capability of the subject. Her criticism is that by rendering the subject as constitutively endowed with the capacity to deliberate and follow through on its intentions, one ends up suggesting that agency is an ability independent of the conditions that engender it. Such an account of agency would imply and reinstitute the individual as eventually coming to exist at a guaranteed and accessible distance from the norms and practices that one relates to by accepting, appropriating, or opposing them.[18]

With this critique of agency, while holding to agency's continued possibility and daily practice, we can now frame more precisely the challenges that Butler poses to moral philosophy. These challenges to agency direct us to examine how we think about agents and projects of social and political change in relation to categories and criteria that might guide their deliberations, evaluations, and judgments. How we understand norms and social conditions as open to be changed by subjects as agents of such change raises the question—even if it is a question that can never be answered fully theoretically—of how we discern, among the effects that ensue, which categories guide our deliberations, evaluations, and judgments of actions, projects, events, and changes.

Butler's work poses a challenge to how we are to theorize these distinctions and criteria, insofar as they are often grounded in frameworks that take intentions and deliberations as the core for understanding human action in history. It is precisely these traditional notions of intentional action and deliberative choice that are undone by Butler's theorizing subject formation in terms of performativity and action and change in terms of resignification. In order to understand the challenge of rethinking ethical agency and criteria for deliberation outside of frameworks of intentional subjects, in the next several pages I examine the potentials for agency as Butler offers them, drawing on Foucault, psychoanalysis, and Derrida's notion of citationality. In particular, I will examine Butler's concept of resignification and the difficulties that Butler addresses in negotiating histories of these signs and the agency in question. The problem of agency emerges as how to understand the link between a necessary gap and willful, intentional action. The ensuing challenges to moral philosophy from this account of agency probe the limits of accountability, especially as intentional agency cannot fully ground accountability and the question of how to theorize critique and social change.

Against understanding subjectivity as an achievement of self-consciousness and autonomous agency, Butler's work argues for thinking of subjectivity as an unending process of formation that never culminates in full independence or self-sufficiency. Instead, becoming a subject means to be formed and undone in relations to others and norms in ways that one can never fully reflectively grasp. Despite the important role that Butler attributes to social norms in subject formation, individuals are not the marionettes of those norms. Rather, Butler accounts for subject formation in subjection to norms as being irreducible to either a deterministic or an arbitrary relation to these norms. One key concept of these debates as well as of Butler's attempts to explain her account of subject formation has been the notion of performativity. The original concept of performativity comes from J. L. Austin's speech-act theory, through which Austin introduced the performative as a way to consider how an utterance can create a reality. One of the most famous examples for such a performative speech-act is the pronunciation of two people as married. In *How To Do Things with Words*, Austin considered several ways in which the performative can fail.[19] Derrida subsequently offered a deconstructive reading of these failures to demonstrate that the performative works only insofar as it always also mobilizes its own failure, since it cannot ensure its own success.[20] Derrida and Austin both consider performativity solely within the context of philosophy of language, but Butler—while drawing on their work—goes beyond them to mobilize performativity to theorize subject formation. For her reworking of performativity, two aspects are key: first, performativity is not performance, and second, performativity offers a way to understand how social norms and schemes of intelligibility form subjects.

Butler laid out her concept of performativity for the first time in *Gender Trouble*, taking up Nietzsche to argue "that there need not be a 'doer behind the deed,' but that the 'doer' is variably constructed in and through the deed" (*GT* 181). Butler argues that what we have in the first instance is the deed or action and that we ascribe it only belatedly, in considering an action, to a doer or agent. Even more radically, for Butler there is no agent as such prior to the deed, but the agent is an aftereffect of the deed. The agent is a peculiar effect, insofar as this effect (the agent) is taken to be the cause and source of what becomes its own origin (the action). The challenges to conventional accounts of subjectivity and agency result from the implications of this account of performative subject formation, because one can no longer try to trace back from actions to the intentions beneath them and evaluate agents according to their intentions. An ethics of the pure will is, in other words, no longer possible. Moreover, consequentialist accounts that focus on the effects of actions equally come into question, insofar as the concept of responsibility still relies on tracing effects and actions back to their authors, who are then held accountable for them. If indeed the links between intentions, actions, and effects are reconceived as a field of phenomena that is not preceded and controlled by agents but through which agents become constituted, then neither intentions nor agents taking into account effects of their actions can any longer be the basic principle of responsibility.

This challenge to the conscious agent nonetheless does not mean that one would have to subscribe to a monistic account of imagining that acts create subjects ex nihilo. For our considerations about subject formation and agency, the key insight from Butler's concept of performativity is that acts cannot simply be traced back to agents and the intentions that preceded them. There is no original or authentic self or individual that only later enters into relations with others and comes to act on a social scene. Rather, Butler's account offers a rigorous way of considering how social norms, practices, and institutions need to be taken into account as co-constitutive of subjects as well as of their acts. The difficulty for moral philosophy and more specifically for reflections on questions of accountability and political and social agency is then to think how this co-constitution requires but also allows a thorough reworking of our conceptions of individual responsibility and accountability.[21]

An avenue into such a rethinking lies in mobilizing the account of how norms and their repetition are at the heart of how we come to be conscious and deliberating subjects. To understand subject formation as orchestrated by norms, normalization, and subjection, as Butler elucidates further in *Bodies That Matter*, does not mean to argue that subjects are fully determined by these norms. Butler clarifies in *Bodies That Matter* that performativity is the reiteration of norms by which one becomes intelligible as a subject (see *BTM* 94–95). The performatively emerging subject is the product of the repetition of the social norms that confer intelligibility. It would be to mistake the core idea of performativity to understand this subject as one of *performing* the repetition of norms, as if in a theatrical performance in which one comes along as such-and-such an individual and enacts another particular role on the stage that then enacts, "seduces to life," this stage persona. Instead, the repetition of norms is "what enables a subject and constitutes the temporal condition for the subject" (*BTM* 95), and this repetition occurs in a ritualized form, constituting the subject over time. As Butler has repeatedly argued, this mode of subjection does not make subjects into puppets determined by norms; instead, subjection brings about unruly subjects because of the excess and indeterminacy of meaning, power, and agency as norms work by producing their own failures. The points of resistances that these failures produce are not the conscious acts of subjects, but these gaps and breakages are the condition of possibility for directed action and transformation.

There are three different sources Butler draws on to explain the workings of these gaps and resistances and to mobilize them. First, she engages Foucault's conviction that there is no "outside" to power but that power relations always also proliferate and produce that which escapes them. Second, drawing on psychoanalysis, Butler argues that subject formation works by bringing about passionate attachments and the unconscious that are not simply continuous with social norms. Rather, "the unspeakably social endures" (*CHU* 153) unconsciously but insolently and continues to interrupt and traverse the conscious subject and seemingly fixed social norms. Third, taking up Derrida, Butler considers the iterability and citationality of signs and norms, which temporalize the process of subject formation and seize upon the temporality, historicity, and changeability of norms as well as of subjects and their identities. Butler speaks of resignification to explain the particular mode through which certain terms, signs, and identities are reclaimed, changed, and mobilized in new and unforeseen ways.[22]

Drawing on Foucault, Butler offers us a way of understanding power's self-subversion by explaining how the effects of subjectivation exceed their occasion and so "undermine the teleological aims of normalization" (*PLP* 93). Foucault argues that in order to understand the much greater scope of power in modern Western societies in the ways that power produces subjects through social regulation and normalization, it is necessary to turn away from finding power exclusively in repressive sanctions. Instead, we must consider how power is administered through various instantiations of norms and stipulations, rather than working within a narrow conception of power as the exercise of punishment and blunt force. This social administration of power works through practices of regulation by producing and dividing the normal from the abnormal. That which counts as "abnormal," such as the insane, the sexually aberrant, the criminal, does not preexist its regulation and becomes subsequently an occasion and object for normalization. For Foucault, the power relation in normalization produces and reproduces the abnormal as that which is to be continuously regulated.

Normalization is not simply a repressive social regime but actually brings forth a flourishing "dark underside" of the normal. The regulatory and productive power of social norms implies that neither the normal nor the abnormal—and hence no agency—is outside of power, regulation, and normalization. Even if the regulatory power of social norms produces their own subversion, these occasions of subversion are never beyond the reach of the social power and norms to which they owe their existence. Consequently, this proliferation of resistances, considered alone, might seem to trivialize the difficulties of social change and political and ethical agency. However, Butler offers a more complicated account by incorporating insights from psychoanalysis. In *Contingency*, *Hegemony*, *Universality*, she explains that she aims to articulate "a theory of agency that takes into account the double workings of social power and psychic reality" (*CHU* 151) and that a strictly Foucauldian analysis cannot "appreciate the instabilities that inhere in identificatory practices" (*CHU* 151). Drawing on psychoanalysis thus allows Butler to consider both the complexity of psychic life and those instabilities that ensue from the ambivalences of our relations to social norms and practices insofar as they produce attachments and identifications. With psychoanalysis we can understand subject formation as a process of subjection that is not simply externally imposed but fueled as well by the subject's investments in this subjection.[23] The resulting challenge for moral philosophy is that desires—and in particular the desire to live well—become ambivalent and can no longer directly provide a critical perspective on social norms and processes of normalization.

Although desires cannot ensure a critical perspective on regimes of normalization, the unconscious life of attachments and identifications is not simply continuous with the conscious life of desire. By considering social practices and norms as forming the subject through identificatory practices, Butler elaborates an account of how normalization brings forth a divided subject. That which does not conform to normality neither is annihilated nor preexists the subject as such; rather, what does not conform to normality is produced and reproduced within the subject: "[T]he unconscious is . . . a certain mode in which the unspeakably social endures" (*CHU* 153). As the subject emerges through its subjection to rules and norms, it is never fully fitting, never fully reducible to these rules and norms, but constantly undone from within. With psychoanalysis, Butler theorizes how norms address and bring about attachments as well as sustain (albeit not in an easily accessible manner) that which threatens the coherence and normality of the subject. These attachments are formed by means of identification and by taking up and becoming passionately invested in the positions and practices that are socially and psychically available. These positions or practices cannot be generalized as being liberatory or oppressive, as in the case of queer people who end up joining groups that aim to "heal" "aberrant sexual orientations" or women who seem to participate in their own disempowerment and oppression. The strength of Butler's account is that it does not explain these constellations as occasions of false consciousness or delusions. Rather, the difficulty lies in the confluence of social normalization and psychic investments and identifications. Consequently, the potential that disrupts the normalization cannot be mobilized easily but also always threatens to disrupt both the subject as well as the social horizon of its formation.

The efficacy of norms' ordering social relations relies on a self-subversion and repetition by reproducing that which resists not only in terms of certain subjects who are on the fringes of what counts as normal and acceptable, but within the subject itself. In her argument, Butler not only adds the dimension of the unconscious and the split subject to Foucault's analysis of the proliferation of resistances, but further contends that the relative stability as well as instability of the subject and the subjecting norms and normalizing forms of social power rely on the repetition of this formative process: "The Foucaultian subject is never fully constituted in subjection . . . ; it is repeatedly constituted in subjection, and it is in the possibility of a repetition that repeats against its origin that subjection might be understood to draw its inadvertently enabling power" (*PLP* 94). In the repeated inhabiting and appropriating of the norms and practices that animate this subjection and subject formation lies the potential for change, for repeating the norms and practices in not quite the same way they arrived. Insofar as the regulating norms and practices are actualized and sustained only by being rehearsed and enacted, this repetition is precisely where the possibility of change and reworking is located.

The difficulty in considering this possibility of reworking and resignifying norms and practices in terms of agency arises when we attempt to think about precisely how this agency is possible, if agency also comprises the capacity to deliberate and decide what to do. Additionally, we have to keep in mind that an analytical account of agency poses the question of evaluative criteria that might guide this agency in deliberation and decision-making but that a theory of agency is not a substitute for further critical examination of this problematic normative dimension. The potential for reworking norms and practices does not say anything yet about how to evaluate the different projects that might aspire to bring about change, but it very clearly poses the question of normativity as a challenge to moral philosophy in considering how it mobilizes particular accounts of the subject and agency.[24] Butler's interventions allow for refocusing the issue of agency as a critical question by considering agency as constituted in relation to social norms and as an issue of a broader structural reworking, thus dislodging the individual as the focus for agential power.

In this way, the perspective of ethics is dislodged from the narrow perspective of the individual, which is only subsequently generalized into a broader perspective of "each and every individual." Instead, because the individual as such is not recuperable as a monadic unit and starting point, the question of social ethics becomes co-constitutive alongside the question of individual ethics. In particular, within this perspective of social ethics, structural violence becomes a horizon of investigation that inquires into violence precisely insofar as its occurrence is not reducible to frameworks of intentional acts of individual agents. Such inquiries ask how violence is exerted through institutions and practices that administrate and proliferate unlivable lives and systemically allow certain lives to be treated as dispensable. This does not mean that such considerations put an end to holding individuals accountable; rather, we have to understand that systemic problems cannot be solved by a symbolic act of individuals being held accountable for their roles in exacerbating and exploiting the systemic problems. Rather than individual agency being treated as a preestablished condition of ethics, it is a persistent question and problematic that is conditioned and exceeded by social, economic, and political practices and institutions. The potentials of individual agency are never absolute but become possible when the practices and institutions that we take for granted come into question.

Our relationship to norms and practices and the terms and discourses in which we are bound up entail a necessary gap or ill fit insofar as no individual is reducible to a set of norms or names. Such necessary misrecognition, however, does not yet ensure a particular reworking of these norms or names and the social contexts that subtend them. This necessary misrecognition makes it *possible* that the norms and practices through which we become recognized can *possibly* be taken up differently and changed, but this necessary misrecognition by no means *is* or ensures critical assessment of social norms and social change. Political action and concerted efforts to change our circumstances are not necessary outcomes of being at odds with the norms, as Butler indicates when she asks, "What are the possibilities of politicizing *dis*identification, this experience of *misrecognition*, this uneasy sense of standing under a sign to which one does and does not belong?" (*BTM* 219). One both does and does not belong, both is and is not—this is the strange experience of one's being able neither fully to embrace nor fully to refuse the name, the position, the sign that one comes to inhabit, under which one comes to find oneself interpellated. The key to politicization seems to lie in this "*experience* of misrecognition," which Butler describes as "uneasy" and which demands a response. The possibility of politicization is, then, bound to "[taking] up the political signifier (which is always a matter of taking up a signifier by which one is oneself already taken up, constituted, initiated)" (*BTM* 219). Butler offers that the political potential may emerge in a certain kind of taking up, assuming, and accepting the signifier that one did not choose and whose history one comes to inherit or in whose history one begins to find oneself (sometimes strangely) implicated. But to be able to assume that unchosen name and situation by which one was chosen, in ways that mobilize political potential and agency, a certain alienation and estrangement through that situation seem to be necessary.

This account of alienation as mobilizing the possibility of a critical perspective, I argue, should not mean that political agency is reduced to a very narrow existential foundation of politics. It also does not yet say anything about the kind of politics that might ensue. But it seems correct to me that experiences that put us at odds with any set of accepted governing norms and interpretations are necessary to be able critically to engage with them. This critical engagement is not yet a particular value judgment and means in this instance nothing more than that one queries the governing norms and that they lose their unquestionable status. This means that there is a kind of unsettling, a possibly painful—at least "uneasy"—experience that one has to undergo and that keeps political life alive but is also the crux of any politics that strives to ameliorate politically the conditions of life. As Butler remarks, "That there can be no final or complete inclusivity is thus a function of the complexity and historicity of a social field that can never be summarized by any given description, and that for democratic reasons, ought never to be" (*BTM* 221). The trouble—and often painful experience—is that not only is this impossibility of final inclusivity, the necessary movement of exclusions and struggles over the negotiation of these delimitations in the social, a systemic phenomenon, but there are actual persons living and undergoing these exclusions and struggles. The task is to hold both perspectives in view as one asks precisely what this "politicization"

means, how we come to grapple with the impossibility of final inclusivity without giving up the possibility of change and ameliorating the violence of exclusion.[25]

We can now formulate more clearly what might be cast as the "problem of agency" with regard to Butler's theory of subject formation and the challenges her account poses to moral philosophy. First is the problematic of how to understand agency as the ability to act willfully and deliberately. Second is the question of how to reflect on principles that orient or ought to orient our actions without rendering moral philosophy an endeavor of grounding a normative framework of abstract principles.

Until her more recent publications—*Giving an Account of Oneself* in particular, but also *Undoing Gender* and *Precarious Life*—Butler's focus in engaging questions of agency seems to have been twofold. First, her starting point has been—and continues to be, even in these later works—that one cannot understand agency outside of relations of power and the formative effects of social norms. Second, she has repeatedly attempted to formulate how undoing a voluntaristic conception of the subject and agency does not entail the abolition of agency. Her accounts aim to demonstrate precisely why a theory of subject formation that argues that there is no subject prior to or outside of formation by norms does not mean that the emergent subjects are predetermined by these norms. The challenge ensuing from these accounts is how to articulate the relation between the gaps and unforeseeable effects traced to this point and the capacity intentionally to bring about certain effects that have a distinct political and ethical character. The inevitable resistances, gaps, and failures of the various repetitions and interactions with norms, practices, and institutions through which we emerge are an undirected and in fact unwilled phenomena, whereas reflected and willed resistance is a directed and conscious act. The question, in other words, is how to theorize agency in relation to these gaps and breaks without resorting to a voluntaristic subject who takes up these breaks in a particular way to turn them against the contested norms and demands, which would then be legible as an instance of agency.

As Saba Mahmood has incisively argued in *Politics of Piety*, it would be problematic to consider agency only through the paradigm of resistance and the subversion of dominant norms and institutions. She explains that such a move presupposes and reinscribes a particular liberal framework that presumes a particular universal desire for freedom from social regulation and conceives of agency only insofar as individuals come to act in opposition to social frameworks. Understanding agency strictly in terms of resistance, according to Mahmood, "elides dimensions of human action whose ethical and political status does not map onto the logics of repression and resistance."[26] I would add that conceiving of agency solely in terms of social change runs a similar danger by reifying either a blind ideal of progress or an equally blind ideal of constant change. Mahmood asks that we think agency rather with respect to a broader spectrum of aspects such as "modes of being, responsibility, and efficacy."[27] My own argument is in part in line with Mahmood's for understanding agency within a broader subject-formative framework, as I am arguing that we need to consider how Butler's challenges to thinking agency make possible and necessary a rethinking of responsibility and critique as key to moral philosophy. But eventually my argument focuses on a different concern from Mahmood's, since I am concerned with the question of deliberate and critical action, which remains an important aspect of understanding agency within moral philosophy. A difficult task ensuing from Butler's arguments is to reconsider agency and deliberate and critical action without falling back into centering on the intentional will of the subject as the primary source for assessing agency and subsequent issues of accountability.

As an aspect of this reconsideration of agency, it seems important to approach resignification as an effect of the repetition of norms and practices that is not already resistance in the sense that Mahmood calls into question here. Inhabiting norms works by citation and repetition of these norms and involves a resignification—or does so if we agree that in this process of inhabiting, taking up, and citing the normative frameworks is an appropriation that does not repeat these frameworks utterly identically but instead infuses them with life in different contexts at different times. Resignification is at work whenever norms are embodied, inhabited, and practiced, even if this resignification is not mobilized in terms of resisting or subverting dominant norms. However, Butler's earlier publications do seem to imply an understanding of agency that suggests at least a very close tie between resignification and resistance by virtue of the situations that Butler has drawn upon for her theoretical accounts, such as the example of Rosa Parks and the civil rights movement or that of queer activism. More recently, especially in *Giving an Account of Oneself*, Butler has turned explicitly to theorize modes of self-formation and the role of relations to others while continuing to argue that none of these relations are formed beyond the realm of social norms and relations of power.[28] In the following two chapters, I take up some of Butler's later works alongside the work of Emmanuel Levinas and Jean Laplanche in order to propose a rethinking of responsibility both as a mode of subject formation and as a concept of moral conduct. My argument in this book, however, is that a theoretical consideration of ethics is not reducible to questions of self-formation. Particularly Butler's work on subject formation through normalization and her challenges to theorizing agency allow us to rethink critique as a key concept that raises the relation between justice and power as a horizon for ethical deliberation.

In arguing for deliberation as retaining an important role in critique and agency in the context of moral philosophy, my concern here is somewhat different from Mahmood's engagement with Butler. Mahmood argues for understanding agency in relation to ethical self-formation as a practice of inhabiting available social and otherwise normative frameworks.[29] For me, the question of agency as a matter for moral philosophy is not confined to questions of resistance but is more generally about what it means for the subject as "I" when this "I" comes to deliberate, decide, and act in relation to others, to situations, to customs and institutions. So the challenge is first to reflect on the ways in which self-relations are formed and practiced through acting in particular ways in relation to others as well as to particular social surroundings. Second, and crucially, the challenge is to theorize the formation of self-relations without reinscribing the self-relation as a site of authenticity as well as without turning the self-relation into a pure effect of the impingement of social norms and demands. Further, we need to consider the ways in which we can account for critical action without reducing agency either to mandatory resistance or to voluntaristic individual choices. In other words, the two challenges to agency that Butler's work delivers to moral philosophy are first the question of self-relation and deliberation, without returning to stark opposition between social norms and the individual, and second the question of accounting for critique and criteria while falling into neither a foundationalist nor a relativist account.

The focus and terms through which Butler has examined agency have shifted considerably over the course of her publications. In one of her early pieces entitled "Contingent Foundations," one of the debates within *Feminist Contentions*, Butler insisted that "agency is always and only a political prerogative,"[30] emphasizing the political aspect of being able to act with power, of being recognizable in one's aspirations as political contender, and of agency as delimited by relations of power and social norms. More recently, she has been reflecting on agency as a mode of self-constitution that does not need to be political in any strong sense, even if it is always constituted within political and social frameworks. In her essay "What Is Critique?" she inquires into subject formation as a "burden of formation" that is negotiated at the intersection of social norms and ethical demands and that, with regard to Foucault's notion of "arts of existence," is understood as "a cultivated relation of the self to itself."[31] In one of her latest works, *Giving an Account of Oneself*, she rearticulates the intertwinement between subject formation as an effect of the operation of norms and subject self-formation in relation to these norms. The reflexive relation that any subject can have to itself is always already constituted and traversed by these very norms in ways that are never fully knowable to the subject: "It is one thing to say that a subject must be able to appropriate norms, but it is another to say that there must be norms that prepare a place within the ontological field for a subject" (*GA* 9). That said, a certain distance from norms is necessary, which requires at the same time that one comport oneself toward those norms.

Butler also reminds us of another kind of distance from these norms by which we are always already constituted, namely, the distance that occurs in one's unknowingness of how precisely these norms structure oneself. This distance, in the sense of one's unknowingness about oneself, is at the same time also a lack of distance that continuously traverses one's ability to emerge at a distance from those norms in a critical relation to them. As Patricia Purtschert argues, critique figures in Butler as an ethical practice insofar as the subject's lived self-relation in relation to social norms becomes a question for the subject.[32] With this double perspective on social norms and subject formation, critique is located at the intersection of politics and ethics as a practice, or in other words, as a mode of agency.

Rather than understanding Butler's earlier accounts of agency as having been reversed, overcome, or perfected by her more recent accounts, we can see that the earlier accounts still figure within her more recent formulations by offering an analytics of how social norms produce subjects and delimit agency. In order to consider questions of self-formation, it remains important to analyze what kinds of acts and subjects become recognizable within the given conditions and are legitimized by a dominant set of epistemological frameworks. Moreover, agency cannot be theorized as a practice of self-formation without reflecting on the complicating challenge that Butler's work poses by arguing that the ways in which we are formed through social norms and processes of normalization constitutively cannot be fully known by us.

Yet the problematic of agency does not stop here at the level of not being able to know in what ways one is entangled and formed, blinded by, and invested in the social norms to which one comes to relate. The question of agency is more complicated, if we take seriously Butler's argument that the agent that is identified as the source and cause of an action and its effects is a belated construct and that the effects of actions reconstitute both the initial action as well as the agent to whom the action is attributed. Butler does not eliminate the intentional subject but she has consistently argued that the intentional subject and its intentions cannot fully control the action and its effects and meanings. In her contribution "Contingent Foundations" in *Feminist Contentions*, Butler contends that the act exceeds the agent, which in turn exposes the problematic of agency because the effects of an action can inaugurate effects themselves in places and ways that had not been foreseen. Nevertheless, when Butler argues that "the action continues to act after the intentional subject has announced its completion,"[33] she invokes an *intentional* subject that is able to reflect on its action and consider it completed.[34] The subject, however, is dispossessed of its act, as the action always goes beyond the subject.

Precisely because the agent is always exceeded and dispossessed by his or her act, it becomes even more pressing to reconsider what it means to hold someone accountable for what he or she does and what categories other than accountability we might find at the heart of moral conduct. Insofar as Butler's deconstruction of conventional accounts of the subject and agency raise debates framed with political and ethical urgency, her accounts have demonstrated how the subject and agency are more than simply ontological conceptual constructs. What is being deconstructed are entities and metaphysical residues still at the very core of our understanding of what makes ethics and politics possible. In this way Butler's arguments become critical interventions for moral philosophy, because they reveal how theorizing accountability relies on a certain account of agency and the subject to be in place already. The challenge that ensues here is how to rethink agency without giving it up, in order not simply to uphold responsibility and accountability as moral philosophical concepts that are premised on theories of agency, will, and intention, but to mobilize the critical intervention for a rethinking of these concepts and the ways in which they structure social realities.

PART TWO

Responsibility

THREE

Responsibility as Response: Levinas and Responsibility for Others

Subject formation in relation to responsibility and moral philosophy pertains to the question of what it means to think about the formation of the subject as an ethical subject or, in other words, as an ethical agent. It is possible to approach this question of ethical agency through the issues of the will and intentionality, as described in the last chapter, in order to outline how questions of responsibility can guide decision-making and deliberation as modes of intentional action. But rather than taking such an approach, I would like to begin this discussion by reflecting on the consequences for thinking about responsibility if we take into account that we become self-conscious individuals who act and respond only in and through relations to others.  If we think about the formation of the "I" in relation to responding to others, and if this question of responding becomes not only a question of responding but also one of responding *well*, then this relation to others in which the "I" emerges as the one who responds is a relation of responsibility.

By considering responsibility in terms of responding, Butler's *Giving an Account of Oneself,* in conversation with Emmanuel Levinas—especially in his *Otherwise Than Being*[1]—offers a way of thinking responsibility as not primarily or exclusively restricted to the sense of being held accountable for one's actions. The aspect of responding to others becomes important for Butler somewhat differently from for Levinas. For Levinas, the encounter with the other can never be reduced or sublated into consciousness; it precedes all empirical social and political realities and therefore can never be known by the self-conscious subject who is formed through the encounter with the other. For Butler, the self-conscious "I" is also characterized by a constitutive opacity or constitutive impossibility of full self-knowledge; this opacity results from how none of us can ever fully tell the story of our own origination and so can never account accurately for all factors that form us from a distance. For Butler, unlike for Levinas, it is precisely the implication in social realities that renders the subject partially opaque to itself in the ways in which social norms condition its formation and the ways in which its desires and attachments are formed in relation to others. On the one hand, such an account of subject formation that takes place in partial blindness in relation to social norms and in relation to others poses a problematic for theorizing responsibility. On the other hand, as I elaborate further in this chapter, such an account and the ensuing problematic also proffer an occasion for rethinking the concept of responsibility through understanding it as a response to an address and, in particular, as a response in relation to others.

In *Giving an Account of Oneself,* Butler insists that the notion of the other is not reducible to the sociality of norms (see, e.g., *GA* 24). There is a qualitative difference, she argues, between the fact that norms implicate us in social contexts and the fact that we are always, willingly or unwillingly, in relations with others. These relations with others are, however, not outside social and cultural horizons that are constituted through social norms and are continuously traversed by these norms, because in those encounters we continuously negotiate these norms. In Butler's earlier works, the other had become very quickly assimilated into the agent of the law, to become the embodied demand of the social norms and personified social regulations. In *Giving an Account of Oneself,* Butler returns to this idea of interpellation and the subject's emergence on the basis of an openness to being addressed. Further, she explicitly considers how our relations to others and our being addressed by them are different from the addresses and demands that norms and laws deliver. Central to Butler's considerations is, in parallel with her earlier work, an insistence that we are not first alone in the world and then subsequently encounter others and the demands that are made upon us, but that being addressed constitutes us as subjects from the very beginning. Moreover, this situation is one of being called to respond despite a crucial incapacity to respond fully adequately and in an utterly timely way. Engaging with these aspects, Butler turns to the thought of Levinas, who was concerned with formulating how the subject is brought about only by a demand of the other and with arguing this situation of subject formation as an inevitably ethical one.[2]

Levinas formulates this coming to consciousness as an event that happens through a kind of unanswerable demand in relation to the other. This scene more specifically in Levinas is one of being accused and taken hostage by the other, and this being taken hostage characterizes in his terms precisely the situation of responsibility. Especially in Levinas's *Otherwise Than Being*, the terminology of persecution is closely intertwined with if not constitutive of responsibility. Butler tarries with this proximity of persecution and responsibility but does not offer the same affirmative use of persecution and being taken hostage; rather, she uses the language of exposure, openness, susceptibility, and vulnerability to the other. Insofar as Levinas's usage of "responsibility" is not without troubles, I would like to consider him in conversation with Butler's work to reflect on the role and status of responsibility in subject formation in terms of responsiveness and responsibility towards others, which cannot be reduced merely to responsiveness to and responsibility toward norms and rules.

It is important to keep in mind that the "responsibility for the other," as Levinas offers it to us, is also not a full account of responsibility within the realm of moral philosophy, since he articulates a responsibility that is preontological, which we can represent only by betraying and which, as he tells us, cannot be turned into a model.[3] "Responsibility for the other," at the core of Levinas's thought, is a responsibility that is more primary than and precedes all conscious deliberation and intention. For moral philosophy, however, responsibility also implies questions about how to guide deliberation and decision-making. Even so, this relation of responsibility as a condition of the emergence of the moral subject comes to frame the horizon in which moral philosophy considers questions of responsible action. In

Levinas, this latter kind of responsibility is tied to the question of justice and laws and emerges only on the basis of a prior exposedness and responsibility toward being addressed by an other.

The other is at the core of Levinas's project of dislodging subject-centered thinking. The subject emerges only as overwhelmed and interrupted by the other, and importantly, this encounter has an ethical valence because it brings about the subject as an ethical subject. Prior to the encounter with the other there is certainly no ethical subject, and even more radically, without this overwhelming of an encounter with the other, we cannot even speak about subjectivity. In theorizing the subject as emerging through primary responsibility for and to the other, there can be no subject other than through being enjoined by the other outside all possibility to choose or decline this responsibility. Levinas argues that the subject cannot be taken as preestablished ontological reality and he offers an approach that insists on "the priority of the other."

However, in taking up Levinas and this "priority of the other" in endeavors to theorize social, ethical, or political relations, we encounter a challenge not simply to shift the site of ontological stability and coherence on itself from the subject-self to "the other" by introducing "the priority of the other." The radicalism of Levinas's thought is that neither "the other," "others," nor an "I" can be recovered as ontological entities preceding the encounter. Thus we have to be mindful that making "the other" a central issue for theorizing subject formation runs the risk of reestablishing the subject at the center of thought—only now as "the other." So the difficulty in engaging with and writing about Levinas and subject formation lies not only in the complexity of Levinas's thinking. Levinas inquires into and brings into crisis the notion of the self-conscious subject as autonomous by exposing the subject and its consciousness as nonoriginal and fundamentally dispossessed because it is constitutively and irrecoverably traversed and troubled by the encounter with the other. In Levinas, this "other" is nearly more enigmatic than the troubled subject. While the "other" is certainly related to those others that one encounters and to one's own being as an other to others, nonetheless the other is in Levinas also closely related to the otherness of a divine other.

Whereas Butler can offer the encounter with the other as "belonging to an idealized dyadic structure of social life" (*GA* 90), for Levinas the encounter cannot be an idealized version of a social reality, because the other is not

any specific and definite other person and such a return into the social to him, it seems, would mean to reinstitute a centering on the subject that he attempts to undo. In my opinion, Butler can take the encounter as an idealized version of the social encounter without being reductive, because, unlike for Levinas, who rejected these theories, psychoanalysis and the unconscious play an important role in Butler's thinking.[4] The other as another person, in Butler, is always also traversed by an otherness inside the individual that is not contained in the subject, as I cannot be said to possess "my" unconscious. But this otherness of the unconscious is neither presocial nor beyond the social—at least this is so in the way Butler has engaged psychoanalysis, from Freud and Lacan in *Subjects of Desire* to (most recently) Jean Laplanche in *Giving an Account of Oneself*.[5] I return to Laplanche in Chapter 4 to inquire further into the consequences of this psychoanalytic dimension for thinking about responsibility in the context of moral philosophy. In this chapter I would like to focus on a consideration of Butler and Levinas in the encounter with the other and our openness to others as fundamental for thinking about responsibility.

Reading Levinas more pronouncedly than Butler does, as giving us an account of how the subject emerges as a moral subject,[6] I will argue for the importance of attending to the gap between an account of the formation of the moral subject and an account of responsibility in terms of responsible action and moral conduct. Since Levinas notoriously frames the scene of the subject's emergence as one of accusation and, even more, of it being persecution and being taken hostage by the other which brings about the subject as responsible for the other, I discuss this scene with regard to the Nietzschean critique of becoming a moral subject through a violence that then becomes endowed with moral value.

Further, I would like to address a common concern about Levinas's theoretical framework that is somewhat different from the Nietzschean critique—or perhaps pinpoints a particular aspect of the Nietzschean critique. This common concern about Levinas is that his version of the primary ethical encounter yields a normative version of self-sacrifice or a prohibition on self-defense in the face of an aggressor. While I discuss some problems that Levinas poses, in particular regarding the rhetorical dimension of *Otherwise Than Being*, one strength of his thinking, it seems to me, is that it opens the field for an inquiry into the relation between subject formation and moral philosophy. This strength, to my mind, lies in how his thinking makes very clear the importance of interrupting attempts to deduce normative injunctions and rules for moral conduct from inquiries into subject formation. One dimension of marking and mobilizing this gap for critical inquiry becomes available by putting Butler into conversation with Levinas in order to examine the role of social norms in conditioning possibilities for the encounter and responsibility. So, on the one hand, we will attend to the discontinuity between giving an account of subject formation and an account of coordinates for responsibility, and on the other hand, we will inquire into the consequences that framing subject formation in a particular way has for delimiting the question of moral conduct. In particular, I will examine the role of ambivalence in relation to aggression and suffering and argue for a dislodging of responsibility from accountability and of ethical deliberation from self-justification in order to explore understanding responsibility as being primarily a matter of addressing and responding.

Ambivalent Addresses

While Levinas's criticism of the common notion of the self-reflexive and self-present subject as the foundation of the subject—and especially the moral subject—can be understood as being compelled by an ethical commitment, it would be too hasty to claim that he is writing primarily moral philosophy. He is concerned with articulating the "otherwise than being" from which we must begin if we want to consider the subject as an individual and as an agent and which will continue to traverse any account of moral philosophy.[7] In *Otherwise Than Being*, he considers ethical language as the language to which a phenomenological attempt is compelled if it tries to disarticulate the subject's primacy and priority as the starting point, aim, and principle for philosophical inquiry (see *OTB* 116). Philosophy that takes the subject as the principle for philosophy is bound, for Levinas, to philosophical approaches that privilege the individual and that begin from a right of the individual subject to self-preservation. In such approaches, according to Levinas, the "autonomous individual" becomes the principle for thought and as such is precisely not called into question by philosophy but is continuously reinscribed as its origin and condition that makes thought possible in the first place. The problem for Levinas with privileging the subject is that there is no openness toward the other in this kind of thought as well as in this kind of subject, because any encounter with an other turns only into a matter of reaffirming the self of the subject.

The terminology that Levinas uses to wrestle with this issue and that traverses his text in *Otherwise Than Being* is that of the *arche*, which means both principle and origin, and in contrast to that, he introduces the *anarchical*, the nonprincipled and nonoriginal. So a philosophy that begins with and grounds itself in consciousness will yield a subject that "is always a self-possession, sovereignty, *arche*."[8] Such a subject is a vision and version of the subject that fundamentally remains closed off from the other, because others are first encountered as threats to self-sovereignty. The conceptions of responsibility and justice that such philosophical approaches subsequently yield are founded on and aiming toward maintaining and achieving the subject's independence over and against others. Levinas does not argue that such a view is contradicted—or affirmed—by our experiences, but he insists that we can never arrive at thinking an ethical subject adequately if we begin with this self-sovereign consciousness.

That said, if Levinas was mainly concerned with thinking "ethics as first philosophy,"[9] we still have to ask what it means to conceive of a first philosophy and what it means to conceive of that first philosophy as "ethics." Levinas writes:

> Ethical language, which phenomenology resorts to in order to mark its own interruption, does not come from an ethical intervention laid out over descriptions. It is the very meaning of approach, which contrasts with knowing. No language other than ethics could be equal to the paradox which phenomenological description enters in when, starting with the disclosure, the appearing of a neighbor, it reads it in its trace, which orders the face according to a diachrony which cannot be synchronized in representation. A description that at the beginning knows only being and beyond being turns into ethical language. (*OTB* 193 n.35)

Earlier in *Otherwise Than Being*, Levinas offers that "ethical terms [are] accusation, persecution, and responsibility for the others" (121). This "ethical language" is a language into which phenomenological description turns in the face of the paradox of trying to capture that which is beyond or otherwise than what can be rendered into something that can be known. The situation of what is "otherwise than being," its description, and the "ethical terms" used to capture it remain, as Levinas asserts, distinct from knowledge and unable to be properly represented in discourse. Levinas offers a critique of thinking that begins with ontology, but there seems to be a certain foreclosure of critique that his text performs, a certain hermeticism that is inscribed through the intensity of performing the emergence of the "I" that is not an autobiographical "I." It is and is not quite the "I" that we all share insofar as we all take it up to refer to ourselves, because the reports of the "I" in *Otherwise Than Being* describe how this first-person perspective, this "I" emerges. Yet these are not descriptions of experiences that all of us could be said to have had, since "[t]hese are not events that happen to an empirical ego" (*OTB* 115). Levinas aims to give an account of the coordinates that make for the framework in which experiences of an "I" become possible at all. Yet through the use of "I," the text produces this "I" as a site that refuses the reader any possibility in remaining at a comfortable distance from the text. The "I" in *Otherwise Than Being* never quite addresses itself to an audience; rather, it seems as if any reader's "I" is at stake and usurped (maybe, in Levinasian terminology, even to the point of being taken hostage and emerging in responsibility for this textual other).[10]

This discourse of the "I"'s emergence is neither a prescription to nor a description of the philosophical subject, because it is a discourse that speaks beyond and prior to all philosophy.[11] The vocative, the address that this discourse mobilizes carries a double dimension, insofar as this address constitutes the impossibility of the "I" as both an ethical and an ontological relationality to the other. In this address ethics and ontology are fused and yet not quite, because that originary address that disrupts and brings about the subject is precisely what remains irreducibly foreign to the conceptual discourses of both ethics and ontology. On the one hand, we are encountering a connotation of "I cannot" that describes this "I"'s incapacity which will delimit the field of this "I"'s possibilities—the "I" simply cannot and will not slip away from the responsibility to the other. On the other hand, we are encountering an ethical connotation of an "I cannot" that leaves open the "I"'s ability to do that which the "I" is coming to understand as an *ethical* impossibility. The question arising then is precisely how the descriptive aspect and the ethical aspect are intertwined. It appears as if the descriptive aspect arises to be addressed by developing a certain persuasive normative force that does not prescribe but instead seduces by a certain fusion of descriptive and prescriptive discourse.

Insofar as any discourse as a rhetorical act cannot help but aim to persuade and bring about assent, then we cannot fault descriptive discourse for acquiring and performing prescriptive demands. If it is not possible to remove the performative reentry of the prescriptive from discourse, this means only that it becomes crucial that a reflection on precisely this rhetorical dimension accompanies the discourse and opens it up to critical engagement. One way to such an opening might be made possible by reading Butler's considerations on address and transference. The category of address allows Butler to engage the scene of subject formation in Levinas with regard to a rhetorical quality that not only traverses the notion of the encounter with the other but also renders this scene as a theoretical account. The critical dimension of the category of address lies in how it allows us to question at the same time the content of an account of subject formation, on the one hand, and the relation and discontinuity between content and the rhetorical force that reaches beyond the text itself, on the other hand.

The ethical valence of the rhetorical dimension lies in its quality of posing an interruption insofar as the rhetorical aspect is not reducible to nor dissolvable into communicable content. By inquiring into the rhetorical in conjunction with psychoanalysis and in particular by bringing the notion of address and transference together, Butler's considerations enable a critical angle for examining the inevitable transference of desire that is at work in framing and sustaining discourses through the structure of address. Before engaging Butler and Laplanche on transference and responsibility in the next chapter, I would like to focus in this chapter on Levinas's formulation of responsibility for the other as mode of subject formation. In *Giving an Account of Oneself*, Butler's Levinasian account of the encounter with the other becomes supplemented and transformed as the scene of address enters as "the rhetorical condition for responsibility" (*GA* 50), because the encounter with the other is established in the form of an address, and the structure of this address becomes crucial to establishing and sustaining us in relations with others.[12]

Reading Levinas and Butler together on subject formation through the encounter with the other that is an address and that brings about the subject being as responsible for the other makes it possible to dislodge responsibility from accountability, which means that the primary meaning of responsibility does not come from a scene like the Nietzschean one in which an action is attributed to me and I am held responsible for this action. Theorizing responsibility as accountability begins with the notion of a subject who seems already to have done something of which it is considered guilty and about which this subject ought to have known better and acted differently. However, the Levinasian description of the "approach" by the other as being constitutive of the emergence of the subject which, for Levinas, compels the use of "ethical language" means that "responsibility," as a conceptual term, captures primarily the modality of the subject rather than a particular modality of actions. In other words, "responsibility" is moved into the realm of subject theory and away from the question of how to act in a given situation. This does not mean that "responsibility" no longer has any meaning with regard to this latter aspect—after all, one of the main claims underlying this book is that the accounts we give of subject formation have consequences for the accounts we come to give of moral conduct, because the former delimit the possibilities and trajectories of the latter.

As Butler demonstrates in *Giving an Account of Oneself*, the question of subject formation is not outside the scope of questions with which moral philosophy concerns itself. That said, examining Levinas with respect to the relation between subject formation and ethics, Butler does not read him directly as a moral philosopher. Rather, she reads him as offering an account of ethical subject formation, whereby ethics for Butler seems to pertain primarily to relations to others and especially in terms of responding to an other. I would like to emphasize more strongly the discontinuity between an account of subject formation and responsibility in ethical theory or moral philosophy while equally taking up Butler's insistence on not considering the moral subject and its emergence as already settled prior to entering into the realm of moral philosophy. Arguing against a seamless transition between an account of subject formation and an account of moral conduct, I elaborate below that it is important not to read Levinas's intervention all too quickly as moral philosophy. Rather we have to trace Levinas's account of subject formation carefully in order to open the field for an inquiry into its implications for moral philosophy. The next task in this section is, therefore, to disentangle this scene of the subject's emergence with regard to the face, the address, and the urgency of the other's demand, in order to ask precisely how the subject is formed through the response and in responsibility. I specifically examine the extreme asymmetry of this situation, which entails both an active overwhelming and a being overwhelmed. Finally, I ask what understanding of responsibility materializes here and what the nonnegotiable obligation that ensues from being overwhelmed by the other means for the question of freedom and agency.

The responsibility for the other that springs from the encounter with the other is explained by Levinas in *Entre Nous* as a proximity to and sensibility of being affected and enjoined by the other's vulnerability and mortality. This enjoining encounter with the other is the immediacy of the face that issues the command "You shall not kill" as being "the fact that I cannot let the other die alone, it is like a calling out to me" (*EN* 104). The face is the ultimate exposure of the other's helplessness and destitution, and in the encounter with the face, the death of the other figures as that which I cannot let happen. At the same time, this possibility of the other's death is precisely "in some way, an incitement to murder, the temptation to go to the extreme, to completely neglect the other" (*EN* 104). In this statement, the relation to the face emerges here as disorientingly ambiguous. While it is the face that relays the inescapable impossibility of silencing the demand of the other, the face also registers as an instigation to abandon and murder the other. All in one moment there is the responsibility for the other, the impossibility of just passing by the other, and the impossibility of not answering the cry for help, but at the same time this does not mean that the course of action is predetermined; the impossible always remains possible. The possibility that one will pass by, that one will remain silent, or that one might even inflict violence on the other remains real. While the other's demand cannot be silenced, the other's life remains precarious; the other can be killed.

The other's death is not only a possibility but also a temptation: "The other is the only being I can want to kill. I can want to" (*EN* 6). Levinas tells us that one can desire to murder the other, but it turns out that the actualization of this desire is the precise moment when the other has not been grasped: "[T]he other has escaped. . . . In killing, I can certainly *attain* a goal, . . . but then I have grasped the other in the opening of being in general, as an element of the world in which I stand. I have seen him on the horizon, I have not looked straight at him. I have not looked him in the face" (*EN* 9–10). Whereas one can want to kill the other, in doing so one will have evaded the face; the other will have been rendered into a faceless object. All that one achieves then is to carry out a violent act, but one will still have not been able to obliterate the other as the face that prohibits murder.[13]

The ambiguity at the heart of the relation to the other is that the face delivering the prohibition on killing is that very instance that also makes possible the wish to get rid of the other completely—and, even more so, this face *incites*, instills a desire, Levinas argues, to rid oneself of the other in the hope that the burden of responsibility for the other would then disappear. So not merely does it remain possible that one might not respond to the other adequately, that one might forget and neglect the other, but with the encounter of the face, Levinas delimits the scene of subject formation as instantiating both an ultimate responsibility and the temptation to murder. But how is it that the injunction not to kill works to tempt one to pass by, to kill and silence the other, whether from neglect or through a more overtly violent act? What is this weakness and helplessness of the face that it incites to murder? What is this call for responsibility that it tempts one to annihilate the other who delivers this call? The temptation to let the other die, to abandon the other, is instigated by the inescapable demand for responsibility. The challenge that Levinas presents here lies in an understanding of the common origin of the call for responsibility and temptation to murder, which is a crucial scene for Levinas that frames the horizon for subsequent considerations of how our constitutive relationality and openness to others figure.

This coincidence between responsibility and aggression might seem counterintuitive, and one might very well expect that the temptation to kill would exist independently from a relation of responsibility and that responsibility in fact emerged to counter this temptation—and thus is quite distinctly different from this temptation to murder. We can therefore read Levinas as criticizing an understanding that would begin with a primary aggressiveness that then gives rise to a bridling of this aggressive human nature and that this bridling is then subsequently identified with responsibility. If we follow Levinas, we begin with responsibility, but it is not an unambivalent responsibility, because the emergence of the moral subject is marked by the emergence of a desire for violence. Levinas alleviates neither the temptation nor the vastness of the responsibility for the other in his account. As Butler sums up in *Precarious Life*, this unalleviated situation means that "the face operates to produce a struggle for me, and establishes this struggle at the heart of ethics" (*PL* 135). Levinas is capturing, at the heart of subject formation, the struggle between the call of the other and the temptation to forsake the other. This means that the awakening to the face of the other is constitutively an awakening to being conflicted, and if the temptation to violence is issued by the face itself, then there is not only no subject but also no responsibility that could be pure and uncompromised. Hence if one wanted to purify theorizing subject formation within this conflict, one would simultaneously eradicate the very condition of the subject's awakening and attending to the call of the other.

For Levinas, it seems that becoming an ethical agent and a moral subject involves also the formation of an active desire to injure. Unlike Nietzsche, however, who argues that this active desire is then belatedly internalized in response to a countervailing environment, for Levinas there is no active desire that precedes the conflict in the subject. Nietzsche and Levinas seem to converge, though, in the view that emerging as a moral subject—as someone who comes to ask "what ought I do?" and "how ought I respond?"—is crucially bound up with struggles that are internal to the subject. For Levinas this struggle is not, as it is for Nietzsche, one of self-aggression, but it is a vexation in which there is intriguingly no room for self-ueberatement, because the other's demand overwhelms and enjoins prior to self-reflexivity. So even in the scene of being enjoined by the other, there is no "I" who could berate herself, and the demand, strictly speaking, overwhelms before there is an "I" who could be overwhelmed. The demand and address of the other radically exceed the subject precisely because they precede the subject. Responsibility hence concerns what reaches beyond and breaks with the internal struggles of the self, even if such struggles are crucial to ethical deliberation. But for Levinas, not only is there a departure from the concern with oneself and one's self insofar as the exteriority of action turns us towards the world and others and away from our internal vexations; the very point of departure in Levinas from which responsibility emerges is a situation where the self is undone by the other. Responsibility, in other words, emerges as what remains irreducible to and propels one beyond self-reflexive questioning of the moral self.

There is no time for the subject when and no place for the subject where there is no responsibility. There is no time or place when or where the subject has not already been approached by the other: "The unlimited responsibility in which I find myself comes from the hither side of my freedom, from a 'prior to every memory,' an 'ulterior to every accomplishment,' from the non-present par excellence, the non-original, the anarchical, prior to or beyond essence" (*OTB* 10). Precisely because the address absolutely exceeds the subject, "responsibility" in Levinas's account can no longer be thought of primarily in terms of one's accountability for one's actions and choices. The responsibility for the other is not a responsibility that one could have chosen, to which one could have agreed; the other overwhelms, and the "I" cannot even remember being overwhelmed and enjoined.

But this responsibility for the other is also without limit insofar as it is precisely not open to negotiation. Strictly speaking, the scene of the encounter with the other precedes consciousness. Consciousness thus can only belatedly and never adequately reconstruct and grasp this scene that conditioned its own possibility. This situation delimits a predicament for moral philosophy regarding responsibility and agency, because to emerge as an ethical agent is not separable from being unable to know whether one has not already yielded to this temptation to neglect the other. Levinas's account of ethical subject formation is radical because there is no subject who could remember and decide before the encounter with the other. If, then, the face is itself not only the prohibition on killing but also the incitement to kill, the emergent subject can know of its responsibility always only belatedly. Hence one's responsibility radically exceeds one's ability to account for oneself and to assume this responsibility consciously, because one has become responsible for the other's death before there was even an "I" that could have accepted or refused this responsibility and before there was an "I" that could have acted mindfully.

This "before," this "prior to every memory," denotes a strange temporality, because this scene of enjoinment as the "non-present par excellence" is not a nonpresence in the sense of a past that once was present and now is no longer present. It is a past that has never been present, but as such, it also has never been past. Levinas speaks of a "diachrony par excellence," which means that this "past" is not one that could be remembered, recollected, and re-presented in memory. A past that could be remembered would mean that consciousness could master this memory and return to itself that which always already happened—namely, the dispossession by the other. At the same time, it is not as if we are here reaching the point of origin of the subject, because the encounter is the *anarchical*, the nonoriginal, past of the subject. So not only is this nonpresence impossible to remember and synchronize in memory, but this nonpresence, while not being present and having never been present, is precisely *not absent*. It signifies that which cannot be surpassed and that continues to interrupt the present. The nonpresent as that which cannot possibly be assimilated into the presence of a temporal continuum is that which interrupts this continuum. In other words, the encounter with the other, the address by the face, is the moment when temporality as the progression of a present breaks down. The address has always already happened, and any response is coming irrecoverably too late, but nonetheless, precisely because of its belatedness, is only ever so much more urgent.

The problematic that we come to grasp here is one that arises out of the interlacing of the question of subject formation and moral philosophy, because responsibility and the constitutive relation to the other are bringing forth the subject precisely through the limitlessness and impossibility of this responsibility. The problematic, more specifically, is that the other's demand of one's presence is unlimited—unlimited both with regard to its beginning as well as with regard to what is demanded of the emergent subject. The other demands everything of the "I"; on the level of this dyadic encounter, there is no room for negotiation, for one's own plans, for the inconvenience of the other's call, not even for taking interest in one's own survival. Because of the irrecoverability of this diachrony, the reaction of the subject—the answer to the summon of the face—necessarily "misses a present which is already past of itself" (*OTB* 88) and which befalls the subject: "My presence does not respond to the extreme urgency of the assignation. I am accused of having delayed" (*OTB* 88–89). Levinas insists that even without having possibly been able to have acted otherwise, the address by the other arrives as an accusation. The "I" is accused of a nonaction, of having delayed, of not having been there for the other, of being too late—yet this passivity is not the passivity of a willful and voluntary "letting happen." The address in the scene of the encounter figures not only as a demand but necessarily also as an accusation, because the responsibility is older than the subject itself and cannot be suspended.

This accusation that Levinas inscribes as being at the core of subject formation is disturbing, because the subject emerges as always already accused of something that it did not will, that it *could not* will. The subject therefore emerges only under the burden of a responsibility to which it can never answer adequately.[14] Responsibility thus is radically severed from imputability on the basis of conscious and voluntary action. There are no deeds that precede the scene and for which the subject then becomes held responsible and accountable. Responsibility in the Levinasian formulation arrives as a responsibility for others that is impossible for us to assume by giving an account of what we did or did not do. Responsibility in Levinas peculiarly precedes the possibility of being able to will and act.

Butler approaches the unlinking of responsibility and accountability differently from Levinas, as for her the constitutive opacity that disorients the perspective of the "I" stems from both the dispossession of the "I" by virtue of social norms and a kind of primary relationality to others. Responsibility as accountability is brought into crisis by Butler, as the "I" can never fully know and adequately narrate and account for either its origins or the origins of its actions. The dimension of the social dispossession of the "I" that undercuts the possibility of attaining and producing full self-knowledge is that this "I" is never anyone's "I" alone, and as such—as well as in being recounted and rendered intelligible in discourse—the "first-person perspective" is always bound by, interrupted, and dispossessed by the social norms that confer intelligibility. As Butler explains: "[T]his interruption and dispossession of my perspective *as mine* can take place in different ways. There is the operation of a norm, invariably social, that conditions what will and will not be a recognizable account, exemplified in the fact that I am used by the norm precisely to the degree that I use it" (*GA* 36).

This dispossession by social norms is precisely that which I can never render transparent to myself as I speak, because I can make myself understood—paradoxically—only insofar as I undergo this dispossession, which cannot be made into a narrative or an account of the "I." The dispossession by the social norms on which we depend, as they govern our social frames of intelligibility, is not the same as the second dimension of the constitutive opacity due to our relations to others, a dimension that Butler offers by drawing more directly on the psychoanalyst Laplanche than on Levinas. There is an openness and exposure in being touched by others that are unwilled and that we cannot will away and that are, as Butler demonstrates, bound up with passionate attachments and desires that we can neither fully control nor render fully transparent to ourselves. The disorientation in and because of the relation to the other traverses and undermines the possibility of accounting for it, because any account is always addressed and given to an other. Accountability is, as Butler shows, not what can serve as a response that would enable and ensure responsibility. Yet the consequence to be drawn from the predicament of accountability is not that responsibility becomes a moot endeavor. Rather, the limitations of our ability to give an account urge theorizing responsibility differently as well as theorizing accountability and holding individuals accountable for actions which remains important for political and ethical reasons, as Butler insists.

In our considerations about theorizing responsibility as a key concept for moral philosophy and in relation to subject formation, there are two aspects that I would like to mark so far. First, for Levinas responsibility enters at first as a complicated mode of emergence of the moral subject. It is the mode of a particular relationality to the other through which the subject emerges as a moral subject. This relationality is grounded in a constitutive and unwilled openness to the other, and this openness carries an ethical valence insofar as the openness to the other renders us responsible for the other. This responsibility is therefore neither chosen nor willed by the subject and is, moreover, a responsibility of a peculiar kind because it can be neither declined nor fully answered. Second, I would like to suggest that as a consequence of this primordial responsibility for the other that Levinas elaborates, responsibility as a key concept in moral philosophy, in terms of the problem of responsible action, becomes transformed as we take into account the predicament of responsibility on the level of subject formation. More particularly, one task is to inquire into the nature of these consequences that are framed by these predicaments of the irrecuperable belatedness that inheres to responding, the impossibility of ever fully knowing how precisely to respond well, and the impossibility of controlling the effects.

One consequence that has already begun to take shape in our discussion so far is that responsibility is tied to a necessary ambivalence out of which the question of responsible action arises. Further, we have to rethink responsibility not by beginning by understanding responsibility primarily in terms of imputability and accountability, but by approaching it as responding responsibly to others in particular situations.

Nietzsche's Critique: Tormented Relations between Ethics and Suffering

While Levinas opens possibilities for rethinking responsibility through considering the relation between subject formation and moral philosophy, the scene of subject formation through being overwhelmed by an unfulfillable demand of the other that brings forth the subject as responsible for this other is not unproblematic. The Levinasian account can especially not so easily be invoked to respond to the critiques of moral subject formation that Butler puts forth in *The Psychic Life of Power* through drawing on Nietzsche and Freud. In particular, it seems that Levinas's scene might end up in an eerie proximity to the scene that Nietzsche criticizes so passionately, namely the formation of the subject through a history of internalization and valorization of punishment and subsequent responses of guilt and self-beratement. Freud later affirmed Nietzsche and reformulated this formation of the moral subject as a development through a particular kind of narcissism that he termed "moral masochism."[15] If Levinas's severing of responsibility from the accused's affirming the accusation does not mean that the subject is absolved from that accusation and its responsibility, then we have to ask whether and in what ways this scene of accusation is different from the scene Nietzsche and Freud have offered in describing the formation of the "I" as orchestrated by the attachment to and internalization of guilt. While it is not hard to read Levinas's account of subject formation as a kind of moral masochism, the question is whether there is a way of reading Levinas that allows an interruption of these cycles of moral masochism.

An interruption of moral masochism would be possible if we were to find in Levinas's account a way of reading for responsibility and answerability different from internalized guilt. One such attempt could perhaps take its departure from the fact that in the Levinasian account the accusation remains impossible to assume for the subject and therefore remains exterior to the subject and cannot be internalized, even while it nevertheless continues to disrupt the subject in its being. Yet why is it that the address that initiates one's coming to be an ethical subject comes back around to having to be an accusation? In other words, the question remains why responsibility even—or perhaps precisely—as a mode of subject formation cannot be severed from accusation, be it an accusation in the Nietzschean or in the Levinasian form.

While Butler does not respond to this question directly, *Giving an Account of Oneself* allows an articulation of a reformulation in response to both positions, the Levinasian one and the Nietzschean one, when Butler asks, "Can we say that the experience of being imposed upon from the start, against one's will, heightens a sense of responsibility?" (*GA* 99). Butler goes

on to consider how responsibility might emerge as a response that is different from the Nietzschean internalization of rage in response to experiencing violation. In distinction from both Levinas and Nietzsche, Butler considers that being overwhelmed by the other is an impingement, a possible violation, but she refuses to circumscribe this violation as a generalized form of an accusation. So in Butler there is a violation that delimits the question of ethics as a question of how to respond to violation otherwise than by guilt or retribution. Yet, importantly, this violation with regard to its role in subject formation is neither dignified nor justified as an accusation but instead "delineates a physical vulnerability from which we cannot slip away" (*GA* 101). Nonetheless, to arrive at this conclusion, Butler's own account first takes us through Levinas's account of subject formation and responsibility in response to accusation and persecution.

For Levinas, as for Nietzsche, the ethical subject emerges in response to an accusation; however, unlike in the Nietzschean account, the accusation cannot be internalized. The accusation in Levinas remains exterior precisely because one cannot assume responsibility in the sense of being able comprehensively to know and fully stand in for one's actions. This accusation reaches beyond that for which one could possibly assume responsibility by offering a coherent and reliable account of one's actions. This situation, in which there is responsibility despite one's radical inability to be responsible, seems irresolvable, but perhaps it is precisely this irresolvability that presents us with the breakdown of the narcissistic chains of moral masochism.

In this scene, where one must assume the responsibility for the other without being fully able to do so, one responds despite one's inability in the face of the accusation. In that moment of one's response to the accusation, what is at issue—from the perspective as the responding agent—is not one's guilt, as that which one must attempt to alleviate, correct for, or refuse. Instead, what is at issue is the other and the enormous urgency of the other's call which awakens the moral subject to the fear for the other's death. This fear troubles the subject to the extreme, and only in the back of this fear for the other does the "I" come to be disturbed about its inability to know what violence it might have already inflicted, even if only by coming too late. Perhaps in this way Levinas takes us beyond the narcissism of moral masochism precisely because in this being touched by the other, the question of one's own moral quality does not occur to the agent. One's own virtuousness is irrelevant not because the "I" *knows* that this question of its own moral quality *ought* not occur to it, but rather this question *does* not occur because the encounter with the other and the question of how to respond well troubles the emergent agent beyond being even capable of thinking about how this fear might be a compromised exercise of exonerating itself. In other words, the accusation very strangely does not come to raise questions of one's ethical quality and how to prove it, but instead opens one up to the question of how to respond to the other in a way in which the issue of the response is the other and not oneself.

The scene of address as an accusation can remain at an angle to Nietzsche only insofar as what Levinas gives us is a way in which the accusation cannot be returned into the cycles of moral self-evaluating. It seems to me that we can see here how Levinas takes up terms that carry a moral, evaluative connotation and aims to disjoin them at the same time from their usual moral weight by radicalizing them to the point where their usual signification breaks, so that through these terms we encounter a prior situation of the subject's emergence. In an earlier essay, entitled *On Escape*, Levinas argues regarding shame that we can disarticulate shame as an emotion from the moral order of guilt and understand it as revealing about a more general condition.[16] Within the moral order, shame implies that "one feels ashamed for having acted badly, for having deviated from the norm" (*On Escape* 63). So the moral interpretation would read shame as a symptom that originated from a specific wrongdoing or transgression. Levinas offers a critique of the moral interpretation of the phenomenon, but his critique differs from Nietzsche's and Butler's critique of morality, which questions how our moral codes and feelings develop out of social relations and power differentials that become normalized and sedimented as criteria for moral worth. Instead Levinas turns our attention to a temporal rivenness and disidentification of the self that shame reveals: "Yet shame's whole intensity . . . consists precisely in our inability to identify with this being who is already foreign to us and whose motives for acting we no longer comprehend" (*On Escape* 63). The phenomenon of shame points us toward not being at home or at one with oneself while being unable to escape fully from oneself. From this insight, Levinas reformulates shame as the condition of our "basic nudity" (*On Escape* 64). Moreover, we can then understand this nudity as "the need to excuse one's existence" (*On Escape* 65).

So here the analyses of *On Escape* and of *Otherwise Than Being* converge in the condition of nudity as exposure and the need to excuse one's existence which offers us the exposure as a situation of being accused, while there is no act for which one could be accused; rather, one's entire existence seems to emerge under accusation. Equally, there is no clear site from which this accusation actively issues. Through the radicalization of our understanding the phenomena, Levinas brings us to the point where the implication is that there must have been an accusation. But just as the emergent subject is necessarily tardy, we as readers come too late, and it remains impossible to narrate the subject's origins adequately. In articulating shame as nudity and subject formation in the accusative as radical exposure, Levinas offers the condition of responsibility as bringing forth a nonidentical subject that cannot return to itself and that is constitutively opened towards the other.

One way to describe this approach might be to say that it mobilizes difficult terms—accusation, shame, persecution—for a preontological account of the subject in order to wrest them away from their weighty histories. The problem with this approach, however, is that these histories of prior usages haunt these terms, but these histories are eclipsed and can in this new usage no longer be addressed as a problem. Yet Levinas's approach is enormously productive, as it raises the question of an original violence that operates through the very terms and metaphors through which we frame our discourses on ethics and subject formation.

Returning to Levinas's account then, our query has to be directed towards the link between this unassumable accusation and the election it comes to figure in order to understand how Levinas attempts to dislodge ontology by ethics, which is yet at the same time beyond the domain of the practical. Precisely because the accusation is an accusation before which one's ability to assume responsibility fails, Levinas tells us that this accusation is both an election and an impossibility to decline to be addressed by it. This inescapability of being summoned to responsibility institutes, in Levinas's terms, "subjectivity [as] being hostage" (*OTB* 127). It is hard at this point to defer the recurring question of what this terminology of violence means for subject formation and ethics. If, as Levinas claims, ontology cannot be thought in terms other than the "ethical," and if this "ethical terminology" is that of being persecuted, being taken hostage, and suffering, then the question of what this means for an ethics of nonviolence becomes inexorable—inexorable and strangely violent itself. How are we to answer? Are we to answer? How to answer without foreclosing on the limits beyond which Levinas attempts to push us, without passing by too early, without yielding to the temptation to close the book before the last page? How are we to respond *responsibly* as we have turned that last page? What does it mean to theorize in the face of the thought of Levinas?

Although the "I" is hostage to the face, this is a strange coercion, because the subject is being taken hostage by the expression of the other's suffering. Subjectivity, as being hostage, is enjoined not by greater physical force but by being ruptured and interrupted, by being wounded by the other's suffering which demands a response and which at the same time signifies the impossibility of an adequate response and even incites violence. In the encounter with the face, the other is "given over to my responsibility, but to which I am wanting and faulty. It is as though I were responsible for his mortality, and guilty for surviving" (*OTB* 91). So consciousness emerges as an insufficient, faulty consciousness—as bad conscience (*mauvaise conscience)*—because in the face of the other's suffering, one's mere existence attests to one's belatedness and to one's possibly having taken the other's place.

Bad conscience in Levinas has interesting resonances with Nietzsche insofar as this bad conscience is also a faulty consciousness and is bound up with a peculiar innocent guilt as well as a guilty innocence. As well as Levinas, Nietzsche offers us accounts of a primary openness to accusation that appears as constitutive for subject formation. There are, however, several differences between Nietzsche and Levinas in how this bad conscience is brought about as well as in what role bad conscience performs in their accounts. Whereas in Nietzsche there seems to be an underlying critique of those systems of morality in whose service bad conscience is brought about, in Levinas that which overwhelms and brings about the faulty consciousness and bad conscience ends up being identified with the good, because being overwhelmed by the other was neither willed nor achieved. Even in attempting to reach an account of morality and responsibility beyond bad conscience, this introduction of the good remains uncomfortably within the reach of Nietzsche's critique of the ascription of value to bad conscience.

Despite their similarities, there seems to be an important difference between Levinas and Nietzsche, insofar as in Levinas there is no broken contract, no missed payment, but instead it is the fear of the other's death that gives rise to this bad consciousness and bad conscience. The emergence of obligation in Nietzsche is steeped in repaying one's debt and in the memory that is being inscribed by means of suffering punishment and eventually in bad conscience coming from the internalization of this punishment. Subsequently, conscience and the ability to make and keep promises are formed through a valorization, so that it seems, as Butler argues in *The Psychic Life of Power* (74–75), that arriving at the ability to promise depends on a promise that must have already been broken.

While the scene Levinas offers us is extremely violent, the violence of the accusation, of persecution, of being taken hostage is disarticulated from the destitution and fragility of the other that brings about the fear and bad conscience. This destitution and fragility bring about an ambivalence of responsibility, aggression, and bad conscience about the irrecoverable belatedness, but without any time for self-beratement. What is remarkable in Levinas is that there is no promise, especially no broken promise, that brings about the address and accusation. What is broken is time, which is also at work in that we cannot stop the death of another. We can merely postpone this death—and then only sometimes. We cannot promise that the other will not die, only see to it perhaps that they will suffer less. The absence of the category of the promise in Levinas, it seems to me, is explainable because for him temporality works through responsibility. The challenge might indeed be to think of responsibility without promises—no promises, but still and only responsibility. This responsibility in Levinas is traversed both by an inevitable belatedness and by an irrecoverable past and concerns fundamentally a very present urgency of responding rather than, as in the Nietzschean promise, announcing an action to be taken in the future.[17]

While Levinas introduces guilt as well as responsibility alongside an accusation, this guilt is not turned into the reality that in Nietzsche feeds into a cycle of responsibility as accountability and justice as retribution. Rather, in Levinas, this guilt is a peculiar kind of guilt. As Levinas writes, "*It is as though* I were responsible for his mortality, and guilty for surviving" (*OTB* 91; emphasis added), indicating that somehow one is responsible and guilty, but not quite fully; it remains "as if." One is not guilty in the sense that the guilt could be attributed to an "I," because there is no self-conscious subject who could account for these deeds. This does not mean, however, that the subject emerges in innocence and is thus released from the burden of this responsibility. Quite the contrary. The impossibility of evading this responsiveness to the other opens the possibility of a subject as an individual without reinstituting the individual as a self-sufficient and sovereign individual.

The priority of being affected and enjoined by the other constitutes an openness toward and dependency on the other that is not simply the negation of independence, because being traversed and wounded by the subject is so fundamental that it cannot possibly be recuperated. Hence this co-constitutive openness and dependence on being addressed by the other cannot be left behind like clothes that the subject has outgrown. Because the subject is continuously implicated in the scene of the address, the subject's openness toward the other neither depends on nor turns into a "natural benevolence or divine 'instinct'" (*OTB* 124) nor "some love or tendency to sacrifice" (*OTB* 124). Not only is responsibility severed from accountability by Levinas, but responsibility is equally as little about love as it is about self-sacrifice.

For Butler, as for Levinas, responsibility does not depend on sympathy or a prior relationship to those for whom we come to be responsible. Rather, while the fact of our openness to being addressed and touched by others is not yet responsibility for Butler, responsibility nonetheless becomes possible out of and depends upon this address and on the dispossession by the other in the address. In distinction from Levinas, Butler emphasizes being addressed by the other as disorientation and dispossession; unlike in Levinas, the language of accusation, beratement, and interpellation is in Butler tied to the realm of the social and functions to offer a critique of the roles of moral and social norms in subject formation. In particular, the terms of interpellation and accusation are the categories of *The Psychic Life of Power* in which she interrogates how power operates to establish the social conditions that compel the formation of the subject as an individual through another response, namely the one of turning equally toward an authority as well as on oneself.

Butler does not frame the encounter with others in a generalized accusatory and persecutory terminology, yet the scene of the encounter in Butler also does not become originally or predominantly the site of love, affection, and benevolence. The encounter as the scene of subject formation is characterized by the ambivalence of a proximity that is overwhelming the "I," even impinging on it, while also enthralling and continuously undoing it. In this emphasis on ambivalence in subject formation, Butler's account, in my opinion, is less indebted to Levinas than to psychoanalysis and especially, in *Giving an Account of Oneself,* to Jean Laplanche. Levinas and Butler both stress that the encounter with the other is not a scene of subject formation that at one time inaugurates us, but instead the "primary" encounter continues to traverse and make itself felt in the encounters we have with each other. Butler differs significantly from Levinas in not relying on a presocial, preempirical, or preontological condition but on her understanding of the unconscious as both individual and social. Conversely, in distinction from psychoanalysis, but drawing on Levinas, Butler casts the encounter with the other as having an ethical valence insofar as she understands this susceptibility toward the other and the dispossession by the other as bringing about an explicitly ethical responsiveness that becomes a condition for responsibility as responsible action.

In Levinas, however, not only is the encounter an ethical responsiveness, but he uses—although this use by no means coincides with our common use of the term—"responsibility" to describe the encounter that yields the subject as accused. Susceptibility and dispossession are in Levinas tied to an extreme passivity and, through this extreme passivity, tied explicitly to suffering: the suffering of the other, by the other, and for the other. In the following pages, I would therefore like to engage with this passivity to address concerns of the stipulation of an ethic of self-sacrifice but to go beyond this concern as well. It seems to me that besides enabling an approach to responsibility from an angle other than its link to accountability, Levinas and Butler allow us to break the link between suffering and justification without writing suffering out of an account of the formation of the ethical subject.

In Levinas this interruption of suffering and justification emerges through his account of the extreme passivity in subject formation. This passivity is another major difference between Butler's account of subject formation, with its proximity to psychoanalysis, and the Levinasian account, as psychoanalysis considers the drives as a primary and ineradicable active openness toward the world. For Levinas, in distinction from Butler and psychoanalysis, there is a passivity that is more passive and prior to any kind of passivity that could be contrasted with activity. For the purposes of the argument here, without eliminating the differences between psychoanalytic approaches to theorizing the subject and the Levinasian account, I would like to concentrate on a certain convergence in the critique of the subject as self-conscious and on an insistence on formation that is beyond the subject's control and even beyond what any of us could possibly recover at any point.

The encounter with the other, as Levinas offers it, affects and overwhelms the "I" beyond its ability to grasp, understand, and respond adequately and brings about the "I" in a sensibility or openness to the demand of the other that is characterized as an "ultimate passivity."[18] One is not awaiting the call of the other, but one cannot help but be susceptible to it. This sensibility figures as a passivity whereby the subject is being overwhelmed and interrupted by the other in such a way that the response to the call of the other becomes a *for the other* that resists appropriation and sublation into a *for itself* of the subject. This passivity is, as Levinas emphasizes, the passivity of suffering: "In suffering, sensibility is a vulnerability, more passive than receptivity; an encounter more passive than experience" (*EN* 92). The passivity here seems unable to turn into receptivity or activity because it is an undergoing that is the exhaustion of vulnerability. Perhaps one could understand this as a being pained that constitutes a sensibility that resists yielding sense.

Responsibility here is not assumable, but it is also characterized by a susceptibility to the other that is prior even to a passivity of a willing undergoing. This ultimate passivity is cast by Levinas as an endurance that is suffered by the emergent subject. While Levinas refuses any attempt to mitigate this undergoing as suffering, he also categorically refuses any attempt to valorize suffering by making sense of it and by justifying it. The question "What does suffering mean?" that one might be tempted to ask exposes precisely in what way suffering is extreme passivity and beyond the grasp of receptivity, insofar as the question "What does it mean?" has to fail.[19] Ascribing sense to this suffering is that which is impossible; suffering is an undergoing that does not make sense and that remains useless to understand. This undergoing of suffering is useless, without returns for the subject or the other. This suffering is for nothing—for nothing that one willed and for nothing that one could get out of it—it is simply for nothing. In the face of the other's call, suffering is inseparably bound to "the unjustifiable character of suffering in the other, the outrage it would be for me to justify my neighbor's suffering" (*EN* 98). The limits that all attempts of theodicy and anthropodicy meet here are striking: the suffering of the other is unjustifiable, and all attempts to justify it are outrageous.

This issue is tricky territory, nonetheless, because the uselessness of suffering does not and cannot mean that one does not have to engage with and attempt to understand and trace sufferings past and present in the name of opening a future in which these sufferings will not have to be repeated. It must be possible to inquire into and attempt to understand the circumstances while equally refusing to make sense of suffering. In her essay in *Precarious Life* entitled "Explanation and Exoneration, Or What We Can Hear," written in response to the terror attacks on New York City and Washington, D.C., in 2001, Butler demands that it must be possible for ethical and political reasons to engage in explanations while refusing to justify that which one seeks to understand. The underlying question in her argument is whether it is possible to refrain from turning a succession of events into a chain of causally related actions. More precisely, Butler argues for refusing to offer an explanation by searching for causal relations between events and through finding single agents whose actions can be intertwined through categories not only of "cause" and "effect" but also of "choice" and "fault." Explanation is about understanding the parameters of a situation under which particular actions and effects become possible without thereby justifying, condoning, or welcoming the violent act of killing innocent people.[30] This demand for the possibility of critical inquiry and understanding implies a refusal readily to inscribe suffering into a logic of sacrifice through which suffering and destruction are turned into an affirmation of a higher cause. The address by the other does not in any way justify justifying the other's suffering as a response, nor does it justify the subject's suffering as a response. As responsibility is severed from accountability in its first instance, so suffering is severed from justification.

Suffering is disjoined from justification insofar as suffering neither justifies counterviolence nor is the distinctive mark of moral conduct. Responsibility that brings about the moral subject through an encounter with the other does not lead us into moral philosophy through stipulating an ethic of self-abnegation or self-sacrifice. But in what ways, then is there a subject emerging through this scene who is an ethical agent? In what ways is this unlimited responsibility, the accusation that is election, the suffering that is ultimate passivity not the sign of an ethics of self-sacrifice that glorifies self-abnegation? Our suffering, as Levinas insists, is not *our* suffering in the sense of suffering for our own sake; suffering is instead inflicted by the pain over the other's suffering as a result of our vulnerability to the nudity and destitution of the face. The suffering of the other does not stipulate or allow for self-sacrifice as compensatory act. There is no room left by Levinas for self-assertion at the cost of the other. The moral subject awakens broken-hearted and terrified about its own belatedness and the violence that it might have already inflicted.[21] But this does not mean that self-sacrifice could be a place of refuge for the subject. In Levinasian thinking, there is no possibility for me to be absolved from the accusation under which the moral subject comes into being. Even in attending to the other, responding cannot be an exercise of self-exoneration; the "I" cannot *choose* to substitute and sacrifice itself, as in that very choice this "I" would return its actions to itself at the expense of attending and responding to the other. One's choice to sacrifice oneself in response to the other's demand would still be an act of self-preservation—self-preservation carried ad absurdum whereby one would assert oneself in the very act of extinguishing oneself, slipping away from the demand of the other, from the demand of one's *presence*.

The fear for the other that traverses the subject through and through is the moment of breakage of the subject as self-sufficient, constituting the subject as shattered and enjoined by the other. This enchainment to the extreme as a moment of extreme incapacity, as a moment of rupture, is the very moment when a new kind of freedom breaks open. The subject awakens to this freedom in "ethical awakening and vigilance in that affective turbulence" (*EN* 146). Not only is this turbulence that of not being able to know the violence that one's existing might have already inflicted on others, but the call for one's presence, for one's nonindifference, still instills within this call the temptation to wish for the death of the other. It remains possible and—outrageously—tempting to foreclose on one's openness and vulnerability toward the other.

Death cannot ensure meaning and sense, either as a sacrifice or as an ultimate reference of fear. While the death of the other and the fear of the death of the other play an immense role in Levinas, I would like to suggest that the ethical responsiveness that he offers us nonetheless opposes deriving an ethic of death and dying as much as it opposes deriving an ethic of self-sacrifice or self-preservation. Responsibility at its heart is about responding to the other. Responding to the other is what brings about the subject, and yet this responding to the address of the other is also what remains all but unproblematic in Levinas, because in responding the subject is individuated through being taken hostage by the other. The question that is pushed to its limit, then, is how to formulate the notion of responsibility for moral philosophy in relation to this horizon, where responsibility and the subject of moral philosophy must undergo a preontological persecution.

Individuation that brings about the subject as self occurs, according to Levinas's account, through the untransferable substitution for the other, because "under the accusation by everyone, the responsibility for everyone goes to the point of substitution" (*OTB* 112). This substitution for the other seems to be undergone by the subject as the other besets it. Substitution is precisely not an activity of self-sacrifice, because this unlimited responsibility for everyone under which the subject finds itself renders impossible any return to itself. The subject emerges first in the accusative, as "me" in "*me voici*" ("Here see me"),[22] in response to the initial and ongoing demand and the concurrent demand of responsibility. The first person in the accusative turns into the "I" in substitution, as the "Here see me" becomes a "Here I am." Levinas seems to offer us this emergence of the subject through accusation, through suffering persecution by the other, and finally through substitution for the other as responsibility for the other in order to get rid of any trace of a willing, sovereign, and active subject. The emergence of the subject is rendered an undergoing to the extreme. The response "Here I am" cannot be the "I" for itself, but figures as the breaking point where the "I" exists solely for the other's sake. This for-the-other is for the other to the extreme; "the self is absolved of itself" (*OTB* 115), but in and through that which it did not will itself and which it cannot possibly assume. The "I" emerging in unlimited passivity is the inversion of identity as self-coincidence and self-possession under the responsibility for each and every other, and Levinas asks, "What can it be but a substitution of me for the others?" (*OTB* 114).

Unlimited responsibility—What can it be but a complete substitution of me for the others? Levinas takes us even further: "We have to speak here of expiation as uniting identity and alterity" (*OTB* 118). This expiation is by no means an achievement of the "I"; this expiation is prior to will, choice, and achievement. Levinas gives various idioms for this unlimited responsibility: being under accusation by everyone, substitution by the other as for the other, and expiation. In this succession of formulations to characterize extreme passivity, Levinas is not offering an argumentative transition between these formulations, and perhaps this is the moment when the argument breaks down, perhaps it is the very limit of making sense of Levinas and within Levinas. It is something different to think about a limit as a point of breakage rather than as a limitation, because a limit reached in thinking does not necessarily need to interrupt thinking but can also mean an unbroken progression by reversal. A point of breakage might in fact be the moment when thinking, when theoretical progression, is interrupted and exhausted by that which it attempts and wishes to grasp but cannot grasp and yet must continue to wish and attempt to grasp. Perhaps this interruption is the moment when thought is being affected in a way that opens it up time and again toward that which escapes it, renewing the life of thought in vigilance and desire for what remains irrecoverably other to it. This does not mean that all interruptions are alike or that there could be a universal absolute that figures as an invariant in escaping all theoretical attempts alike. Rather, there are important differences with regard to in what ways different theories meet their particular limits and specific points of breakage and how these interruptions perform in and through these theories. With regard to Levinas, the question, then, is how to attend to the specific fissure that occurs in the face of the precariousness of the other.[23]

The demand that the face delivers, which constitutes the responsibility of the ethical agent, is the demand not to abandon the other. The demand of the subject's presence for the other is without limits, and it seems that the limitlessness of this presence for the other comes to mean that the subject be present in the place of the other. In this substitution, the other is not assumed, the other's suffering is not assimilated or justified, and suffering for the other cannot claim to alleviate the suffering—it might, but that is beyond one's control. Equally, the subject's responsibility is not suspended, the "I" not exonerated, but as Butler reminds us in her reading of Levinas: "It is important to remember that our ordinary way of thinking about responsibility is altered in Levinas' formulation. *We do not take responsibility for the Other's acts as if we authored those acts*" (*GA* 91; emphasis in the original). Levinas's formulation of responsibility for the other as a substitution for the other does not imply that the subject effaces itself to the extent that there is no self possible anymore at all. But substitution as the extreme moment of being for the other in self-dispossession is the constantly recurrent moment and movement when the subject is individuated in relation to the other and is being dispossessed by the other. This individuality in substitution emerges as an irrecoverable irreplaceability insofar as there is no one who could take the place of the addressed subject. Quietly through the other, the subject is engendered: "I exist through the other and for the other, but without this being alienation" (*OTB* 114).

We exist as ethical subjects only through our relations to an other, and the ethical valence of these relations is not based in our good will, in our sympathy or love for the other, but in our openness toward being addressed by others. While it is always possible to reject and refuse the demands of the other, our openness to the address of the other is a constitutive part of our situation and is nothing we will or could will away. The address in Levinas arrives as demand and as accusation, but he demonstrates forcefully how the accusation cannot possibly be internalized or assumed by the subject as its *own* fault. In this regard one could even say that Levinas takes Nietzsche to task, because despite the critique of responsibility as accountability, there is not much room for the individual's relations to others as a key to responsibility in Nietzsche.

Taking leave from the perspective of the individual, however, Nietzsche's more general critique of morality, as tied to a valorization of violence, fear, and guilt, still gives rise to questions. Even if *I* cannot affirm myself as responsible for the other in an act of asserting and assuming the address and the accusation, this does not yet undo Nietzsche's criticism that morality comes to be bound up with the valorization of the undergoing of violence. It is not enough to point out that the subject does not get to invoke or conceive of its undergoing as anything that makes it a good person, because there is a more general worry that Nietzsche voices, namely, that morality introduces goodness through suffering. Nietzsche's criticism takes on a cultural perspective that is not reducible to the perspective of the individual.

So while Levinas refutes the idea that affliction by the other can ever be anything to which the subject attributes value, he does offer a scene framed within the terminology of great violence (persecution, being taken hostage), and goodness also arrives as election in persecution:

> The one affected by the other is an anarchic trauma, or an inspiration of the one by the other, and not a causality striking mechanically a matter subject to its energy. In this trauma the Good reabsorbs, or redeems, the violence of non-freedom. Responsibility is what first enables one to catch sight of and conceive of value. (*OTB* 123)

It is difficult to negotiate Levinas's account, because it is not a phenomenological account of a real experience but an account that attempts to articulate something that is more primary and "otherwise than being."[24] This otherwise than being, while not appearing itself as a reality of being, continues to structure ontological or ontogenetic discourse that assesses the nature of the realities in which subjects live together, encounter each other, and negotiate demands. In a way, one could say that the "otherwise than being" is the condition of possibility that delimits and traverses the way in which the existence of subjects is structured. However, even before it has been spoken, this claim about the condition of possibility is already wrong, because Levinas attempts to undo and disarticulate the primacy of the logos and the subject that is at work in the framework that renders what conditions empirical reality as an epistemological, transcendental condition of the possibility of this reality. Levinas articulates neither an empirical reality, nor an ontological reality, nor a transcendental a priori when he offers persecution, accusation, and substitution as modes of subject formation.

The problem with Levinas and with the violence that comes to figure so crucially for the horizon of ethics is not simply that nonfreedom figures as violence. Butler engages this aspect of Levinas's argument by figuring it as a dispossession by the other that makes it possible to ask what nonviolent responses might look like. The problem that I am trying to lay out here is not that Levinas associates nonfreedom with a kind of violence and not even that this nonfreedom might be the experience of dispossession, of being overwhelmed, an experience of a certain violation and vulnerability in relation to others that gives rise to the possibility of morality, namely in the form of the question "How to respond responsibly?" The problem with Levinas instead lies where the gap between the violence and the question of responding seems to be closed once the violence of nonfreedom is considered absorbed in "the Good" in a move that is presented as a description of the anarchical, which is prior to logic and ontology and so can be criticized on the grounds of neither.

Matters with Levinas are complicated, though, because this introduction of the Good does not mean that he simply equates suffering with moral value; rather, he decidedly rejects any attempt at justifying suffering. Suffering is never justified as good; instead, for Levinas moral value and the Good arrive outside logics and justification. The Good is introduced as that which seeks out, "chooses," and assigns the subject to responsibility for the other that is the emergence of non-self-sovereign subjectivity. Subjectivity that is different from self-sovereignty is also the result of persecution and of being taken hostage by the other, a claim that cannot easily be written out of

Levinas. What we encounter in *Otherwise Than Being* is the performance of a prelogical and preontological account of responsibility and subject formation that is bound up with an avowedly unjustified, unjustifiable, and outrageous introduction of the Good.[25] The same account offers us the violence of the preontological relation to the other that comes to figure as primary ethicality, which, however, is not morality or ethical action, which requires logic, critique, evaluation, and comparison.

What Levinas offers is a powerful and enthralling though not unproblematic response to Freud's and Nietzsche's critiques of morality as reliant on self-inflicted violence. Levinas dislocates the Nietzschean and Freudian critiques by insisting on the priority of the relation to the other against beginning with moral norms and precepts and against beginning with the subject or the self. Levinas argues that there is an ethical openness and responsiveness toward others that brings us about as ethical subjects, and he rejects self-abnegation and self-sacrifice, as much as any primary right to self-preservation, as betraying that which makes for our ethical openness. That this openness has an ethical character in making us responsible for the other by whom we are touched is not an effect of something that we willed, and therefore Levinas demands that ethical openness cannot be turned into a matter of the self, be it a self-assertion in the name of self-preservation or in the name of self-abnegation. Further, by locating this ethical responsiveness in relation to the other, Levinas offers a mode of ethical subject formation that occurs not primarily in relation to moral precepts and norms. Nonetheless, Levinas remains hard to read, in particular when in *Otherwise Than Being* violence comes to figure as crucial for the emergence of responsibility and the ethical subject and when this violence is inscribed in a generalized form as prior to all social and historical contexts, contours, and specificity.

While I believe that this problem is not marginal in Levinas, it seems still worthwhile to pursue his insistence on a dislodging of the scene of the formation of the moral subject through self-craterment and self-castigation, in particular through the possibilities that open up in conversation with Butler's reading of Levinas. I would like to consider Levinas's dislodging of the moral subject as crucial for moral philosophy, as he offers this dislodging through insisting on a relationality to others that is not merely a relation of dependence and care but is a relationality through an exposure and vulnerability that fundamentally decenters the "I." This decentering is especially productive for a consideration of subject formation insofar as it also frees the moral agent in a very specific way, namely from hyper-self-assertion for the predicaments of responsible action in a world in which we can never be fully in control.

In *Giving an Account of Oneself*, Butler herself affords a kind of dislodging of the Levinasian account that opens up thinking responsibility in relation to subject formation and moral philosophy. After wrestling with the concept of "persecution," she focuses on the understanding of exposure to the other and the unwilled being disrupted by the other as the moment in which the possibility for moral agency arises.[26] For Butler, this horizon of responsibility is tied to attending to a shared susceptibility to each other. In response to considering the possibility of responsibility beyond bad consciousness, she offers that responsibility is about *not* "recoiling from the other, from impressionability, susceptibility, and vulnerability" (*GA* 100). By linking responsibility to our susceptibility and vulnerability to others, she does not offer vulnerability as a value in itself. Rather, vulnerability becomes a sign and reminder that might direct us in search of responsible responses. In thinking about what an "ethics from the region of the unwilled" would look like, she suggests that such an ethics might comprise "tak[ing] the very vulnerability of exposure as the sign, the reminder, of a common physicality and risk" (*GA* 100). Consequently, responsibility as a mode of subject formation that indicates an ambivalent openness and ethical responsiveness to the other comes to afford a precarious moment for an openness to a response that may affirm and answer to this responsibility.[27]

Responding Responsibly, Deliberations, and Social Predicaments

If our openness toward being addressed by others constitutes us in a relationship of responsibility, and if this situation of our becoming is not yet an account of moral philosophy, what, then, are the consequences of this situation of being addressed and responsible? What does the account of the dyadic encounter imply for the key questions from which moral philosophy emerges: "How ought I treat you?" and "What should I do?" The question at the heart of this consideration is how our theorizing responsibility will be further transformed if we do not begin with accountability but still begin with a situation of responsibility, even a limitless responsibility. Precisely how do we move from this avowedly unassumable responsibility to an account of responsible action? To ask this question is also to ask the question of the possibility for a moral principle that might orient our actions.

In order to attend to this question, we must understand that we cannot deduce a set of moral precepts or a code of ethical conduct from the encounter with the other and this dyadic relationality. The for-the-other does not return to the "I," and thus it is impossible to delimit or exemplify the act in which that self-suspension congeals. As Levinas carefully emphasizes, the for-the-other "can only be discreetly. It cannot give itself out as an example, or be narrated in an edifying discourse. It cannot, without becoming perverted, be made into a preachment" (*EN* 99). The concrete situations and actions through which the for-the-other appears are not by virtue of their uniqueness safeguarded from being generalized, narrativized, and advocated as a model or standard. Preaching, which means prescribing concrete conduct, is not impossible per se, but in a way it is always a distortion if not a travesty of that which it attempts to prescribe and stipulate. As soon as concrete action is turned into an example and is ascribed normative force—even if only with regard to its context—the act exceeds its specific and unique context. The exemplary is an example only insofar as it is not absolutely unique but instead demonstrates and illustrates an instance of a generality, implying not only interchangeability but also repeatability. Being repeatable, the example travels beyond the specific instance and operates in the service of a generalization. Being relayed as exemplary and repeatable, the concrete, the discrete is no longer discreetly, but it is invested with a normative voice and force, which implies that one could and ought to follow the example. Yet whatever is rendered as an example is that which cannot be generalized, because the concreteness of the response, of the "here I am" cannot be mastered, claimed, and prescribed in a conscious act.

The problem of normative ethics arises through a normativity that renders the concrete into a model that stipulates a concrete instance as "preachment"; however, not every normative discourse needs to be preachment. Normative discourse is not to be condemned and abolished per se, but the question must be how this discourse can acknowledge this predicament of having to betray the particularity of the scene of responsibility as the scenario from which it emerges. In other words, if it is the case that normative discourse meets its inherent limit in the very responsibility in whose name it is put forth, then the question is: How can normative discourse bear witness to the ways in which it necessarily betrays the particularity of responsibility that it attempts to safeguard? If normative discourse must operate through generalization, what are the ways in which it can attend to its necessarily compromising the uniqueness of the other? The conclusion to draw from Levinas is not that we ought not to have norms and laws. Not only does Levinas's thought not allow for such straightforward normative deductions, but because we are implicated into a world where there is always more than one other, we must constantly craft, create, and enforce norms and laws.

What, then, can we derive from Levinas's thought, if not that we should abandon norms and the laws in favor of some kind of an ethic of the other and for the other? In the following pages I would like to suggest a way to read the emergence of "justice" in Levinas's account as crucial to understanding responsibility as a central term for moral philosophy, not only as a term delineating subject formation. As we move in this book to inquire into the meaning of responsibility with regard to responsible action, one dimension that becomes important is the relation of responsibility to the demand for justice. At the same time, responsibility remains equally tied to and bounded, as well as unbounded, by the prior relationality to the other. I would like to suggest we consider responsibility as the horizon of moral philosophy, namely, as that explicitly of the question "How should I treat you? What ought I to do?" By considering responsibility as this horizon of what should, even *ought*, to be done, my argument attempts to work against efforts to inscribe responsibility as absolutely other than normative ethics. Retaining the question of normative demands as an open and urgent question affords and invigorates critiques of normativity by interrogating these demands in relation to the questions of responsibility, justice, and judgment.

The necessity of normative and judicative discourse and of compromising the unique relation to the other derives for Levinas from the situation that the relation with the other is always already troubled by human sociality insofar as there is always more than one other: "If he [the other] were my only interlocutor, I would have nothing but obligations! But I don't live in a world in which there is but one single 'first comer'; there is always the third party in the world: he or she is also my other, my fellow" (*EN* 104). Levinas refers to this other other as "the third," indicating that the dyadic relation remains prior to the triadic situation and is not surpassed and left behind by the situation of sociality. Every other is and remains an other to me and demands my presence, but because this call is not a single call but a plurality, the demand for justice emerges:

> [J]ustice, here, takes precedence over the taking upon oneself of the fate of the other. I must judge, where before I was to assume responsibilities. Here is the birth of the theoretical; here the concern for justice is born, which is the basis of the theoretical. But it is always starting out from the Face. (*EN* 104)

This is a remarkable passage, as it is in the context of the social that Levinas informs us of our obligation for judgment: "I *must* judge." This obligation to judge is not severed from the more primordial relation of responsibility and thus presents the "I" with the predicament that one *must* judge and compare in the face of the unique and incomparable the faces of all the others that equally confront one. An obligation arises to reflect on the demands of the multiple others, to compare, weigh, and judge them, but at the same time the demand of each individual other is not transformed or alleviated by this obligation. Theoretical deliberation emerges only in the name of justice and is always bound to the primary and ultimate responsibility for each and every other, as well as to the collective. Thus objectivity, intentionality, and consciousness neither precede nor supersede the responsibility for the other, because objectivity, intentionality, and consciousness emerge as a response due only to the subject being summoned and overwhelmed by the other, which is always already a multitude of others. Because of the *ultimate* responsibility for *each and every* other, one cannot single-handedly choose one over the other, one cannot abandon one other in the face of another other. The obligation to judge materializes as an imperative that takes the form of "You must compare because it is incomparable!"[28] Deliberation and theoretical discourse arise and even *must* arise, because the encounter with the face—while remaining the primary and constitutive moment—cannot figure as a call to blind sacrifice for the other.

At issue for responsible responsibility is the question of judging in the form of taking into account and weighing against each other actions that others do against others. While Levinas makes very clear regarding the dyadic encounter that self-preservation does not limit the limitlessness of the responsibility for the other, the question of self-preservation returns here, as deliberation and judgment come to be possible and necessary tasks of the moral subject. The responsibility prior to all judgment denies favoring one other over another other and therefore demands that one regards what one other does to another other. But the obligation to judge, Levinas clarifies, "does not mean the taking account of possible wrongs I may have suffered at the hands of one or the other, and denying my dis-interestedness; it means not ignoring the suffering of the other, who falls to my responsibility" (*EN* 195).[29] Thus, while I am obligated to consider what one person does to another, and while this might mean that others will be called to assess what has been done to me, the latter is not my task and not in my hands.

The entry of the third here comes not to mean for me that in thinking about and weighing what others do to each other, I should or even can enter my own suffering into that equation. The question that this assessment raises is whether there is not a necessity of self-preservation at the heart of being able to deliberate and act. *Must* one not also take care of oneself in order to attend to others? Does one not have duties regarding oneself that arise out of one's responsibility for others, because not taking into account one's own survival might mean to abandon others? Levinas at this point is merely but very clearly saying that the obligation to judge does not imply that it would be up to me to set my suffering over and against others' suffering. This does not mean that one's own situation never matters but that the task of weighing, deliberating, and deciding—importantly—is not primarily a matter of self-justification. Deliberation being dislodged from justifying oneself is the complementary aspect to responsibility being not in the first place about accountability.

The underlying question here is how to act responsibly in a world in which we are always in relation to more than one other. The particular challenge of addressing this question in conversation with Levinas and Butler is that responsibility emerges for us through them as a situation of an unwilled, limitless responsibility for each other. How do we move from this limitless condition to responsible action? And how does the encounter with the other as our primary responsibility continue to play a role for responsible action? To deal with these two questions, I would like to begin by examining the relation between the encounter and the situation of always being among many others as Levinas offers it in *Otherwise Than Being*. In Levinas's terminology, this question is phrased in terms of the relation between the dyad and the triad.

The asymmetry that characterizes the dyadic relationship—in which the face of an other summons me—cannot be converted, developed, or sublated into reciprocity because of the way in which the other always remains irrecoverably other. Owing to the limitlessness of the demand of the other within the dyad, for Levinas there is no room for self-preservation. But this relation is complicated by the entry of the third, and in return "[t]he relationship with the third party is an incessant correction of the asymmetry of proximity in which the face is looked at" (*OTB* 158). What precisely is this "correction"? What does it do to the face of the other? What is the "I" becoming? A few paragraphs later in *Otherwise Than Being*, Levinas writes:

> Synchronization is the act of consciousness, which . . . institutes the original locus of justice, a terrain common to me and the others where I am counted among them, that is, where subjectivity is a citizen with all the duties and rights measured and measurable which the equilibrated ego involves, or equilibrating itself by the concourse of duties and the concurrence of rights. (*OTB* 160)

Synchronization—the act of comparison—marks for Levinas the birth of the subject's agency and activity in response to the demand for justice, through which one weighs and judges the demands of the many others by which one finds oneself addressed. Not only does this weighing establish common ground between the others, but one is also "counted among them." Thus, in a departure from the dyadic relation through which the "I" emerged as displaced and expelled from its place, in this multitudinous relation the others and I share common ground. This ground is the locus of justice, perhaps even the original locus of justice, an assertion that seems to imply that originally—or nonoriginally, anarchically—there is no justice but only responsibility, namely, a responsibility that is prior to justice.

Only with the entry of the third person and the consequent demand for justice, which occasions the birth of consciousness, does the emergent subject become one of the others, and being a citizen of justice's terrain means to have measured and measurable duties and rights. It seems as if, with this act of consciousness that is enabled and demanded by the entry and presence of the third, the dimension of sociality emerges as momentum by which the unlimited responsibility and the "I" undergo an opening that does not undo or cancel the responsibility but instead opens it toward sustainability. Nonetheless, the priority of the dyadic relation continues to make itself felt even in the social situation in which one is facing many others. As Levinas explains, under the auspices of the third, "[m]y lot is important. But it is still out of my responsibility that my salvation has meaning, despite the danger in which it puts this responsibility, which it may encompass and swallow up" (*OTB* 161).

One's survival as emergent self-interest is always in danger of obliterating one's responsibility toward the other. If we follow Levinas's account, the "I" can attend to the other only in an incomplete way that will fully adequately take on the limitless demand of responsibility that the face conveys. One has to compare, judge, and act, one has to decide for one against another, and one has to consider what it takes to sustain one's own life—but these considerations are not outside the horizon of responsibility. Considering and weighing what to do remain troubled (and troubling) by the possibility of already having forsaken the other, by the possible and tempting foreclosure on the other, and by the impossibility of fully controlling the situation to which one's deliberations, decisions, and actions can never quite fully attend.

Ethical deliberation emerges for us in response to the situation of sociality, which is that we always find ourselves in the midst of multiple others. Furthermore, ethical deliberation, as it concerns itself with responding responsibly, is not about a "justificatory logic," although it will always run the risk of turning into a project of self-justification. Butler's critique of a responsibility that takes hold only through bad conscience is that bad conscience is itself problematic because "it recoils from the other, from impressionability, susceptibility, and vulnerability" (*GA* 100). Taking Butler's critique in light of Levinasian thought, we can formulate more precisely that when ethical deliberation becomes self-justification, it turns into an exercise in assuring ourselves about the goodness of our actions and in return makes us immune against others' demands and criticisms. By unclenching the demands of self-justification, the possibility of another kind of ethical deliberation emerges—one that is not, or at least not as tightly, subject to Nietzsche's critique of conscience as "knowledge" of the good only through the internalization of punishment that results in a bad conscience that then demands justification in advance of any possible failure of promises. Ethical deliberation beyond bad conscience in this light is about weighing demands of others that arise out of concrete situations, and ethical deliberation is even concerned with justification in the sense of giving reasons that allow and inform decisions. Giving reasons and deliberating, however, should then enable decisions rather than simply bolstering decisions that have already been made on the basis of justification. Approaching deliberation beyond a preoccupation with self-assertion renders decisions, as well as the one who offers these deliberations, open to criticism rather than preempting criticism.

There is no guarantee in this process that one will not become self-defensive or that one's attempts to explain might not end up being perceivable only as attempts to justify oneself. We cannot preclude this possibility of failure precisely because ethical deliberation and ethical judgment are not solitary activities; rather, as responses to particular situations and others, they are another address in themselves. As Butler reminds us:

> [J]udging another is a mode of address: even punishments are pronounced, and often delivered to the face of the Other, requiring that Other's bodily presence. *Hence, if there is an ethic to the address, and if judgment, including legal judgment, is one form of address, then the ethical value of judgment will be conditioned by the form of address it takes.* (*GA* 46; emphasis in the original)

Ethical deliberation is not radically different from making judgments, but in fact always, and even importantly so, is implicated in and bound up with the activity of judging. Since that is the case, it seems important not to consider ethical deliberation as an activity removed from others or in relation to others only insofar as I over here deliberate what to do in response to some others over there. When we consider deliberation, it is key that we consider what ethical deliberation means and how it works precisely in relation to the scene of the address and in relation to the intensity of our unwilled openness to being addressed and touched by others. We then have to seek to recognize what kinds of addresses and encounters deliberation and giving reasons for decisions engender.

Butler's argument about understanding judgment as a form of address has, it seems to me, important consequences regarding judgment in its ties to ethical deliberation. Moral judgment in its proximity to legal judgment is a particular kind of judgment that is rendered after an action or a set of actions has taken place. Moral judgment in this sense evaluates past actions and approves, condones, or condemns them (see *GA* 44–49). There is also a second dimension to moral judgment, which conceives of moral judgment as practical judgment that precedes the action that it then deliberates, evaluates, and eventually approves, condones, or condemns as a course of action to be taken. In this form, moral judgment is closer to political judgment than to legal judgment and makes a claim about what ought or ought not to be done.[30] The rhetorical function of the explanations and justifications that are provided alongside this judgment is to induce the action that is offered as something that "ought to be done."[31] Judgment as this kind of practical judgment, Butler reminds us, is not outside the scene of address but is itself a mode of address.

At this point we can discuss two aspects that have to be taken into account in any attempt to formulate a theory of judgment in moral philosophy. First, in disarticulating responsibility from accountability and rearticulating it through being addressed by others and responding to others' demands, as Butler insists we must, we need to consider legal judgment and condemnation as modes of address and ask what ethical requirements this implies for how judgments are rendered. Second, with regard to deliberation and practical judgment prior to acting, we must take into account that any conscious act we consider and carry out remains traversed by our being dispossessed and disoriented by the touch of the other and by a constitutive unknowingness.

This unknowingness about our own actions, which we can never quite fully control, means that action and freedom are possible only in the form of an unfaithful leap, a necessary betrayal of the primordial responsibility that arrives through the dispossession of the "I" in the encounter with the other. As a consequence, there is a disorientation and disjointedness that are introduced between our ethical responsiveness and our acting ethically responsibly. The primary responsiveness cannot ground or even really orient our actions beyond making very clear that there is a predicament inherent in ethical deliberation—or that it is precisely this predicament that gives rise and particular urgency to ethical deliberation: responding and acting are demanded of us, and yet any response will be belated, never fully knowable or controllable, thus rendering it impossible for us to be absolutely responsible. In attempting to respond and act responsibly, one paradoxically fails one's being called to respond, because one's ability to act and know, one's coming to say and stand as "I," is irrecuperably breached by a double failure: one is at odds with the other because one is arriving too late and because to act also means to distance oneself from the other, and one cannot ever come fully to assume the responsibility for this failure.

This failure of becoming fully accountable has accompanied us throughout this chapter. While often the main concern has been to understand responsibility other than primarily as attributing deeds to an agent and holding the agent accountable, now the main concern is to ask what can guide responsible action and what the consequences are if the responsibility of the encounter cannot ground the "I" and its action as responsible. Considering the consequences of the ambivalence that ensues from this situation of being responsible without a grounded subject prior to its becoming responsible, Butler suggests that this constitutive limitation of assuming responsibility implies an insurmountable need for forgiveness that none of us can evade. Yet the ambivalence of the failure is precisely that the need for forgiveness does not abolish the demand for responsibility. Rather, responsibility has to do with acting as being conscious of limitations and then becomes a question of how to sustain the possibility of responsible action precisely in the face of those limitations.

While the limits of responsibility as accountability may clear, these limits more generally remain problematic in our thinking about responsibility, because to argue that I cannot fully know and stand in for what I have done does not mean that the consequences of my actions are no longer relevant. While we can never fully know the effects and especially the hurtful effects that we may have inflicted, we nevertheless remain responsible for our actions. This relation between responsibility and unknowability means, as Butler argues, that we will remain irremediably in need for forgiveness.[32] Butler offers that as one becomes conscious of this unknowingness and this dependence on forgiveness, it is precisely this knowledge and this acknowledgment of the limits of knowing and acting that might "constitute a disposition of humility and generosity alike, since I will need to be forgiven for what I cannot have fully known, and I will be under a similar obligation to offer forgiveness to others who are also constituted in partial opacity to themselves" (*GA* 42). Obligation here reemerges in Butler's account, in this way similar to Levinas's, precisely from the region of the unwilled. If we cannot ever act fully responsibly, the implications for thinking about ethical theory are, however, not that responsible action and moral philosophy are no longer possible . Instead, it is the failure to become fully responsible that opens up the possibility for ethical life and for an inquiry into morality.

In an interesting gesture in her discussion on politics, power, and ethics, Butler inquires into ethics as that which emerges through the failure to become fully self-transparent and self-aware regarding one's actions and obligations. Ethics, under the auspices of failure:

> would center perhaps on a certain willingness to acknowledge the limits of acknowledgment itself, that when we claim to know and present ourselves, we will fail in some ways that are nevertheless essential to who we are, and that we cannot expect anything different from others. This involves, perhaps paradoxically, both a persisting in one's being (Spinoza) and a certain humility, or a recognition that persistence requires humility, and that humility, when offered to others, becomes generosity.[33]

The interesting question here with regard to Levinas is the role of persistence in one's being, perhaps even the necessary persistence in one's being, and in acknowledging the limits of the livability of the for-the-other. Although there might not be a primordial right to one's own survival that one can invoke as a precondition for and championing of one's attending to others and risking oneself for the other, there might be an emerging obligation that will continuously be troubled by the anarchical relation that the subject always already has to compromise. But because there are always more and other others who demand one's presence—others present, past, and future—there is no ultimate ground for justifying or even prescribing how one is to offer one's presence and one's actions.

Because responsibility is about responding, however, and about returning an address in the response to sustain the encounter with others, we can say that there is an emerging obligation to sustain the conditions of the possibility of responsibility. Sustaining the conditions under which responsible action becomes possible is also a question of subject formation. Responsible action is not possible if our relations with others and becoming a moral subject in our relations to others are no longer possible: "[W]e do not survive without being addressed, which means that the scene of address can and should provide a sustaining condition for ethical deliberation, judgment, and conduct" (*GA* 49). Within this question of sustaining the condition for responsibility, we return as well to the question of the social conditions under which responsibility arises. As noted earlier, our encounters with others do not take place outside social realities conditioned by social norms. So alongside Butler's thought on social norms and subject formation we can now pose the question of social norms in terms of the Levinasian account and ask how his account of the scene of the encounter becomes transformed by theorizing the relation of responsibility as conditioned by social norms, their demands, and their seduction.

For Levinas, the scene of the encounter with the other remains outside and prior to the realm of the socially and historically concrete, although the dyadic encounter traverses all of our encounters with others. In *Giving an Account of Oneself*, Butler marks her divergence from the confines of Levinas's argument, which inscribes the dyadic encounter as a transcendent, preontological reality, when she explains that for the purposes of her inquiry she will take the dyad to be an idealized form of thinking the social encounter with others:

> One can argue that it is the voice of no one, the voice of a God, understood as infinite and pre-ontological, that makes itself known in the "face" of the Other. And that would surely conform to many of Levinas' own claims about the primary address. For the purposes, though, we are treating the Other in Levinas as belonging to an idealized dyadic structure of social life. (*GA* 90)

This move attests to Butler's concern with social and political questions and introduces the demand that conceptual frameworks need to aid in thinking critically about the social realities in which we find ourselves. The question of the relation to social frameworks allows Butler to introduce into this discussion of subject formation in the encounter with an other the question of social norms that adjudicate intelligibility. What are the conditions under which someone can appear as an other with a face that delivers the ethical demand? While it is not within the individual's control to allow or hinder someone to appear as a face, the enjoining power of the face is adjudicated and graded and scaled by social norms and appearing as a face at all is delimited by social norms of intelligibility.

Levinas does not completely obliterate the social and historical contingencies of the concrete situations of our encountering an other; he tells us that representation, interpretation, and comparison are necessary and are even called for: "An objectivity born of justice and founded on justice, and thus required by the *for-the-other*, which, in the alterity of the face, commands the *I*. This is the call to re-presentation that ceaselessly covers over the nakedness of the face, giving it content and composure in a world" (*EN* 167). Levinas distinguishes between the demand of the other that engenders and commands the "I" and that is not open to interpretation and the requirement to interpret and compare the incomparable others precisely because there are multiple others and because each other commands the "I" uncompromisingly. Precisely because of the unlimited responsibility for *each* and *every* other, one cannot disregard the sociohistorical particularities, the historically contingent constellations of power relations, of violence inflicted on one other by another other.

But the question of social conditions also plays a role different from what Levinas imagined, namely with regard to who can appear as a face at all; as Butler clarifies in her reading of Levinas, there are differences in the possibilities of whether images of faces can appear and if so, with which demands and messages. For Butler, not just any image of any face seems to appear as a face in the Levinasian sense of that which delivers an ethical commandment. To demonstrate how in some cases faces come to humanize and in some cases their representation is aimed at a dehumanization, Butler points to the representations of the faces (whether hidden or seen) of Afghan women over and against the faces of Osama bin Laden and Saddam Hussein (see *PL* 143). For Butler, thoroughly transforming Levinas's framework, the social and historical particularities that provide norms of intelligibility are not only at issue with regard to the question of comparing and judging conflicting responsibilities but are already at work in delimiting whose faces come to appear as faces of others who come to deliver the primary ethical demand for responsibility.

For both Levinas and Butler, one is overwhelmed by the face and one does not control the conditions under which one could and would be overwhelmed, but these conditions are in themselves not unchangeable. For Butler, the norms of intelligibility that condition the encounter with the face are dependent on the social categories and norms that adjudicate the ways in which faces are humanized or dehumanized. This being implicated in conditions of social intelligibility is, as Butler points out, the situation of the "I" being dispossessed by the social conditions of its emergence: "This social dimension of normativity precedes and conditions any dyadic exchange, even though it seems that we gain access to that sphere of normativity precisely in the context of such proximate exchanges" (*GA* 23–24). If appearing as a face depends on social norms of intelligibility, then the dyad is always already interrupted by such norms, which open the dyadic relation towards the social conditions of existence. One consequence here is that with Butler—*pace* Levinas—we return to the questions of social norms, their role as conditions of intelligibility, and their changeability over time. With regard to subject formation and moral philosophy, we then have to attend particularly to the role of "social normativity" not only as a normalization that occurs through institutions or impersonal norms but also as conditioning and traversing our face-to-face encounters with others that are not institutionally mediated.

In particular, a critical examination of Butler's concept of responsibility has to interrogate the difference between Butler and Levinas with regard to Butler's drawing on Foucault to offer an analytic of how social norms and relations of power delimit the conditions and practices within which we encounter others. Only then can we say that offering an account of subject formation as a question for moral philosophy demands attention to an ethic of encounter and address but also, importantly, equally an engagement with critical social theory. The question "How should I respond?" on the one hand requires our asking who this other is to whom and for whom we are becoming responsible, and on the other hand we are required to ask: What delimits the possibilities of who and what can appear as an other to whom we become responsible? Precisely how does "the social" orchestrate responsibilities and the conditions under which we emerge as subjects? Attempting an inquiry here means—as Butler argues and performs—that the "I" has to become a social critic, because "[o]ur acts are not self-generated, but conditioned. We are at once acted upon and acting, and our 'responsibility' lies in the juncture between the two" (*PL* 16).

In this chapter we encounter, through Levinas's thinking, an uncompromisability of responsibility at the level of subject formation. This uncompromisable responsibility importantly breaks with attempts to begin theorizing responsibility from accountability and thus allows us to think about responsibility differently. To that end, we find that we must attend to the limitations of our ability to assume responsibility, which does not lead into irresponsibility but instead demands vigilance and reminds us of a shared need for forgiveness. Our capacity for responsibility depends on an unwilled openness toward others that can always be foreclosed and that from the start depends on which others can appear as others at all. In the Levinasian framework there is an ambivalence at the heart of this ethical responsiveness: not only is it always possible to foreclose on the address of the other, but the very encounter with the other seems even to incite a conflict within the moral subject through which the "I" emerges in relation to others. Responsibility depends on an ethical responsiveness that is bound to our exposure and vulnerability to others that means that responsibility is not primarily a question about one's relation to moral norms and ideals, although moral norms and ideals are certainly not deemed irrelevant, as they frame the conditions of subject formation and ethical action.

With Butler, we have been emphasizing the importance of conceiving of this relation through the category of address and in consequence of conceiving of responsibility as both a response and an address in return. If we say that responsibility and responsible action depend on an address, this means that in order for one to ask "How ought I to treat you?" and "What ought I to do?" someone or something happened first to this "I" as an address. Without an address and an awakening to it, there is no "I" who comes to ask what one should do and who the other and others are to whom one comes to respond. With this understanding of an address as a condition of responsibility, an element of spontaneity is introduced that is not exactly the spontaneity of the will. But this spontaneity is the precondition for will and action and lies in what frameworks are in place that render situations recognizable for posing the question of how to respond well. As a consequence of considering how situations come to deliver an address, our discussions of moral philosophy shift from hinging on the will and intention to the question of how our taken-for-granted frameworks of understanding and doing facilitate or foreclose the ways in which the question of morality and ethics as responsible action arises in the first place.

Further, the address that precedes responsibility and its response implies an inevitable belatedness of responsibility and response. Even so, apart from the temporal peculiarity and limitations arising from this situation, this belatedness functions as a reminder that responsibility never exists in a vacuum but is always bound to particular situations and others. On the one hand, responsibility and the "I" that emerges in the act of responding come irrecoverably too late and are implicated in an unknowingness that radically limits our ability to account for our actions and their effects. On the other hand, insofar as responsibility never occurs outside of specific social and historical situations, this means that responsibility requires interpretation and critique in order to attend to the particulars of the circumstances under which encounters with others demand responsible responses.

Both within and beyond Butler, we can therefore argue that responsibility is not primarily about accountability but about responding to others. And deliberation is not primarily about justifying oneself but about interpretation, about explanation, and about translation. Understanding this aspect of translation in reaction to being done to and having to do is what I would like to explore further in the next chapter by drawing on the psychoanalyst Jean Laplanche. Responsibility is further dependent on critique as a practice that is both theoretical and social, if we agree that the subject is not the unquestioned ground for moral philosophy but has become (or has to become) a question for moral philosophy. Critique is crucial precisely because we cannot deduce principles for moral conduct from accounts of subject formation, at least not without rendering a descriptive account into prescriptive account.

FOUR

Ambivalent Desires of Responsibility: Laplanche and Psychoanalytic Translations

Given contemporary critiques of the subject and of the moral subject in particular, the project of this book is to consider the implications of these critiques for rethinking moral philosophy. If we start with a revised understanding of the subject in terms of its formation, rethinking responsibility consequently becomes a pressing question, since we no longer have the subject unquestionably as that of a self-conscious and self-knowing moral agent. Thinking about subject formation in the place of a theory of the subject means considering the histories and processes of this formation not as external or prior to what this subject is and can be. More specifically, taking up Butler's theoretical work on subject formation, becoming a subject is a continuous process characterized by an irrecoverable dispossession in one's relations to others and to the social norms that condition and sustain one's emergence in encounters with others. One consequence of this approach is, as I argue in previous chapters, that responsibility becomes one of the key concepts of moral philosophy. On the one hand, responsibility is seriously called into question by this theory of subject formation, but on the other hand, responsiveness and responsibility become a crucial link to understand how being decentered in and through our relations to otherness is related to moral conduct in response to others.

In effect, the notion of responsibility undergoes a reformulation that disarticulates accountability as the basis for responsibility. We become responsible not because actions can be attributed to us and we can be held accountable for them but because we are addressed by others in ways that demand that we respond, and respond well. Regarding this reworking of responsibility, one of my concerns in the previous chapter is to elaborate on address and response as crucial to framing our understanding of responsibility. The question "How ought I to treat you?" arises because of our openness and responsiveness to others, and so being addressed and responding constitute a relationality that is formative rather than supplemental to the question of responsibility.

Ethical reflection becomes necessary as we find ourselves addressed by others, and so responsibility emerges in the first instance as a question that implies our relationality to those who address us. This relationality, which lays the ground for responsibility, cannot be recovered by memory or reflection, insofar as the conditions of our relationality precede us and we cannot distance ourselves from these conditions in a way that would allow us to gain full reflective knowledge of them.[1] There are different accounts of this relationality, of our being entangled with others, and of our self-unknowingness that can be offered, and the differences between these accounts have implications for what understanding of responsibility in moral philosophy then follows. For the psychoanalyst Jean Laplanche, for example, the "I" is formed in response to an address by the other, as it is in the work of Emmanuel Levinas. However, unlike for Levinas, for Laplanche the address by the other does not deliver an ethical commandment. Rather, while the other's address delivers a demand to respond, it does so through the need to translate this address, because the address is suffused with unconscious meaning and desires. In Laplanche's account, responding and responsibility are determined by how emotions, desires, and fantasies condition our opacity to ourselves as well as our way of relating to others and ourselves.

In this chapter I would like to turn to psychoanalysis and more particularly to the work of Laplanche to return to the notion of desire that has been key to Butler's work from the beginning. Butler engages psychoanalytic theory in her work in various ways to address issues of desire and sexuality, mechanisms of identification and disidentification, and the interrelation between social norms and psychic life in subject formation. Most recently, in *Giving an Account of Oneself*, she turns to Laplanche's work and considers particularly the psychoanalytic notion of transference to examine the nonnarrativizable rhetorical and relational features of communication. Communication works to a large extent through rhetorical and affective dimensions of which we are never fully aware, even while we are in the process of communicating. The ways in which emotions and desires are mobilized in communication limit our control over the effects of what we say and do, but this affective dimension also enables and sustains our interactions and bonds with others. In this chapter I draw on Butler and Laplanche to argue that taking into account desires and being dispossessed by them in encountering others can yield a more expansive understanding of responsibility. It will be crucial to these considerations that whenever we respond to others, these responses are traversed and disoriented by desires and by our past in ways that we can never fully master. This past is never completely past but makes itself felt in the present in ways that we do not control but to which we can and must nonetheless attend and which—if we accept the insights of psychoanalysis—can be reworked in relation to others. Neither, then, are we forever helplessly given over to our dispossession, nor is responsibility the antidote to this dispossession. Instead, as I will argue, we need to understand responsibility in relation to this dispossession and as becoming possible when the effort to gain full control is renounced.

Drawing on psychoanalysis for theorizing responsibility in a philosophical study raises the (perhaps unanswerable and interminable) question of the relation between psychoanalysis and philosophy—and here, more specifically, between psychoanalysis and moral philosophy. Moral philosophy is not contiguous with psychoanalysis, but there is a meeting point between them in that both rely on and formulate theories of the subject and provide accounts of subject formation. Insofar as psychoanalysis offers an account of the subject as being interminably in the process of its own formation, this psychoanalytic account can aid moral philosophy in theorizing moral conduct as an ongoing project that also implies an ongoing problematic of self-formation. I would like to take up in particular some insights into subject formation offered by Laplanche's theoretical elaborations that reflect on the predicaments of having to respond to others without ever knowing fully well how best to do so. Because psychoanalysis and moral philosophy are different theoretical endeavors, it seems to me that these predicaments can become available for interrogation and critical reflection as we move between these two theoretical contexts.

One crucial difference between psychoanalysis and moral philosophy is that, for Laplanche at least, the possibility of psychoanalytical work depends on the suspension of moral judgment. Analysis aims neither directly at determining what ought to be done nor at deeming the analysand's utterances as either good or bad. This approach that deems it necessary for psychoanalysis to suspend both the process of determining what ought to be done and of defining a clear-cut aim for psychoanalysis as such is, as he points out, a contested view.[2] Suspending the desire to delimit steps of action that "ought to be taken" is, for Laplanche, crucial to enabling the process of working through and reworking the psychic material in analysis, because the reworking is done not by the analyst but by the analysand. In particular, this reworking is an undoing of the ego and the unconscious that were formed in response to the external world and an unbinding of primary responses and attachments.

Laplanche's approach differs from those of other psychoanalysts such as Freud and Lacan because Laplanche casts this formation of ego and unconscious in the infant as a "general theory of seduction." This seduction theory describes the formation of the psychic apparatus as the infant's response to experiencing the adult world as one of communicating enigmatic, overwhelming meanings and demands. The infant's response to being overwhelmed by the meanings of the adult world is to translate as best as possible the messages and meanings that others communicate—unknowingly—when they care for and interact with the infant. That which cannot be translated, because it remains enigmatic, is repressed and forms the unconscious as "the other implanted in me . . . forever an 'internal foreign body.'"[3] This otherness, having been irrecuperably overwhelmed by the other, and managing the untranslatable become in turn what opens us from the beginning to others and what conditions our ability to relate to others. Within this background, Laplanche understands the reworking of the primary responses and translations as detranslation and retranslation in the analytic process. This translation process is not aimed at resolving and dissolving the enigma of the other by recovering the enigmatic messages but at reworking one's relation to the enigma of the other that both enables and delimits one's capacity to relate to others. Laplanche and Butler both emphasize that those messages are not possessed by any of us, just as one does not "have" an unconscious, as if one could exert control over it. For Butler, in keeping with Laplanche's position, "the ego is not an entity or a substance, but an array of relations and processes, implicated in the world of primary caregivers in ways in ways that constitute its very definition" (*GA* 59). For her and for Laplanche, the "undoing" that one undergoes in the analytic setting is the undoing of one's sense of self insofar as transference mobilizes these relations that make up the ego by recreating the scenes of address through which these relations were formed.

In her earlier work on subject formation, Butler focuses on modes of address with regard to how we are interpellated and enjoined by normative demands that form us as societal, moral, psychic, and bodily subjects. In her more recent work, particularly in *Giving an Account of Oneself*, she examines the encounter with others as a mode of address and response in relation to others, which introduces the dimension of responsibility in relation to others. If we consider responsibility with regard to norms and bring Butler's earlier and later works to bear on each other, this responsibility cannot be seen as the responsibility conscientiously to fulfill the demands of norms. While we might be held answerable in relation to norms, responsibility in relation to norms means striving for a critical relation to them. Responsibility as responding to others and in relation to others is not external to social realities of norms, but, as Butler emphasizes, the encounter with others and the sociality of norms are not reducible to each other: "[I]t will not do to collapse the notion of the Other into the sociality of norms, and to claim that the Other is implicitly present in the norms" (*GA* 24). Relations to others are not the same as relations to norms, yet in both cases we are dealing with subject formation through being addressed, an address that arrives as a demand that compels a response.

The question of responsibility, as I am arguing it, emerges in conjunction with the question of how to respond *well.* That said, in Laplanche the address by the other does not initiate the addressee into an ethical scene or relation. The address in itself does not convey an ethical commandment or even a message with a particular ethical content, and equally the address is not in and of itself relaying a specific prohibition, ideal, or stipulation. Although the address by the other arrives as a demand of the other that compels a response, as Laplanche emphasizes, this demand is first of all overwhelming and confounding because it remains enigmatic. If we take the Laplanchean understanding of address and response as modes of subject formation in order to illuminate considerations of responsibility, this enigmatic nature of the other's demand is a reminder that the address and the demand of the other cannot serve as the criterion for moral conduct.

The demand of the other is not the criterion for ethics and moral conduct in the sense that knowing what the demand of the other is would translate into the standard for what will inevitably count as responsible action. Sometimes it is even necessary to frustrate the demands and desires of others or necessary that our own desires and demands be frustrated. Psychoanalysis is certainly not a secret key to deciphering the desires of others (or one's own desires, for that matter) to satisfy them better. My goal in this chapter is rather to understand desires and our dispossession by them in our interactions with others as a context for responsibility, insofar as desire and responsiveness are media for elaborating on our relations and on our capacity to relate to others.

Theorizing responsibility as a question of responding, insofar as one comes to ask "What ought I do?," emphasizes the dimension of deliberation, judgment, and decision-making involved in responsibility. However, responsibility and ethics as practices cannot be reduced to deliberation and judgment, even if we conceive of deliberation and judgment as responses that are conditioned by scenes of address that make them necessary. In this chapter I therefore elaborate responsibility as a practice in relations to others and discuss how, through transference, a transformation of our ability to interact becomes possible precisely through these relations.

Desire Transferring Responsibility

In *Giving an Account of Oneself* Butler turns to psychoanalysis and to the notion of transference to reflect on the rhetorical and affective dimensions of giving an account of oneself. To that end, she considers in particular what evades us when we conceive the self exclusively as a narrative, a story, or an account. Even though we can approach the self with regard to its implication in narratives, the web of narratives that constitute our selves is traversed by nonnarratable aspects such as experiences and desires that cannot ever be fully narrativized and hence remain at odds with any narrative rendition that we might give of ourselves. The ways in which we relate to others and how desires are at play in these relations might be exactly what escapes the explicitly narrated but that also conditions and animates the grammar of narrativity. Psychoanalysis can help us in this regard, as Butler argues, because it provides the theoretical tools to understand relationality and desires as traversing and at times even undermining what one aims to render explicit in communicating an account or a story. The psychoanalytic notion of transference is in particular helpful because "transference interrupts the suspect coherence that narrative forms sometimes construct, a coherence that can displace from consideration the rhetorical features of the scene of address, which both draw me back to the scene of not knowing, of being overwhelmed, and also, in the present sustain me" (*GA* 59). In turn, this reflection on transference in relation to communicating with others aids us in theorizing responsibility, because transference allows us to grasp how communicating involves not only conveying information but also acting on others, specifically a kind of acting that cannot be fully thematized in reflection.

The ways in which desires and the rhetorical aspects are at work matter for theorizing responsibility as responding and relating to others, insofar as desires and the rhetorical aspects of communication make fully transparent self-reflective speech impossible. This dimension of desire also implies that in responding to an other, the desires of the responding and acting "I" are not halted or eclipsed. As we see with Levinas, responsibility as a particular manner of responding can be construed neither solely from concerns about the subject or moral agent nor solely from concerns about a single other. There is always a third crucially involved in framing the meaning of responsibility, which is the presence of others, real or imagined, the relations to multiple others. Laplanche and Butler go beyond this aspect of the third by considering how desires and demands in relations and in communication are polyvalent, multiple, and all but transparent to us. While these desires are not impeding and "contaminating" our relations and communications, as that which animates and sustains relations and communications, they are an important, even irreducible, aspect for being addressed, responding, and addressing in return.

In addressing an other, as Butler explains, one is "elaborating a relation to an other in language as I go" (*GA* 50). This elaboration of the relation and of how in the process of this conversation "you" and "I" are altered makes for the ethical valence of the interaction. Butler's argument is surprising not so much for deeming this giving an account as ethically relevant, but insofar as it is not the content of the account alone but the situation of a relation and the unspoken exchange that are key to the ethical dimension of the account. She explains this unspoken dimension of communication further by means of the notion of transference: "In the transference, speech sometimes works to convey information . . . but it also functions as both the conduit for a desire and a rhetorical instrument that seeks to alter or act upon the interlocutory scene itself" (*GA* 50). The desire for which speech is the medium and the dimension of speech as a rhetorical instrument are not reducible to each other. The desire that is at work is, I would like to suggest, the desire to change not only the terms, positions, roles, and preconceptions that delimit how we come to interact, but how I come to interact with a particular other, as the psychoanalytic context suggests a polyvalence of desire.

In the context of transference, desire and address not only act on the other but also end up disorienting me, because desire is not reducible to conscious willing. In relation to this other who is addressed as "you," unconscious histories of desires and relations to others and others' desires—and so my own opacity to myself—are at play: "The 'you' constitutes an object in relation to which an aim of desire becomes articulable, but what recurs in this relation to the other, this scene for the articulation of desire, is an opacity that is not fully 'illuminated' through speech" (*GA* 51). Desires as well as my opacity cannot be rendered translucent but can nonetheless be transformed in relation to an other who is addressed as "you." However, my ability to address myself to "you" as "I" is not simply a linguistic and cognitive skill that we acquire throughout infancy and childhood (and possibly never stop acquiring). Rather, there is a further condition for this capacity that lies, as Butler suggests, in our openness to others that is tied to the formation of the ego through being initially overwhelmed by others. Relating to others, in this view, is not based in my recognizing that "I" am like "you," not even in a likeness of "sharing" this "otherness within us." These qualities can be said to be ones that we have in common, but understanding and acknowledging these qualities as shared does not precede and precondition how we come to relate to each other. The possibility for relating to others lies in this openness that implies a capacity to be addressed and in responsiveness to others that we cannot simply will away.

We find this impossibility to will away our openness toward others in both Levinas and Laplanche. Moreover, as Butler points out in *Giving an Account of Oneself*, both thinkers, despite their differences, understand this openness as a susceptibility and responsiveness to others as constitutive in subject formation. In her discussion of the differences between the two accounts, Butler formulates pointedly that "[w]hereas Levinas asserts a primary passivity indissolubly linked with an ethical responsiveness, Laplanche maintains that there is a primary indissolubility of impression and drive" (*GA* 98–99). Despite the convergence of Levinas and Laplanche in that for both there is a crucial openness and responsiveness to the other and that for both the encounter with the other is overwhelming, for Laplanche the responsiveness and the encounter do not carry an immediate ethical valence, as they do for Levinas. Further, the priority of the other and the other's otherness are not presocial, preontological, or preempirical for Laplanche, but what is overwhelming and enjoining is socially and culturally contingent, although certainly not reducible to consciousness and conscious acts.

In Laplanche, the primary encounter does not circumscribe a time before time and is not a scene of passivity before all passivity, as it is in Levinas. Instead, in Laplanche the primary encounter is the infant's encountering the adult world, and in this regard he considers drives and desires as being crucial to understanding the formation of ego and unconscious. The unwanted address is overwhelming in Laplanche not because it carries an ethical commandment, as it does for Levinas, but because the gestures and utterances the infant encounters are already infused with meanings, desires, and fantasies—especially unconscious ones for which the infant has no register. In Levinas's account of the encounter with the other, there is a constitutive ambivalence because the encounter itself incites one to violence against the other, while at the same time the commandment not to kill is delivered in that very encounter. In Laplanche's account, ambivalence emerges through the overwhelming and enigmatic character of the messages that produce a scene of helplessness, anxiety, and desire that is never fully left behind and never fully recoverable.

In my opinion, the dimension of the unconscious as well as the ambivalence of desire that Laplanche's work offers allow a nontheological account of subject formation without undoing the dispossession by otherness that Levinas elaborates as central in his critiques of the subject and of ontological thinking. Further, Levinas and Butler's reading of Levinas in relation to Laplanche allow us to approach the psychoanalytical accounts with the question of responsibility and to ask how psychoanalytical insights might aid us in reformulating the moral philosophical understanding of responsibility. We can take our cue from *Giving an Account of Oneself* and examine how theorizing desire (insofar as that can ever be possible) provides ethically relevant insights with regard to the opacity of desire that implicitly structures, interrupts, confounds, and animates our interactions. Affective meanings, demands, and fantasies not only constitute a way in which we relate to others but also delimit our affective susceptibility to others' desires and demands. Desire and transference communicate what is not quite possible to render fully discursive and delimit and limit our ability to know and control what effects our words and actions might have on others and what effects addresses and actions that we undergo might have on us. If there is no communication without transference, and if, owing to transference, the effects of our words and actions remain to some extent beyond our control, then the only way to put an end to transference and desire and gain full control over them would be to take oneself out of the interaction—the scenes of address and response—entirely.

If, however, we attempt to understand moral conduct and responsible action in relation to others, then responsibility cannot be situated beyond transference and desire. Rather, we have to work toward, as Butler suggests, "an understanding of transference as a practice of ethics" (*GA* 64) by acknowledging and examining the crucial role of desires in responsiveness and responsibility. Responsibility thus always carries with it a risk of being overwhelmed and of undergoing a dispossession by others as well as a risk of overwhelming others in return. This does not mean that desires or the unconscious could be unambiguously instituted as a criterion for what constitutes responsible actions and ethical life. There is no imperative "don't say this, because it will overwhelm!" that we could deduce, but desire and relationality set the stage for ethical responses. If we understand our relations to others as always being conditioned by asymmetries and ambivalences, then symmetry and harmony cannot serve as communicative ideals, in neither a regulative nor an actual manner. Responsibility in relations cannot mean that the aim is to abolish these asymmetries and ambivalences; instead, responsibility becomes a question of precisely how asymmetries and ambivalences are played out and whether they have oppressive and abusive effects or become fluid and enabling.

Drawing on both Laplanche and Butler, I would like to argue that the asymmetrical and ambivalent character of our interactions is conditioned in relation to the asymmetry of the primary encounter between infant and adult, the earliest encounter with social and power differentials. The asymmetry between infant and adult, for Laplanche, results specifically from the fact that the world around us does not come upon us as neutral, meaningless facts, but that gestures and interactions are always infused with conscious and unconscious meanings, desires, and fantasies. He casts this situation as a "seduction" scene, and his "general theory of seduction" aims to decenter the subject (as well as the role of primal fantasies such as castration) as the backdrop for developmental accounts: "[S]eduction is not to be placed on the same level as other primal fantasies; it is not a fantasy, but a communication situation. Secondly, this communication is neither bilateral, nor symmetrical."[4] Seduction is not about fantasy, but about a particular reality in the form of communication.[5] The reality of this situation is the reality of the message and of its being communicated and thereby overwhelming the infant. The reality of this seduction is different from biological, material, or psychological reality because it is the reality of the message or, to be more precise, the reality of the *enigmatic message* that has been communicated.[6]

The enigmatic message is the dimension of desire and fantasies with which gestures and utterances of the adult world are charged. The example that Laplanche gives to explicate the enigmatic nature of this message coming from the other is the example of the child encountering the mother's breast, which "is a major erogenous zone in a woman, which cannot fail to perform that function in relation to the child. What does this breast which feeds and excites me want of me? What incites me to be excited? What does it want to say to me that it doesn't know itself?"[7] Clearly this example is an inference, because what one thought as an infant encountering the breast by which one was fed cannot be remembered. It is not necessary for Laplanche's theory that there is a breast involved, or even a mother as primary caregiver, since the importance of his theory lies in the erogenous charge of the adults' gestures and in the impossibility of remembering the primary impingement because there was no "I" who could remember. The impossibility of remembering also owes itself to the fact that the message or enigma of the other is not a statement that the infant could not fully understand; rather, in this staging of the scene there is an address that arrives as undecipherable but is nonetheless an address.

The message is overwhelming to the infant because of the greater "knowledge" of the adult, but this knowledge is unmasterable because it comes from the adult's "having an unconscious." No one, however, can "have" an unconscious in the sense of possessing and controlling it. The unconscious cannot be mastered by the adult; rather, his or her actions are infused with unconscious fantasies. Thus the message that is communicated comes to the child not only by means of verbal communication but also by a nonverbal message that cannot be controlled by the one who is transmitting it. So even the one in the active position cannot fully control what she or he is communicating. If we follow Laplanche's considerations, our own understanding of "communication" is reworked. He casts the encounter of caregiver and infant as a "communication situation," but this communication is not an exchange or interaction between two (or possibly more) interlocutors. Although he tells us that "this communication is neither bilateral, nor symmetrical,"[8] which means that at the beginning there was a "communication" in which there is no reciprocity or mutuality, nonetheless something is communicated, even importantly so by being neither cognitively or consciously controllable nor by being discursively rendered explicit.[9] More specifically, the asymmetry of the communication figures this scene as a confrontation; the infant is confronted by the other with a message that it cannot understand but to which it must nevertheless respond.

This account of the formation of the "I" through the seduction through communication is characterized by a radical but compelling asymmetry. With this understanding of the "I," an element of asymmetry, confrontation, and even seduction is always inscribed into our communications insofar as we never fully leave infancy behind. Our past, including our past as infants, continues to condition and traverse the way we relate to others, respond to them, and communicate with them. What was communicated and the terms on which we were addressed as infants were neither determined nor consciously willed by us at that time. From the very beginning we were touched and addressed in terms that none of us could have made or even consented to.

Even though we are not forever completely helplessly given over to being addressed in terms and situations we did not make nor will, the terms and situations in which we are addressed by others and address ourselves to others are also at no point in our lives fully of our own making. The aspect of "seduction," of being carried away, refers us to a responsiveness that we cannot will away, although there may be addresses that go unheard, appeals that go unnoticed, and remaining silent is a possible response.[10] This responsiveness, as suggested by Laplanche, which is formed and reinforced by the address, does not mean, as in Levinas, that the infant is responsible for the encounter or its terms. But in contradistinction to Levinas, there is also no primary responsibility for the other; for Laplanche, however, there are desire and disorientation from the beginning. The encounter with the other, in a Laplanchean view, does not immediately bring about an ethically qualified responsiveness; rather, the responsiveness and its further trajectory are delimited by an emotional entanglement with the addressing other and a passionate attachment to that other.

The emergence of the "I" through this impingement of the other happens through an address that communicates a *demand* by confronting the infant with it. This demand is, more specifically, enigmatic and unknowable, which, as Laplanche lays out, conditions the untranslatability of the enigma of the other and at the same time compels the infant to translate in order to contain the overwhelmingness and to respond as adequately and as well as possible. By translating, the infant transitions from utter passivity—the passivity of being overwhelmed by the other—into activity that is possible only relative to the other's breaking in. Translation is in a certain way a closure, a distancing of oneself from the other, but it also constitutes an attachment to the other, since that which cannot be translated is repressed and forms the unconscious, where the untranslatable continues to live on. The unconscious is, therefore, for Laplanche, "the result of repression bearing on fragments of communications which it, by doing so, makes foreign to the context which is their origin" (PTT 174).[11] This means that through the process of translation, the initial message that came from the other person is displaced and the origin evacuated and relocated inside the subject, where that which could not be translated is retained through the unconscious.

Using these spatial metaphors to describe the unconscious, however, is not quite adequate to capture its function, as Butler in her interpretation of Laplanche makes clear: "The unconscious is not a topos into which this 'too much-ness' is deposited. It is rather formed as a psychic requirement of survival and individuation, as a way of managing—and failing to manage—an excess" (*GA* 54). In other words, the unconscious is not a site where what remains untranslatable is put to rest but a mechanism to deal with the traces of the overwhelming enigmatic messages that do not lead an indolent life. Subsequent addresses by others rupture the murmur of the "I" and reactivate the primary situation of having been overwhelmed, bringing back the traces of the untranslatable.

This reactivation of the untranslatable and of being overwhelmed is the effect of transference, and with reactivation also comes the possibility of reworking the translation of the untranslatable excess that returns. The unconscious and repression are important mechanisms in dealing with "too much otherness" in relation to others. As the unconscious is "enacted" in relation to an other, the undoing of the repression brings to the fore the constitutive dispossession, disorientation, and incoherence of the "I." I can tell stories about who I am, how I came to be where I am now, but I cannot know with certainty or give a definitive account of what made me. Key to this impossibility is that these stories came to be only through my relations to others, and in my attempting to offer a story to another other, it is precisely the presence of this other that interrupts and disorients my story by making me ask: Who am I to tell you this story? Who are you? What does this story tell you about me that I do not say? What are you thinking that you are not telling me? So the other becomes the occasion for the unraveling of myself and my assumed coherence.

Butler clarifies that arguing for an understanding that accepts a fundamental and irrecoverable dispossession of the subject by the other does not mean heralding dispossession, disorientation, and incoherence either for their own sakes or as new virtues of the subject: "The purpose here is not to celebrate a certain notion of incoherence, but only to point out that our 'incoherence' establishes the way in which we are constituted in relationality: implicated, beholden, derived, sustained by a social world that is beyond us and before us" (*GA* 64). As infants we were addressed, cared for, and touched by others before there was an "I" who could register and later recall those instances as memories. We can speculate about and theorize this relationality as a condition of our emergence as conscious subjects, but none of us can recover those relations and give a full account of how one's capacity to relate to others was formed by those primary relations. This irrecoverability of our own origins constitutes an "incoherence" and dispossession of the self-conscious "I" that we never outgrow, control, or even know fully. If "our 'incoherence' establishes the way in which we are constituted in relationality," (*GA* 64) precisely how does this "incoherence" determine how we relate to others?

Because of this incoherence, because of one's being dispossessed, there is always more than the explicit that is relayed in communication, especially as one is being dispossessed by one's own words in relation to an other. As one addresses oneself to another, one's words betray one. One's words always do more than what one knows that one does, because the words carry an address and act on the other. As an address, the force of the argument might indeed become clearer if we reformulate the last claims as an address: as I address myself to you, my words betray me. I always say, or rather do, and thus communicate more than what I know that I do. Not only do I consciously aim to act on you, attempting to persuade you, but in relation to you as I speak, I articulate more than I know; my words become the medium for desires and an accumulated array of emotions, relations, addresses, and responses. But this dispossession not only bespeaks my incoherence and relays potentially overwhelming messages but also repeats that which conditions this incoherence, making it available for a possible alteration.

In particular, the kind of "self-disclosing speech" that one practices in giving a narrative account about oneself is, as Butler lays out, understood by psychoanalysis as a kind of speech that also "recreates and constitutes anew the tacit presumptions about communication and relationality that structure the mode of address. Transference is thus the recreation of a primary relationality within the analytic space, one that potentially yields a new or altered relationship (and capacity of relationality) on the basis of analytic work" (*GA* 50–51). The "tacit" underpinnings that condition the mode of address and our relations cannot be rendered explicit by a mere cognitive effort; rather, they become accessible as they are "recreated." All the implicit histories' relations, addresses, and responses—what we often call "emotional baggage"—are at work when transference is at work, and perhaps, to the extent that there may be no communication without transference, all communication is traversed by primary situations.

Indeed, there may be no address without acting on another, without desires and emotions communicated in the back of what is explicitly articulated. One implication of this is that the meaning of altruism is relativized if my relating, addressing, and responding to an other relies on and makes these actions, in the back of all intentions, also partly about me, about my relation to the other and otherness. In return, in being addressed I cannot help but become the recipient of meanings that are not articulated and that are not really about me, or that are about me only insofar as it was in relation to me that they surfaced for the other. What the other addresses to me is equally not only about me but about the one who addresses him- or herself to me.

Bringing these considerations on transference to bear on our concept of responsibility, we can understand better how responsibility is one mode of responding and interacting with others that is complicated by how desires traverse our relations with others. Responding and responsibility are thus not reducible to conscious deliberation, moral judgment, and consciously determined action. Responsibility is about responding to concrete others in concrete situations as well as about our capacity to relate to others. This capacity is constituted by a relationality that is not an abstract given but instead is shaped through the array of addresses, responses, and relations that form our ego and unconscious and that is continuously reshaped in transference. Our ability to respond well to others, our ability to ask the question of responsibility—"How ought I to treat you?"—depends upon our relationality and responsiveness to others. And this responsiveness and capacity to relate are elaborated and sustained in relation to others. In relations and interactions, part of responding responsibly is determined by whether reworking the way we relate to each other becomes possible or whether this possibility is foreclosed.

So how and where one will pose the question "How ought I treat you?" is neither fixed nor fully in one's conscious control. How and where I come to ask this question "How ought I treat you?" are constantly changing because how this question occurs to me depends on my capacity and manner of relating to others in general, which are continuously reworked in transference. This change or elaboration is not a linear process with neither a real nor an ideal end point with regard to which one could then mark and measure one's progress. To think about transference as an ethical practice does not mean that we all ought to "psychoanalyze" each other. Rather, it means that the question "What does the other want from me?" introduces a vexation into ethical deliberation, because one cannot fully evade the disorienting "touch" of the other. This vexation in turn becomes the occasion for the possibility of elaborating and reworking our relations to others and our capacity to relate to others.

Disorientation and Responsibility

We are disoriented by the encounter with an other, dispossessed of ourselves from the beginning, and this disorientation and dispossession delimits and sustains our capacity to relate to others. This account of the formation of the subject through a dispossession by the other allows us, I suggest, to understand that this dispossession can also become the site for altering and developing the way we relate to an other. If the capacity to relate is an important resource for responsibility and ethical reflection, we still have to ask how these insights can furnish a more substantive understanding of how this disorientation and dispossession in relation to an other can shape our practices. In what follows, I would like to offer a discussion of benevolence derived from Butler's and Laplanche's discussion of transference that is conditioned by the suspension of assuming a position of knowledge about who the other is and what is best for the other and by the suspension of normative judgment.

As part of this argument, I would like to suggest that we can understand the return of judgment through its complicated relation to this suspension of judgment and "knowledge" that is also a suspension of desires to solve the problems of the other for the other. Responsibility in transference is aimed neither at substituting oneself for the other nor at creating a narrative or "solution" for the other. As Butler emphasizes, "At its best, the transference provides . . . a holding environment and offers a bodily presence in a temporal present that provides the conditions for a sustaining address" (*GA* 59). In reflecting on transference, so runs the argument of this section, psychoanalytic theory can instruct theorizing responsibility by complicating the notions of benevolence and free speech in relation to others, precisely because who the other is to whom we respond is a question to be posed continuously rather than a known given.

In psychoanalysis the conscious subject undergoes an undoing, but this happens in a very specific way. First, it is an undoing that turns to the past and is interested in "going back over" that past not to gain better knowledge of this past or to abolish this past by rendering it fully present but to reopen it for a certain "resolution," to make it more workable through the process of transferences. Second, this turning and going over the present translation of the past are made possible through psychoanalysis insofar as it offers "a place for speech, for free speech, but not, properly speaking, the place of an exchange. There is an essential dissymmetry in the relation" (TPA 227–228).[12] Free speech, as Laplanche offers it to us, is not a matter of reciprocal exchange; rather, free speech mobilizes transference and detranslation, which disorient and interrupt any presumed mutuality. Free speech produces and heightens the asymmetry in my interaction with an other to whom I address myself, because the effects of the address on the other are unforeseeable. Free speech involves a risk, namely the risking of oneself as one dares to speak without knowing exactly what the effect will be.

Free speech in analysis and the dynamic of transference allowing for a detranslation and retranslation of an enigmatic message become possible in analysis, according to Laplanche, under the conditions of a concern for the analysand's good. Psychoanalysis, as Laplanche argues emphatically, "does bring experience and knowledge—that of the method—but also a radical refusal to know the good of its patient, to know the truth about his good" (TPA 228).[13] Psychoanalysis is not completely unknowing regarding the analysand; rather, the knowledge and experience that psychoanalysis brings are in framing and enabling the possibility of being undone by and in the presence of the other. The space that allows for free speech, though, is created through the analyst's refraining from making particular judgments regarding the analysand's good. The analyst is even actively to refuse to "know" when this knowledge is desired by the analysand.

In order to consider the implications of this kind of free speech beyond analysis, we have to ask what the implications are of this characterization of "free speech," of reopening the relation to the originary encounter with the enigmatic other by being overwhelmed by the demand of the other beyond the analytic setting. What happens as we move to consider less clearly circumscribed situations of encounters between individuals? What does it mean in that more general setting to respond in a way that enables critical speech rather than forecloses it? One presumably goes into analysis trusting or at least hoping and willing to assume the analyst's goodwill in becoming the recipient of one's speech. This presumption, however, cannot always be made in situations outside analyst's office, where aims, expectations, and roles are often less explicit and where the asymmetries of power and knowledge are differently complex from in the analytic setting.

Certainly not all situations of responding and responsibility are alike, and to insist on the importance of address, encounter, and transference for thinking about responsibility does not mean to imply that all situations, relations, and encounters are reducible to a common structure. The limit in providing a general theory of how to respond to others is the generality of the necessity to attend to the particularities of any given situation, because they will be decisive in thinking about what it means in that particular situation to respond well. Nonetheless, "attending to the particulars" remains a vague notion, and it is by no means self-evident precisely what these "particulars" are that characterize the situations or encounters in which ethical deliberation and action become necessary. One difficulty in recognizing and analyzing such situations results from the circumstance that there are no pure facts, but instead situations and events are already endowed with meaning and how we encounter and relate to others depends on our epistemological, ethical, and cultural frameworks and predispositions. Theoretical work aims at offering an occasion for reflecting on these frameworks, accessing and assessing them, and possibly allowing for their alteration. Theoretical reflection at its best might be able to initiate an encounter with an other—be it only a textual other—that does not leave us unchanged and might even open up a space for reflecting, reworking, and eventually responding.

Responsibility as responding to others becomes possible insofar as we are in a relation with others and sustain that relation, even if these relations are highly mediated or indirect. The problem is that often this relational dimension to responsibility is evacuated, eschewed, or emptied of the overwhelming and disorienting character of being addressed that precedes and necessitates a response. As Butler and Laplanche lay out, being addressed by others and interacting with others imply asymmetries and confrontations by being undone and disoriented by the other and by one's own reactions in the face of the address, all the while still having to respond.

One problematic that this disorientation of responsibility introduces and heightens is the question of who the other is. Not only does the other arrive as a message or an enigmatic demand, but one is addressed by others and addresses them in return in the form of response. To address an other transforms this "other" into a "you," which not only introduces the question

"Who are you?" into reflections on responsibility. Moral philosophy is further concerned with and even draws on an impersonality, a generalization, and perhaps even a necessary evasion of the "you" to demonstrate responsibilities to others beyond our proximate relations. Through this problem of who the other is, the question of responsibility raises the issue of recognition.[14] In other words, if the question of responsibility is conditioned by the question of *how* to respond *well* to another, to you, then theorizing responsibility as responding to an other will also have to ask who this other is, who this "you" is, and what relation there is between them. The question "Who are you?" ties responsibility to the question of recognition, where recognition is a crucial aspect of what it means to respond *well* to an other. In the following I would like to draw on Laplanche's work to problematize the assumption that as soon as the other is addressed, the other is simply "you," a tangible potential partner in dialogue.

The question "Who is the other?" seems at first to be a merely epistemological question, but it carries ethical valence when we consider that it marks the "I" 's openness to the other and potentially mobilizes this openness as availability to the other. At the same time, that which exposes me to the other is in return possibly overwhelming, precisely because the question "Who is the other?" is not merely a soliloquy—"I wonder, who is the other?" When extended to the other as "Who are *you?*" this question takes on the character of an address. The problem in this shift, however, is intricate, as Laplanche's comment on the strangeness of the other elucidates: "For every one of us it is difficult to give an account of this strangeness, and to face it. Think of it in terms of grammar. In grammar, you say, the first person is the person who speaks. The second person is the person to whom I speak. The third person is the person of whom I speak. But who is the person who speaks to me?"[15] In his essay "Responsabilité et réponse," Laplanche makes this argument in a similar fashion but is more explicit on the impossibility of identifying the other who addresses me: "But who then is the person who speaks to me? Because that certainly is neither I, nor you, nor he" (*Mais quelle est donc . . . la personne qui me parle? Car ce n'est assurément ni je, ni tu, ni il*).[16] What Laplanche indicates here is that the other by whom I am addressed is not readily identifiable as "you," which appears strange indeed, as, particularly in personal encounters, it seems quite obvious that you are the one by whom I find myself addressed.

For theorizing responsibility, this confounding moment regarding "Who is the other?" seems to pose a serious problem, because if the other is so very unknowable—faceless, one might even say—if there is no "you" who can address me, then how is there the possibility for a relationship? At the same time, this refusal to identify the other is interesting, perhaps even crucial, for theorizing responsibility in the context of understanding translation and transference and of a deferral of judgment. If the other is not you, then the ontological and epistemological questions "Who are you?" "Who is the other?" and "How can I know you and what need I know about you?" "How can I know the other and what need I know about the other?" are not external to the question "How ought I to treat you?"

Insofar as you are other to yourself, it becomes impossible for me readily to assume that you are this "you" who I think is addressing me. If we accept that in all our interactions transference and countertransference are at work, then we might say that in every communication the asymmetries are not as clear-cut as they might seem at first and that daring the "you" in addressing another person means in fact risking two "I"s. Even in responding to you, I will not only expose myself to you in the fragility of my "I"; I depend on your response, but at the same time my response is another address, namely, you finding yourself addressed by a demand, by my demand for your response.

What seems like a dyadic relationship between a "you" and an "I" is, however, at no time an exclusively dyadic relation after all, because there are always already other others disorienting this dyad in various ways. All dyadic relations are disoriented by social norms and frameworks that condition the terms and situations in ways that we cannot fully control. Moreover, although the disorientation that Butler and Laplanche discuss is socially and culturally specific, this disorientation is not reducible to the works of social norms but introduces the enigma of the other as also bound up with a sexual, erotic, desirous, and unconscious dimension. The question of responsibility is therefore not reducible to responding to demands by others, but responsibility and our responses are framed by finding ourselves addressed by others and situations that demand responses. While the address entangles us with an other, it is not a dialogic relation that is instituted; dialogue or mutual understanding does not ground our responsibility toward others. Instead, our translations of the enigmatic messages and responses to the other as well as the social and cultural schemes that delimit our interpretations and understanding of the world around us provide the framework for responding subsequently and for limiting what we can know.

The predicament is not simply that what we can know is limited and that in some respects we remain unknown to ourselves. Butler demonstrates that these limitations do not obviate responsible conduct per se, but they can inform and invigorate our sense of responsibility. Acknowledging our own irresolvable opacity and understanding that it results from our being entangled in relations with others, from being exposed and responsive to others prior to conscious reflection, can become a resource for responsibility and make us more thoughtful, more careful. But this acknowledgment cannot guarantee that we will not do and say things that later turn out to have been irresponsible. One worry, as Butler points out, about beginning to theorize responsibility from its limits is that the consequence will be the destruction of responsibility, because if one could not have known the consequences of one's actions, then the possibility of holding someone accountable for his or her actions remains limited. The worry continues that to insist on our opacity ends up "giving license" to any and all behavior (see *GA* 19–20). Butler's aim in *Giving an Account of Oneself* is to demonstrate how the contrary is the case and that the limitations of our capacity to know have very specific implications for moral philosophy, because we can know how these limits are conditioned.

While this not knowing can work to make us more careful, it remains important to keep in mind that this newly won carefulness can always turn into a silencing mechanism that undercuts critical questioning in the name of care and attention to those who are addressed. The ethical valence of not being able to know becomes problematic when this kind of responsiveness and responsibility consolidates hierarchies and reentrenches social norms. This not being able ever fully to know can in return, however, also imply an enabling insight, namely, that one can and must dare to address others.

That irrecoverable incoherence and unknowingness obviate the possibility of responsibility is a conclusion that mistakes the limitation of knowledge for an impossibility of any knowledge. As a consequence, such a misunderstanding then turns the argument that we are limited in what we can know into a justification for not even attempting to know anything about others, our obligations, and the effects of our actions. This argumentative shift is problematic because it surreptitiously transposes an epistemological quandary about the possibility of ethical reflection into a moral justification for the omission of ethical reflection. The epistemological question certainly has ethical valence, because our constitutive opacity marks our fallibility and circumscribes how the unflinching stipulation of an obligation to know can come to exert violence in the name of maintaining the possibility of moral conduct. At this point two worries converge—namely, the worry about theorizing responsibility on the basis of stipulating a knowing subject and the worry about theorizing responsibility by theorizing the limitations of our ability to know. These two worries converge into one large concern that the approach to responsibility will frustrate and exhaust rather than renew and orient our capacities to deliberate, judge, and act responsibly, which also, but certainly not exclusively, require the ability to denunciate and condemn actions as wrong and reprehensible.

The question for a moral philosophical account is whether focusing on the limits of what we can know can offer sufficient orientation for determining our responses to the recurrent question "How ought I to treat you?" In his review of Butler's 2002 Adorno Lectures (a considerably shorter version of *Giving an Account of Oneself*),[17] Friedrich Wilhelm Graf offers reservations about the robustness of Butler's argument that the acknowledgment of our constitutive opacity to ourselves can bring about and foster "self-acceptance (a humility about one's constitutive limitations)" and "generosity (a disposition toward the limits of others)" (*GA* 80). Graf worries that in the end we are left with nothing but a "rhetorical plea" for this acceptance of our and others' limits. He wonders whether it is possible to derive a theory of "strong recognition" from a "theory of the weak 'I.'" I would like to take up Graf's reservations here, but not in order to "fix the problem" by offering a supplement or by inquiring whether his criticisms are warranted; Graf's concerns are important because they provide an occasion to examine how this concern delimits an underlying problematic or question about what we expect and require of moral philosophy.

What is it that we assume a strong theory can achieve that a "weak" theory cannot? That it can offer normative principles? Or grounds for normative principles? Or more substantive accounts of what this generosity of granting others their opacity means? Perhaps the underlying concern is that the possibility of substantively orienting responses to "How ought I to respond? What ought I to do?" cannot be proffered by the "theory of the weak 'I,'" because it rather limits, undercuts, and questions these orientations as they emerge. The "weakness" is the function of critique. The plea for more generosity is indeed an important plea—and perhaps insofar as theory does not seamlessly necessitate practice, theory might in a way always end up as a plea, a set of arguments that seek to persuade but cannot ensure or control their own intended and unintended effects. Insofar as a theoretical inquiry—as critique—examines limitations of our knowledge, it then has to be careful not to turn a logical "you have to" into a moral "you must" or a logical "you cannot" into a moral "you must not." The plea remains the limit of what the critique of the subject can responsibly offer. Perhaps moral philosophy cannot say more but must at the same time desire to say more and factually always ends up saying more. These predicaments cannot be abolished, but reflection on them not only is possible but also becomes necessary as critique of the possibility of moral philosophy and of its limits. Attending to these limits, and in particular to the predicament of having to respond while absolute certainty and knowledge remain unattainable, can then orient our practice toward a kind of mastery that is of necessity a weak mastery in the face of the impossibility of fully knowing.[18]

It is impossible ever fully to know the effects of one's actions and words, past and future, and if one accepts the psychoanalytic view, then this impossibility of knowing the effects of our actions and words owes itself at least partially to the fact that our actions and words are infused with unconscious meanings and fantasies. In communicating, one can never fully know whether an utterance or a gesture might reactivate overwhelming encounters in the other to whom one addresses oneself. Interacting with another, therefore, cannot be based on full knowledge of oneself and one's own actions; rather, it must aim for a mastery that is self-critical and self-reflexive. Laplanche offers us "a mastery which recognises its limits and acknowledges its own testimony [that] is something different from one which strains itself and, in the end, fails" (TPA 233). This means that the inability to know does not sever responding to the other from the weight of responsibility but instead reframes the notion of responsibility as a response that performs and requires an acknowledgment of its own fragility and limitations. How can any answer recognize its own inner limitation? Perhaps by not acquiescing and eliminating the question to which it responds but by instead holding the question present, thus avowing that it is not the ultimate response to that which demanded this response.

Continuing to ask the questions of how to respond well to the other, who the other is, and who I become in the face of the other occasions and orients the possibility of critical reflection. This possibility of critical reflection is in part facilitated through transference, and with Laplanche we have examined the interlocutor's solicitude and deferral of judgment as creating stability and an environment that allows for the possibility of free speech. However, for moral philosophy in conversation with these insights drawn from psychoanalytic theory, the problematic arises that in many of our encounters, though constituted by asymmetries, it might remain unclear how these asymmetries are distributed; they might be fragile and shifting, not easily revealing precisely how they relate to the model of analysand/analyst or the model of infant/adult. This is not to say that there will not be assumptions made about who "knows more," but outside of these very particular situations, these roles and positions will no longer be so clearly delimited, which means that the questions "What does the other want from me?" "Who is the other?" "Where is the other?" are not attenuated but heightened by the asymmetrical relations.

In *Fearless Speech*,[19] Foucault offers a different understanding of the asymmetrical conditions of interactions, and through this interpretation he allows us to think further about how the differences in power and possibilities outside of analysis might reintroduce judgment and criticism whose suspension Laplanche has argued as crucial for analytic work. As Laplanche does, Foucault introduces a notion of free speech that becomes possible precisely because there is an asymmetry in power and knowledge. He argues that free speech, *parrhesia*, is available only to the one *not* in the power position: "Someone is said to use *parrhesia* and merits consideration as a *parrhesiastes* only if there is a risk or danger for him in telling the truth" (*FS* 15–16). Risking oneself is, for Foucault, constitutive of the possibility of engaging in free speech. This risk is intertwined with the courage necessary to risk oneself in addressing oneself to the other by *saying the truth*, which is a truth "capable of hurting or angering the *interlocutor*" (*FS* 17).

Free speech occurring in analysis seems to be at an angle to the defining trait of Foucault's free speech as having to be "criticism of the interlocutor or of the speaker himself" (*FS* 17). This criticism in the Foucauldian version takes the form of a statement of what one does or has done and then a statement of what one *ought to* or *should* do or have done; *parrhesia*:

> may be the advice that the interlocutor should behave in a certain way, or that he is wrong in what he thinks, or in the way he acts, and so on. Or the *parrhesia*

> may be a confession of what the speaker himself has done insofar as he makes this confession to someone who exercises power over him, and is able to censure or punish him for what he has done. (*FS* 17)

Free speech in Foucault instrumentally involves offering evaluative judgments and, it seems, even moral judgments. The approach of psychoanalysis in dealing with such statements being offered by the analysand requires from the analyst not to return or affirm these judgments, since these moral judgments are seen as being detrimental to analysis, and therefore psychoanalysis considers these as precisely the material to be worked through and untied, unbound.

For Laplanche, free speech is facilitated by withholding and suspending judgment about what ought to be done in the context of analysis. If we take Laplanche as representing free speech "in analysis" and Foucault as representing free speech "outside analysis," then it seems as though outside analysis free speech is necessarily bound to judgment and inside it there is no way judgment should ever reenter. However, there is a convergence of Laplanche and Foucault insofar as the way judgment performs as an address to the other person depends on the position from which one speaks and not only on one's intentions. On the one hand, we can take Foucault as a reminder that judgment and criticism need not be detrimental to interactions but are actually crucial in our relations to others. On the other hand, we do well to be reminded by Laplanche that judgments are not all there is to interactions and that they might curb rather than foster the possibility of thoughtful and critical reflection. With both Laplanche and Foucault, we can reflect, beyond analysis, on how asymmetries in our interactions are conditioned not only by unconscious desires and transference but also by power.

Frank speech and criticism not only presuppose a power relation but also produce asymmetries that cut across what might seem the obvious power positions. Criticism can also prevent or delegitimize the possibility of a critical rejoinder preemptively by ascribing to those who are addressed as "others" the position of power, which then means that they cannot have access to free speech or that if they offer criticism, they are using the prerogative of the powerful but that there is no virtue of free speech in their speech. What began as critique then ends as moralistic discourse. But if judgment is to have value as an ethical practice in critical discourse, the relation between judgment and responsibility will be an important question, as is what then becomes of accountability.

Reworking Accountability as Translation

In this and the previous chapter I argue against defining responsibility primarily as a question of accountability. Responsibility is not reducible to asking what one's obligations are and for which actions one will be held accountable if one omits them or fulfills them poorly or improperly. Such an approach frames understanding responsibility as measured by criteria for appropriate fulfillment of obligations and by standards for attributing actions to agents. However, such an approach cannot take into account responsibility as a response and its role in subject formation. Instead, theorizing responsibility with accountability as a starting point takes the subject as a settled precondition for the question of responsibility, and the version of the subject that such a theory implies is one that can know what it ought to do and ought to will and that can and will act accordingly.

In *The Genealogy of Morals*, Nietzsche criticizes precisely this assumption of taking the knowing and willing moral subject as a given entity. Responsibility, he argues, becomes, after a long process of formation, the prerogative of the promising individual who will not change his will, delivers on his promises, and thus is accountable and able to account for his actions. Nietzsche offers a genealogy that conceives of the ability to promise and the privilege of responsibility as formed through being held accountable and punished. The moral subject is thus formed only belatedly and retroactively as a cause of its actions upon the occasion of being held accountable for them. Responsibility, in this account, emerges after external norms are internalized and one comes to hold oneself accountable to them prior to acting. As a consequence of Nietzsche's criticism, introducing responsibility on the basis of accountability is rendered problematic.

The aim of my argument so far has been to take up these insights and to argue responsibility as a key category for moral philosophy but to approach theorizing responsibility not from a question of the attribution of actions to agents and not by deriving obligations from moral norms, their knowability, and the possibility of willing and acting accordingly. Instead, I attempt to understand responsibility as being conditioned by having been addressed and by our responsiveness to others and as a question of responding well to others. This approach, however, does not yet explain what happens to accountability, whether we should get rid of the notion completely or whether it remains important for moral conduct and, if so, how it would then reenter.

One problematic that Nietzsche's criticism raises and that Butler takes up is the question of how there can be accountability if self-knowledge about our actions and intentions is always limited and traversed by an unknowingness about the conditions of their formation. With the grounds for accountability in question, practices of judgment and punishment come equally into question. Is the establishment of accountability prior to the judgment and punishment what renders practices ethical? Is it for that reason that accountability is so often considered as crucial for moral conduct, because without accountability there cannot be responsibility or responsible judgment? Being held accountable and holding others accountable do not, I would continue to argue, establish grounds for one's responsibility. Nonetheless, these practices continue to be an important part of ethical life precisely because they refer to the past and past actions insofar as this past and its consequences matter in the present. But arguing that accountability has to be established first in order to give just cause to rendering judgments and punishments is problematic, not because accountability, judgment, or even punishment are to be denounced per se, but because this argument tends to presuppose that judgment and punishment could settle the past and with it the temporal rivenness of ethical life.

The difficulties that rethinking accountability poses become particularly clear with regard to broader political dimensions such as transitional justice and efforts in the politics of truth, reconciliation, and reparation. Discussions about accountability in its legal, political, and personal aspects run up against a crucial quandary in the relation of justice and forgiveness and the possibilities and limits of both.[20] My considerations about accountability here address a much narrower set of questions of how our opacity to ourselves as agents does not render accountability impossible but allows us to rethink accountability by attending to responsibility as responding and to this inability ever fully to know others, ourselves, or the conditions and consequences of our actions. Hence I set aside the discussions on forgiveness and the politics of reconciliation in order to focus more specifically on the temporal aspect in responsibility through responsiveness and accountability.

In this attempt I would like to shift our perspective from thinking about accountability primarily as a problem of attributing past actions to someone, possibly to oneself as wrongdoing. Instead I am primarily interested in how accountability arises as a problem over the irrecoverability and unsettledness of the past and how we might understand accountability as a particular mode of responding to being undone by this past. By drawing on Butler's and Laplanche's insights into judgment, transference, and translation, I would like to examine the possibility of understanding accountability as a practice that allows an attending to and a reworking of the ethical predicament that arises when past actions and their consequences give rise to ethical questions in the present.

While we can certainly know about our actions and their consequences, this knowledge remains limited because of our constitutive unknowingness. This unknowingness is conditioned in various ways, as Butler lays out, namely, by our relation to social norms, our relation to others, and our relation to temporality, which constitute a dispossession that we cannot become fully conscious of. It might seem that this unknowingness regarding our own actions undermines the possibility of thoughtful and deliberate decisions and accountability for these decisions because this unknowingness introduces irrationality and irresponsibility into our actions. This irresponsibility characterizes our actions insofar as responsibility requires knowledge and reflection. If, however, there is a constitutive limitation to this knowledge, then there is a necessary irresponsibility or fallibility that makes responsibility possible, if to become responsible is to respond (and certainly, not responding is also a response). Without the suspension of the requirement to know completely "What ought I to do? How to respond well?" we could never act because we can never fully know. Responsibility is not reducible to the knowledge about what to do, but ethical reflection and deliberation as practices striving for such insight and knowledge are crucial for the critical potential of responsibility.

This moment of suspension hence introduces a moment of irrationality and irresponsibility, a moment of spontaneity in action that is not reducible to reflection, which seems to undermine our capability for ethical reflection and action as well as the possibility of being held accountable and holding others accountable. Any account of intentions and reasons remains a belated account, an aftereffect and rationalization of affects, motivations, and decisions which can never conclusively establish the "truth" about one's considerations and actions. Beyond the irreducible spontaneity and affect in willing and acting remain our unwilled responsiveness and openness which precede and traverse our conscious willing and acting. My aim here is to argue that we can acknowledge the unknowingness and irrecoverability of past intentions and that we continue to be accountable and hold others accountable. To this end, we need to understand how our unknowingness, rather than our capacity for reflective knowledge, grounds accountability and continue to ask how accountability can function as a practice of reworking that enables rather than curbs ethical reflection and responsible action.

In *Giving an Account of Oneself*, Butler suggests that rather than knowledge or intentions, it is our constitutive opacity that grounds accountability: "[W]hat conditions our doing is precisely that for which we cannot give a full account, a constitutive limit, and that this condition is, paradoxically, the basis of our accountability" (*GA* 111). This claim might seem counterintuitive, but I would like to suggest that approaching the question of accountability by asking about its basis renders different responses from if one seeks those grounds by asking about justification. Our opacity establishes the necessity, importance, and relevance of giving an account, not despite our unknowingness but because of our unknowingness. The basis for accountability is not that I can justifiably be expected to be able to render an account of myself and my actions because I was able and am able to know myself, my intentions, my deliberations, my actions, and their consequences with certainty. Rather, my knowledge about myself, my intentions, my deliberations, my actions, and their consequences is constantly traversed and limited by my unknowingness, but this limitation, while not abolishable, is not unchangeable. Moreover, the past has not simply passed away, and if the past is to provide a resource for responsibility, then attempting to give an account for what I did, whom and what I responded to, who I became, and what became of my actions can become instrumental in enabling ethical reflection that aims to bring about a truth about my intentions and actions not for truth's sake alone but because their consequences matter.

So in other words, accountability and judgment are not posited as grounds for moral conduct in themselves but become available for critical reflection by examining them as specific practices of moral conduct that are part of ethical life but that are by no means the exclusive foundations of ethical life. As Butler points out regarding condemnation and punishment, the ethical dimension of judgment and punishment is conditioned by the relation between the one judging and the one judged and the kind of address that the judgment comes to be: "Condemnation, denunciation, and excoriation work as quick ways to posit an ontological difference between judge and judged, even to purge oneself of another" (*GA* 46). The ethical problem in judging and condemning someone's actions arises, Butler argues, not because judgment in itself is ethically suspect. Rather, the problem arises when the severing of the relation between judge and judged becomes the aim or the presupposition for rendering a judgment or punishment.

Butler emphasizes the complexity inherent in making judgments by equally refusing to condemn making judgments in the name of an ethics beyond judgment as well as refusing to accept making judgments as an ethical value in and for itself:

> Although I am certainly not arguing that we ought never to make judgments—they are urgently necessary for political, legal, and personal life alike—I think that it is important, in rethinking the cultural terms of ethics, to remember that not all ethical relations are reducible to judgment and that the very capacity to judge presupposes a prior relation between those who judge and those who are judged. (*GA* 45)

Judging, holding accountable, and being held accountable become problematic when these practices are performed in a way that the relationship of judge and judged is foreclosed on, severed, or disavowed, so that these practices in themselves are no longer considered as responses and as addresses to the other, even—or particularly—if the intent is to condemn a set of actions rather than the person. In fact, if subjects are indeed formed performatively and there are no subjects preceding actions and fully independent of them, then it is no longer possible to assume that one could so easily hate the deed but love the doer; actions and subjects are not so easily separable. An attempt to rearticulate judgment as an ethical and legal category would have to break with taking this disjuncture between agent and action as the premise and instead formulate how precisely practices of judgment might enable such a separation.[21]

Making possible this separation and sustaining the relation to the other seem crucial to framing judgment and accountability as ethical practices that allow the forging of the possibility of a different future without striving to obliterate the past. The past then becomes a resource that informs and strengthens ethical deliberation and responsibility. The problem that I have elided to some extent so far, however, is to determine exactly what constitutes that which we come to call "the past." Even outside the discussions about what "history" might be, how history relates to memory and to a collective and an individual dimension, "the past" as referring to past actions and experiences is not a simple or stable referent. To think about the past and one's relation to it points us to ask how the past is constituted affectively and cognitively through representations, discourses, and addresses and through that which can be remembered as much as that which remains repressed, forgotten, and irrecoverable.[22] So simply to say that we need a "critical relation to the past" does not solve the quandaries, because the question is exactly what one is relating to in this relation to the past and precisely how this relation might be enabled as a critical one.

Turning to psychoanalysis is helpful here because it offers conceptual frameworks for understanding this relation to the past as vexed, not easily recoverable, and affective in ways that resist narration. The critical relation to the past cannot be achieved without the work of undoing the present, which requires an undoing of the ground that the past has come to inhabit, a ground that one might not even be aware of being tethered to.[23] Accountability in these terms becomes that practice by which an undoing and reworking of how the past lives on are made possible. This does not mean that the past is simply rewritten at will. In fact, the incoherence of the subject is perhaps what allows the possibility of separating a set of actions from its agent and the possibility of reopening and reworking one's relation to the past, which is as much about one's relation to oneself as well as to others and to social norms.

To explore this undoing, it seems useful to turn once again to Laplanche's reflections on transference and the process of detranslation that risks an undoing of the self by reactivating an overwhelming past. Detranslation is a process in which one loses control over that which has been managed by the present translation. Through translation, Laplanche explains, the untranslatable excess of the originary confrontation with the other is retained but is also managed in a way that prevents this past from obliterating a future for the "I." Laplanche describes translation as "a movement forward in time through first going backwards."[24] In other words, translation is the process that holds the overwhelming past in check and allows the "I" to move forward. But translation does not obliterate the past trace of the enigmatic message. Since translation is a kind of coping mechanism for reacting as well as possible to that which exceeds one's capacities to deal with the other's messages and demands, the translation itself remains preliminary and subject to revision.

While in the analyst's office detranslation and retranslation are particularly facilitated, this clinical setting is not the only place where this process of undoing and reworking happens. Rather, if transference is, as Laplanche suggests, at work in all our interactions, then this process of detranslation and retranslation potentially happens all the time. What is specific about Laplanche's view, however, is that the past that needs to be retranslated and is reactivated in transference is the past of the primary seduction, and the untranslatable is registered through the enigmatic signifier. As Laplanche explains in his lecture "Psychoanalysis, Time and Translation," the messages the infant receives from the adult world are "messages perceived as enigmatic, that is as a 'to be translated'" (PTT 175). As a response instigated by the encounter with the other, translation not only orchestrates the formation of the "I" and the unconscious over and against the enigma of the other, but also is the means of "entering into time . . . which is at once a taking oneself forward and a leaving behind" (PTT 176).

Translation thus points us to a duality inherent in the temporality of becoming a subject. To emerge as a subject through translation as a response to the enigmatic address by "taking oneself forward" entails a movement toward the future. This movement is prompted and also limited by the enigma of the other, which will remain to a certain extent untranslatable and live on as that "upon which the auto-theorisation of the human being seizes but which it cannot reduce except in an unstable and asymptotic fashion" (PTT 174). "Taking oneself forward" is always characterized by "preliminarity" and imperfection, by a not-yet that renders retranslation necessary, while the original of the address which has to be translated can never be fully recovered. At the same time, as there is a return of the past in translation, the moving into the future through the response, the translation also requires a "leaving behind." This leaving behind is peculiar because that which is left behind does not fully disappear, and at the same time one never had direct access to the messages that then come to constitute one's past and live on as such only through being left behind. The past is present as the past only insofar as it is not settled.[25]

In our considerations regarding accountability and responsibility, the past in question is not the same as in psychoanalysis. The past that accountability reaches for is, if we accept the psychoanalytical account, certainly riven by one's early infancy, utterly irrecoverable by memory, but in considering how we become accountable for our actions, that which constitutes the untranslatable rest does not necessarily have to center on sexual messages that the infant neither caused nor wished for. Instead, the past in question with regard to accountability is tied to, even though it is not necessarily solely caused by, my actions. Despite these differences between the past central to psychoanalysis and the past central to the question of accountability, Laplanche's reflections are helpful for theorizing accountability because they provide a conceptual framework for understanding how we are partially unknowable to ourselves because our past, which continuously conditions our formation, is never fully accessible to us. For theorizing accountability in relation to such a limited knowability of the past, Laplanche's insights offer a way to consider what it is about the past that cannot be fully thematized in reflection and how that irrecoverable past nonetheless requires responding to it and dealing with it.

By presenting what he calls an "obligation to translate,"[26] Laplanche's elaborations allow us to rethink how one comes to be compelled to deal with what one did not wish for, did not make, and could not even know or fully comprehend. Laplanche describes the necessity of dealing with the untranslatable as an obligation, but, as I would like to demonstrate, this peculiar form of an obligation allows for and necessitates a reformulation of the very notion of obligation. This obligation is strictly heteronomous: "Once more, it's an *obligation* that does not come from the receiver. It's an *imperative* which is brought to him by the work itself. It's a *categorical imperative:* 'you must translate because it's untranslatable.'"[27] The obligation comes from the message itself and assumes its categorical force, paradoxically, only because it is unfulfillable and irresolvable. The resulting translation and response do not put the address and the situation of the address to rest, but one comes to be responsible for the translation that one has produced. This responsibility, however, does not emerge as a question asked to establish whether or not one has produced a faulty translation for which one is then to be faulted. Instead, the responsibility for the translation is a responsibility to retranslate continuously, because the message cannot be fully translated and is, as Laplanche puts forth, in fact untranslatable. In other words, this responsibility is conditioned by the necessity of having to respond in one way or another. The relation between responsibility and accountability that is established here is one in which accountability and the giving of an account become the occasion for a new translation that opens the possibility for responding and responsibility in the future.

In this approach to accountability and responsibility, we attend to the past and are asked to reevaluate our relation to the past, to account for this relation, and to become accountable, insofar as the past continues to matter for the present and in order to renew the capacity to respond in the present. It seems to me that part of the demand for accountability is motivated by an effort to ensure that we do not treat our actions and their consequences as irrelevant. In this light, asking for accountability to be a retranslation, a reopening, and a reworking of the past might at first seem like proposing a project of revisionism. But going back over one's past deliberations, positions, decisions, and actions and considering them in the changed context that their consequences and the new situation have yielded does not mean a change to the "facts" of the past. Instead, this going back is a return in order to go forward, not by changing the facts but by laboring through one's relation to them and possibly yielding a change in one's position.[28]

The past is available to us, we could say using Laplanche's terms, only in translation and as messages whose original meaning has been lost but that continue to shape our present insofar as they provide the backgrounds and frameworks for our reflections and deliberations. Insofar as the past is not settled, it remains as a kind of "untranslatable excess" that can disrupt present interpretations or translations, necessitating a revisiting and reworking of our relation to the past: "Each important circumstance of [the individual's] life . . . is for him the occasion to call into question the *present* translation, to detranslate it by turning towards the past and to attempt a better translation of this past, a more comprehensive translation, with renewed possibilities" (PTT 176). Implied here is that in every situation of significance, my understanding of the present is ruptured, insofar as that understanding becomes questionable. But what exactly is being called into question? The present *translation* that is called into question is the translation of "the past" that was constituted by the other's address and to which my translation was my response. This response is now in turn called into question as not sufficient and, more explicitly, as not *good enough*, as the reference to the attempted *better* translation indicates.

This "better translation" can be undertaken only by turning to the past, however, specifically by turning to the past in a movement of detranslation, which means that I need to work through the present translation and *analuein*, analyze, and untie it in order to get to that of which it was a translation. In the analytic process, as Laplanche considers it, this movement of detranslation does not stop at the past nor even have as its purpose a full retrieval of this past or a recovery of the "truth" about this past: "The aim here is not to restore a more intact past (*whatever would one do with that?*) but to allow in turn a deconstruction of the old, insufficient, partial and erroneous construction, and hence to open the way to the new translation."[29] Hence the turn to the past here is a movement into the future through attending to the past, insofar as the detranslated material compels but also allows for a new translation, one that can open the present toward a future differently "with renewed possibilities" (PTT 176). The aim is not to produce a new translation that will end the need for all translation, nor can a new translation ever be made without going back over the old one. Similarly, we can argue that through giving an account and being held accountable, it is possible to arrive at a new position in a way that does not require that the old position be forgotten or denied, but that what is necessary is the very labor of undoing the old position by working through the effects that it came to have.

Reworking and changing one's position, one's opinion about beliefs held before, explanations offered earlier, and actions taken previously must be possible and are at times critical, but not all reversals of one's position are alike. If what is precisely not reopened is the question of whether past decisions were the right ones to make in the first place, then the return to the past and the explanations sought in this past end up working merely to justify and bolster one's decisions. To make a reworking possible through giving an account and becoming accountable—in a complicated way, even admitting that one could not foresee the consequences of one's actions—a form of explaining is necessary that does not simply shore up the interpretations, deliberations, and decisions made in the past. Explanations have to work rather like archeological efforts that render past interpretations, deliberations, and decisions open to reevaluation.

If giving an account and attributing actions to an agent work solely in the name of establishing culpability, then instead of fostering responsibility, the demand to give an account runs the risk of becoming unfulfillable and even oppressive and ends up foreclosing on relations with others. Responsibility as responding and acting exposes us to others as well as to the possibility of undergoing and inflicting pain and violence. Offering explanations can, even despite other intentions, perform in ways that attempt to revoke and sever one's relation to others and the potential of an undoing of oneself. At the same time, giving an account can become the site of reworking and of transformation not only of one's positions and actions but of oneself, as Butler considers when she returns to the notion of giving an account of oneself at the end of *Giving an Account of Oneself.*

In her conclusion to this work, Butler offers Foucault's account of himself and his reflections on giving an account as a form of public self-criticism and, in that form, as something different from establishing a conclusive identity or story of this individual: "This account does not have as its goal the establishment of a definitive narrative but it constitutes a linguistic and social occasion for self-transformation" (*GA* 130). Giving an account in this light is not about the production of a coherent and final narrative; rather, the account is relocated in the social realm and redescribed as an occasion for change. This transformation and reevaluation become possible by going back to the past and performing an account of this past in relation to others. I give an account, and this account conditions my relation to past actions and their effects in the present—even though I might not have intended them and might not have caused them intentionally—with the aim of affording a reworking of this relation.

If psychoanalysis is correct, then this reworking is facilitated through transference in relation to others to whom the account is given. The truth or falsity of this account of who and what I am in relation to my actions and in relation to others is not what secures my responsibility or even renders me a moral agent by virtue of producing a reflective knowledge about my self-identity or my "character." Rather, the self-reflection to which the account gives rise becomes the site of my undergoing a dispossession of myself and my actions. This dispossession makes possible a transformation of my capacity to relate to others as well as a transformation not of past events but of how their traces and consequences continue to delimit possibilities for the future.

Although this account can become an occasion for transformation, often—especially in the case of public announcements of someone declaring that he or she "takes responsibility" usually for a series of events that went wrong—the disjuncture between the utterance and its effects becomes very clear when the account and the declaration of taking responsibility do not produce any perceivable change in the further course of action. It would be problematic to institute a norm that requires that giving an account should always lead to a transformation or that renders accountability into a social-therapeutic practice and thereby pathologizes the failure to undergo transformation by giving an account. The disjuncture between the account and further actions and the potential that one might not lead to the other comprise the moment in which the norms conditioning the social occasion for the account become potentially available for transformation as well. Although to "fail" to give an account or to change is not necessarily an expression of resistance, the refusal to give an account can be a mode of resistance that calls into question the legitimacy of the demand for accountability. One becomes accountable in relation to others, and the norms, values, and frameworks of intelligibility that delimit the situation in which one is being asked to give an account are not of one's own making.

So while one's relation to oneself by means of giving an account of one's relation to one's actions is at the heart of giving an account, this self-relation does not precede one's relation to others. Rather, it is formed and performed in the context of being addressed by others and responding to others. In her reading of Foucault's late works, Butler argues that the self-relation that the account performs is caught up not only in personal relations with others but also in the social realm, insofar as one's self-relation is "*published*, brought into the realm of appearance, constituted as a social manifestation" (*GA* 131). Responding by giving an account does not take place outside relations of power and the workings of social norms that determine who can speak and be heard. The norms that govern how accountability is produced delimit the conditions under which an account will be intelligible, as well as when, how, and for what kinds of actions someone will be held accountable.

I cannot unilaterally determine when and how I will be held accountable or when and how others are held accountable. The situations in which giving an account becomes possible and necessary are conditioned by our implication in social and historical realities, but not predetermined by them, as Butler explains: "[W]hen we do act and speak, we do not only disclose ourselves but act on the schemes of intelligibility that govern who will be a speaking being, subjecting them to rupture or revision, consolidating their norms, or contesting their hegemony" (*GA* 132). We can run up against the limits of these realities in various ways: when one finds oneself having to refuse the demands to which one has to respond, when one finds one's responses impossible to be heard, or when one finds one's demands to others refused or going unnoticed. As we run up against the limits of these schemes of intelligibility, what becomes possible are critique and a revision of the norms determining the occasions and subjects of accountability, which are norms not only of intelligibility but of moral conduct as well.

So the status of accountability in moral philosophy and moral conduct, as I argue here, is not to ensure that a subject has self-knowledge about its actions, consequences, and its potential to become guilty. But accountability (or, more precisely, holding oneself and being held accountable) and giving an account remain important practices of moral conduct, because through them we share an unknowingness about ourselves at the same time as our actions of the past continue to have effects in the present. Responsibility is always caught in the peculiar predicament of the impossible synchronicity that is the space in which responsibility emerges and becomes possible and necessary, but by which it is also traversed and undone. Apart from the irrecoverable address that conditions our responsiveness, the concrete past to which actions are responses never purely returns us solely to a moment or situation in the past but orients us as well towards the future, insofar as "How to respond?" is a question that opens up onto future action. So insofar as responsibility implicates us in deliberating and determining how to respond best to the question "What ought I to do?," responsibility is oriented toward a future that it must desire to control—and will have to fail to control. In contrast, accountability emerges belatedly and is oriented toward the past that it must vainly desire to change. Accountability as an ethical practice in the service of responsibility—and so in the service of making possible a future—becomes an effort of and occasion for reworking and transforming not the past in itself but how the past continues to bear on the present and informs ethical reflections, deliberations, and decisions.

Giving an account, understood as an occasion for self-reflection in relation to others, does not constitute a practice untouched by power and social norms but can instead enable a critical relation to power and social norms.

Responsibility, as well as accountability, is caught up in frameworks of power and traversed by social norms in ways that we can never leave behind because we have to respond and become accountable in relation to others in socially and historically bounded situations. And precisely because it is impossible to conceive of moral conduct outside of social norms and relations of power, moral philosophy must become critical.

PART THREE

Critique

FIVE

The Aporia of Critique and the Future of Moral Philosophy

My discussion of responsibility as a key concept for moral philosophy in previous chapters centers on articulating responsibility in terms of responding to others and as a mode of relating and being with others. Responsibility as a question and problematic of moral conduct emerges as a genuinely ethical question because of our condition of being with others. I argue in the two preceding chapters not for disposing of accountability and judgment but instead that our understanding of accountability and judgment changes if we approach these questions with responsibility posed as primarily a question of how to respond well to others. More specifically, I argue for this reframing of the concept of responsibility as a response to Judith Butler's account of subject formation and her critiques of the self-sufficient and self-transparent subject. In conversation with Butler, Levinas, and Laplanche, I attempt to formulate responsibility through the perspective of our relations to others. In these discussions, my focus is on responsibility's specific temporality which opens toward the future through the modes of address and response. So the argument so far is that the poststructuralist critiques of the subject—and Butler's critiques in particular—do not render considerations of moral philosophy obsolete and impossible. Rather, these critiques provide an impetus to rethink central concepts of moral philosophy. Among those, responsibility emerges as a privileged site and moment for a reformulated moral philosophy.

It would be problematic, however, to reduce moral-philosophical thinking to responsibility alone, because social structures, institutions, and political events also require our responses, our actions—and not necessarily only those mediated through our relations to concrete others. It is certainly possible—and important—to consider social and political structures, institutions, and practices through the grammar of responsibility. Through this framework, which rests on our relations to others and our shared vulnerability, the social and political issues become framed as ethical precisely insofar as responding well to others is at stake. It seems to me that attending to the issue of a shared vulnerability is crucial to formulating the social and political aspect of moral philosophy, especially since to a large extent this vulnerability is also something that has to be emphasized as a shared condition in order to give rise to these very ethical commitments and quandaries. However, if the grammar of responsibility comes to be the exclusive paradigm through which we can critically relate to these social and political issues, we then lose the decidedly political dimension at stake both in Butler's work as well as in moral philosophy.

The traditional moral-philosophical problematic of justice circumscribes one genuine intersection between moral and political philosophy, which I would like to explore by mobilizing questions that arise around Butler's work. More specifically, to attend to this political dimension, I would like to turn to critique as a key concept and practice in Butler's works, insofar as critique addresses the problematics of power and social transformation in ways that are not reducible to the paradigm of the relation between individuals as concrete others.

In *Giving an Account of Oneself,* Butler insists on the importance of a critical reflection on morality that takes into account social and historical contexts as the horizon of morality. In her reading of Adorno, she emphasizes:

> his commitment to considering morality within the changing social contexts in which the need for moral inquiry emerges. The context is not exterior to the

> question; it conditions the form that the question will take. In this sense, the questions that characterize moral inquiry are formulated or stylized by the historical conditions that prompt them. (*GA* 6)

Rejecting the idea that the social context is exterior to morality—a distracting exteriority that must be transcended by abstraction—Butler aligns herself with Adorno's claim that moral quandaries are dependent on and delimited by social and historical situations. Moral quandaries in this view are not unchangeable problems and questions that transcend time and place; they emerge in specific formulations dependent on the situations that give rise to moral inquiry. Precisely what determines the moral status of an inquiry and the role and place of critique is a central question that guides this chapter.

The proviso is that—insofar as we want to commit ourselves to understanding matters of morality as historically and socially conditioned—there cannot be an absolute and fully conclusive solution to this question of what characterizes matters of morality as such. Nonetheless, I do believe that it is possible to elaborate productively upon the question of how to understand critique in relation to moral philosophy. Attempting a preliminary response that situates itself at a particular juncture between Butler and Adorno, I work with the discussions that have followed in the (perhaps waning) wake of the so-called Foucault-Habermas debate in order to clarify the aporia of normativity at stake in these debates. This aporia of the impossible foundations of critique helps us understand how critique in the context of ethics needs to be critical in the sense of both an epistemological critique as well as social criticism.

Critique, as Butler elaborates it, aims to understand and interrogate how questions of moral conduct are conditioned by social and historical circumstances and frameworks. More specifically, critique becomes central to moral philosophy insofar as social and historical contexts condition the form of moral conundrums, insofar in turn as these contexts are determined through social norms and structures of power. Moral philosophy as a critical inquiry needs to examine how social norms and power determine situations within which moral questions arise and become available and urgent. In other words, to insist on critique as cutting across concerns of responsibility means to consider in what ways questions of responsibility, in terms of responding to others, never appear outside the reality of a world that is already structured by social norms and practices. Our relations to others are not external to or simply separable relations of power and social contexts, so we need the grammar of critique as well as that of responsibility for thinking about moral philosophy, especially within the context of Butler's critiques of the subject.

If as ethical subjects we are formed in subjection to social norms and relations of power, then being a subject, neither as "I" nor as "other," can alone serve to develop a critical stance in relation to these norms and power more generally as we encounter them. It might, however, very well be in relation to concrete others that social structures come into question for us and we experience them as violent and unjust. It is hard to formulate in a general and abstract way what critique means in Butler's works, because her notion of critique is performed in critical analyses of concrete social and political situations, practices, and institutions. So in attempting to reflect on critique here, we need to understand how concrete situations condition any conceptual and theoretical inquiry into critique. The possibility of theorizing critique in this way may lie in that reflection on these implications is an attempt continuously to open up questions and clarify problematics rather than put them to rest absolutely.[1]

Social institutions and practices are rendered open for critical questioning in Butler's works by her method of examining how social norms adjudicate which subjects and lives become intelligible and socially acknowledged. With this understanding of critical reflection as uncovering what forms of life are rendered abject (falling outside the scope of what is socially normal, acceptable, and supportable) Butler's notion of critique is situated in between critique as an epistemological assessment of the limits of knowledge and critique as politically oriented social criticism. While it is possible to formulate these practices and their aims as an instantiation of responsibility and a particular way of responding, I hesitate to do so. Certainly critique is a form of responding, but I am concerned here more with the undoing, rather than the determining, that critique performs and on which it relies to render normative frameworks and aspirations open to debate. Critique seen this way is a practice that seeks to reflect on how we attain a critical relation to evaluative and moral norms as well as to social norms. Critique thus raises not only the question of the practical conditions that make critical inquiries possible as a personal and public practice, but also how we might reflect on the criteria according to which we make substantive distinctions between different normative political and social projects.

In this chapter I first argue why critique is not reducible to an ethos and in which ways critique allows moral-philosophical reflections to focus on the quandaries that social and political normalization and its criticism pose. Second, I would like to explore the problematic epistemological situation in which all critical thinking finds itself when it aspires to take a critical perspective on historical constellations of power, all the while knowing itself thoroughly conditioned by these constellations. Addressing this problematic, I take up the opposing positions that have generally become affiliated with the Foucault-Habermas debate. Butler's work will be of help in articulating a position that allows us to reassess the epistemological aporia of normativity between power and knowledge. Ensuing from this problematic, not only is normativity shown to be framed as the question of whether critique is all that is still possible in current thinking, but a further question posed is how to refigure moral philosophy such that it rigorously acknowledges the absence and impossibility of absolute foundations and the refusal to settle for contingent foundations too easily. My aim in the third section of this chapter is to use this problematic situation to argue, by drawing on Butler and Adorno, that this question of the continued possibility of moral philosophy situates critique at the crossroads of ethics and politics.

Critique beyond Ethos

In the following reflections, then, I would like to consider critique not just as a form of "taking responsibility for norms and institutions" in the sense of becoming accountable for them in the ways in which they function by taking political action to change them if necessary. Insofar as critique as a practice is concerned with calling norms and institutions into question, with taking them as a kind of address that demands a reflection and a response, critique has much to do with a particular kind of responsibility. Yet, as I point out above, by foregrounding this aspect of responsibility, the critical relation to norms and institutions becomes personally and individually quite morally laden. To understand critique as a kind of responsibility thus privileges ethical self-formation in the endeavor. This foregrounding—depending on how it is mobilized and presented—runs the risk of presenting the engagement with social norms, practices, and institutions as being important precisely because of an ethical self-formation that becomes invested with a pathos of relationality, address, and response. At an angle to an ethos of response, the aspect that I would like to emphasize here is instead the structural and political dimension that critique mobilizes in Butler's work.

In this regard, I would like to suspend the focus that responsibility as responding to others and as a practice introduces, in order to broaden the horizon of a rethought moral philosophy through critique as a key concept. Seen in this light, moral philosophy cannot be reduced to an ethos or a set of guidelines for ethical self-formation. Rather, by raising justice as both a question and a demand, a universalizing perspective of social criticism opens up that introduces an ethical and political dimension going beyond concerns of an ethos or ethical self-formation. Insofar as critique considers the workings of social norms and the claims of normativity, it allows us to shift our perspective from self-formation to social, institutional criticism and the relation between politics and ethics. Undertaking this shift does not mean abandoning the question of subject formation. Instead, rather than foregrounding subject formation as an ethical telos and project, analysis of the practices and situations of subject formation is mobilized as a heuristic to examine the material effects of social norms and relations of power.

Critique, then, is not so much what grounds responsibility in the sense of ensuring the moral correctness of the criteria that guide our responses. Instead, by interrogating how a situation is configured so that it elicits a response in the first place, critique opens and refigures the field for responsibility, for responding, and for determining "What ought I to do?" because in order to act, one needs to come up with an interpretation of the situation. In such an inquiry, we move from an individual consideration to the question of social action when the "What ought I to do?" becomes posed as "What ought we to do?"

The difficulty in this relation between the "I" and the "we" is that the "I" implied in the "ought" is in a sense both already plural and relentlessly singular. On the one hand, the question of what one ought to do is a question that individualizes. No one else can answer this question for the individual "I," if the conclusion that is the decision and action following is to be different from a mechanical following of a rule. But insofar as this consideration of "What ought I to do?" is one that implies a normative dimension, there is a kind of plural implied in this "I." This "ought" is compelling precisely insofar as it articulates a kind of universality or aspiration to universality that is not reducible to a contingent individual instantiation. At least in its aspiration, this "ought" is not purely individual, although it might always turn out to be a radically singular instantiation of this obligation. "What ought I to do?" always works in a generalizing manner, because there is a rule or rationale implied according to which one makes a decision. So it seems that while the individual "I" is the one to come to decide and act, this decision is not random but is conditioned by the circumstances and a reasoning by which the normative aspect of the response transcends the radically individual dimension.

The "I" also becomes or implies an "anyone" who ought to act in this manner given these circumstances. That relation between the individual "I" and the aspiration of "anyone" is one of the contested sites of moral and political philosophy and where ethics becomes political—or, more precisely, is already implicitly political and must become explicitly political in order to remain critical. In other words, because the invocation of a particular course of action as applicable to all can always be questioned, and because at the same time to invoke this "ought" or "must" is to invoke more than an individual predilection, this "What ought to be done" carries in itself an aspiration to validity that it can enact and realize not automatically but only through persuasion or coercion. To avow this bid for power in an articulation of what ought to be means to acknowledge the political aspect of the normative claim that results from the collective and universalizing dimension implied in that claim. This situation in return becomes a site for critical inquiry in the field of moral philosophy, insofar as we ask how we should reflect on and assess different sets of criteria to distinguish between various normative projects and in what ways these criteria should and can be independent of power and persuasion.

This social and political dimension arises in conjunction with the question of who the subject of action is and how this subject—plural and singular—comes about. This subject that asks either in the plural or in the singular what ought to be done is not a subject that could be taken for granted or that precedes the social field within which these questions of moral conduct arise. As Butler reminds us early on in *Giving an Account of Oneself*, it is certainly true that ethical and moral conduct presupposes an "I" who acts: "[T]here is no 'I' that can fully stand apart from the social conditions of its emergence, no 'I' that is not implicated in a set of conditioning moral norms, which, being norms, have a social character that exceeds a purely personal or idiosyncratic meaning" (*GA* 7).

In attempting to inquire into how moral normativity might differ from social normalization, it is important to keep in mind that there is no subject of ethical deliberation that comes into existence prior to or outside norms, both moral and social. Butler's reminder here is that moral norms are not radically other than social norms, because moral norms work in a normalizing manner producing subjects and are not only belatedly appropriated by these subjects. Normative convictions that we come to hold are not drawn from a source that is radically distinct from historically specific conditions and social and cultural traditions. We grow into traditions and are formed by histories and social practices and, for the most part, we do not consciously decide at some point to become a part of some cultures and traditions rather than others. There is no time when the individual exists without having been formed by social and cultural practices in ways that one can never fully understand and critically examine. Social and cultural practices carry and transmit histories and frameworks of how to understand the world, social norms, and moral values. The question is not how we come to operate within sets of moral values and norms but rather how it can be that sometimes these frameworks become open to critical examination and reworking.

Insofar as moral norms always operate within concrete social settings, they work not unlike social norms in bringing about subjects through normative demands and with normative commitments. In addressing the social dimension of norms, critique allows us a different conceptual focus from responsibility, because taken up within the context of moral philosophy, critique asks the question of the relation between power and justice. This question is then not posed only as a question of the moral conduct of individual agents or the relation of an "I" to others, the question at the heart of responsibility. Instead, critique addresses the structural dimension of social institutions and practices, of political and social action, and the predicament of universality that is implied in claims to what ought to be done. This universality of the "ought" in the context of the particularly moral not only concerns itself with the life of one individual or a particular group but generalizes this concern and poses it as a question of justice. At stake, then, is not a formulation of justice uncontaminated by historical and social relations and untainted by politics and power. At stake, rather, is how to attend to the problematic that this situation poses, if we are to give up an ideal and stable disarticulation of the power and moral norms.

With this problematic as a horizon, critique becomes a key concept for moral philosophy every bit as much as it is a limit concept of moral philosophy. In its link to morality, critique is compelled to pose justice as a question and horizon for its critical examination. Yet in posing justice as a question, critique cannot be exclusively subsumed under the aegis of moral philosophy because of the political, legal, sociological, anthropological, historical, and cultural dimensions of asking what justice might mean. Insofar as a critical account of justice has to examine these dimensions, which belong to fields other than moral philosophy, the endeavor to give a critical account of moral conduct and justice as political and social issues compels the moral-philosophical considerations to reach beyond a narrow delimitation of moral philosophy. Moral conduct always remains determined by the particulars of the situation to which action responds and within which social justice might come to mean something quite particular under the given circumstances. Hence what projects might become articulatable and feasible depends crucially on their social and political contexts. If moral philosophy is to continue to reflect conceptually on issues of moral conduct and social justice, and if moral philosophy remains committed to being critical, then it must enter into conversations with other fields of scholarship, because it is not possible conclusively to adjudicate questions of moral conduct and social justice in a reflection on abstract principles.

While the principles of moral conduct and of justice cannot be conclusively articulated by moral philosophy, it can very well reflect on this very predicament. This reflection is part of what critique entails, namely disentangling and confronting the aporias that structure the reflective endeavor. Returning to the differences between critique and responsibility as ethical concepts, responsibility is not to be emptied of the social and political dimensions that emerge if we formulate responsibility as a question of responding to and taking responsibility for social conditions and political action. But figured through the modes of address and response, responsibility points to an interrogation of power and history and thus to its joining forces with critique.[2]

Insofar as critique inquires into the consequences of normalization, social forms of power, and the social and cultural frameworks that determine which addresses are recognizable as such, it is not quite reducible to responsibility, if responsibility is to retain its relational characteristic as a response that constitutes a kind of ethical subject. Responsibility foregrounds the subject of ethical action, even if the subject is thought primarily through its relationship to the other. At stake in the inquiry into critique are two concerns with a different focus from that of responsibility in relation to others and responsibility as mode of subject formation: first an ethical and political concern regarding the role of power and social norms in the formation of the subject, and second an epistemological concern raising the question of the philosophical role of reflections on subject formation and its political implications.

This epistemological concern is directed against a fusion of ontology and morality and against an ontological foundation from which one would then deduce normative criteria.[3] Such a position is problematic because in this framework the elaboration of ontological realities takes the place of a critical inquiry into normative consequences. How we understand subject formation has consequences for how we understand moral conduct. However, we cannot posit a generalized relationality as an ontological reality and then derive from that a criterion for moral conduct, because then we can no longer ask how this "relationality" is produced in the first place, through which forms of social patterns and practices that govern understandings of what relationality means.

Butler's critiques of the subject not only call into question the presupposition of a particular self-conscious, self-willing, and self-transparent subject in accounts of moral philosophy. Her critiques are more far-reaching. Her aim is not limited to substituting a fragile, opaque, and relational subject for the discredited version of the subject; rather, Butler's critique scrutinizes the central and foundational role of the subject in contemporary accounts of moral philosophy. Presupposing any subject on which to build guiding principles for moral conduct is rendered problematic, because if the subject is presupposed, this disables as a question of moral philosophy the possibility of a critical reflection on the subject and its formation.

Butler lays out this problematic conversation with Adorno's insistence that it must be possible for individuals to take up moral norms in "a living way" within the social contexts in which they live and act. If such appropriation becomes impossible, then these norms that operate in the name of morality end up turning into a coercive and violent force that makes life less rather than more possible. Butler emphasizes Adorno's negative dialectics—the nonidentity in the relation between universality and particularity—as being an extremely productive insight into how critique and morality are linked: "The universal not only diverges from the particular, but this very divergence is what the individual comes to experience, what becomes for the individual the inaugural experience of morality" (*GA* 8–9). The experience of morality or the horizon for moral inquiry is delimited and enabled when the individual comes into conflict with the existing moral and social frameworks and when these frameworks become available for reconsideration.

While this way of understanding moral questioning requires a critical consideration of the social context for moral conduct, Butler asks whether Adorno's reliance on individual experience and deliberation does not omit a consideration of "whether the 'I' who must appropriate moral norms in a living way is not itself conditioned by norms, norms that establish the viability of the subject" (*GA* 9). The problem for moral philosophy that Butler frames here is the double role of the subject, as both constituted by norms and as taking them up and critically examining and appropriating them. A problem emerges insofar as the subject as an individual becomes the critical limit and vantage point in determining the breaking points of moral norms and their adequacy in enabling livable lives. Yet this subject as an individual is itself not only always embroiled in social contexts but also constituted through them in ways through which it can never attain full reflective distance. The question then becomes how to account for this formation through norms and how to enable a thorough critique of these norms without already preempting certain norms from critical questioning.

This double bind of critique implies that we cannot unproblematically take an account of the fragility and responsiveness of subject formation, of individuality, and of corporeality as a foundation for moral philosophy and then derive principles that ought to guide moral conduct. In the essay "Violence, Mourning, Politics" in *Precarious Life*, Butler elaborates that the vulnerability of bodies is not a universal characteristic whose meaning could be accessed beyond social conditioning: "[V]ulnerability is always articulated differently . . . it cannot be properly thought outside a differentiated field of power and, specifically, the differential operation of norms of recognition" (*PL* 44). When we articulate principles of respect and recognition, we rely on discursively produced knowledge about the conditions of our lives. If we accept that power is at work in these discourses through which criteria for truth are established, then we cannot arrive at a critical position simply by first offering a theory of subject formation and then deriving normative principles and moral norms from the ontogenetic account. If no ontological account of subject formation can be formulated in a way that does not already perform normatively, namely, in normalizing ways, then critically theorizing subject formation becomes a question rather than a foundation for theorizing responsibility and moral philosophy in general.[4]

Taking critiques of the subject seriously means that moral philosophy cannot recover the subject—neither in the form of an "I," nor in the form of "the other," nor in the form of a "you"—as settled ground for its reflections. However, these critiques do not imply that the subject and that agency are dead, only that responsibility and the address by the other cannot serve as the base for moral-philosophical reflections without the return to an absolute and, with that, to an almost theological structure of argumentation. To conceive of the other and the dynamic of address and response as that which impels and guarantees an ethical demand means to inscribe the other and the other's address as absolute. If a theoretical argumentation introduces an absolute point of reference beyond and before historically conditioned social realities, then by removing the referent of its claims from the realm of contingency, the theoretical argumentation takes a quasi-theological turn. If the other is understood as the grounds for the possibility and urgency of ethics, the ethical argument does not rid itself of a quasi-theological move, for the sources of the normative demand are eventually removed from critical inquiry and end up being a matter of faith (even if, as Derrida insists in his later work, it is an act of faith without religion).[5]

Insofar as critique arises alongside the question of the subject and the refusal to accept any grounds of arguments at pure face value, neither responsibility nor critique can be reduced to outlining an ethos. Moreover, the question of moral conduct is not reducible to the question of our immediate relations to others, because these relations do not yet provide us with the understanding and conceptual tools necessary to address social and moral norms, institutions, political projects, and relations of power. The role of power within questions of moral conduct is precisely what we can continue to consider with Butler through critique as a category for moral philosophy.

Acknowledging social conditions and relations of power as constitutive of subjects and modes of knowledge and thus giving up the possibility of finding a truth beyond socially and historically contingent conditions means that ethical considerations about responsibility have to become self-critical regarding their own contingent sources. In *Giving an Account of Oneself*, Butler explains how ethical considerations require critique, especially when she discusses Foucault's turn in his later works to the kind of self-formation that is performed in responding to the demand to tell the truth about oneself. Butler reflects on the responses Foucault gives in an interview in which he is asked to give an account of his thinking as well as of his reflections on the hermeneutics of the self. In her reading of Foucault, Butler considers the demand to tell the truth about oneself and to give an account of oneself as practices of self-reflection and ethical self-formation in relation to others who become the recipients of the account.

This rendering oneself accountable, when it becomes a self-reflective practice, not only functions in coercive and punitive ways but may also renew the capacity to deliberate, judge, respond, and act responsibly. Yet both the practice of self-reflection and our relations to others that prompt ethical self-reflection are already socially conditioned beyond the proximate others whom one encounters. Therefore, the demand for ethical self-reflection and the terms and categories available for this reflective practice are determined by, although not reducible to, these social conditions and with them, relations of power:

> If the question of power and the demand to tell the truth about oneself are linked, then the need to give an account of oneself necessitates the turn to power, so that we might say that the ethical demand gives rise to the political account, and that ethics undermines its own credibility when it does not become critique. (*GA* 124)

The ethical demand in this context becomes the demand to tell the truth, presumably in response to an other who delivers this demand. In and through these addresses and responses, power is negotiated, and the concrete social contexts determine the criteria and limits of what will count as effective and proper address and response. As Butler argues, because the scenes of address and response are conditioned by social relations of power, critique becomes necessary in order to reflect on the workings of power and of social norms in these scenes and discourses. However, this critique cannot simply presuppose the subject as the agent of this critique and thus inscribe the position of an individual who offers a criticism as being already at a distance from those norms that are to be critically called into question. So rather than returning critique all too quickly to a discourse on critique as an ethical practice, I would like to suggest that we read Butler here in a manner that holds the question of power in relation to but also at an angle to the question of the self as an ethical subject and its formation in relation to others.

This relation between ethical subjectivity and critical engagement with the question of power is key to the credibility of ethics, as Butler postulates: "ethics undermines its own credibility when it does not become critique" (*GA* 124). I would like to suggest that we can read "ethics" here as both denoting the practice of striving for an ethical life, which implies a certain practice of ethical self-formation, as well as signifying the theoretical reflection on ethical practice, which we have been calling moral philosophy. If we accept this reading, then two things are at stake in this claim. First, moral-philosophical reflection has to break with the focus on the subject and take power into consideration; moreover, this consideration of power emerges as that which lends the moral inquiry its credibility. Second, ethics as a practice guided by the question of "What ought I to do? How should I respond?" eventually has to turn away from this "I" to issues of power, even if the occasion and agent of this turning are this "I." Ethical practice thus requires self-reflection as well as a break with the infinite cycle of self-reflexive introspection and reflection to take economic, social, cultural, and political institutions and practices into view.

The argument that ethical reflection and deliberation have to be broken eventually—and to some extent betrayed—in the very name of ethics is not new, especially insofar as this break with reflection is understood as the turn to action. Along with others, Derrida offers an argument along these lines in several of his later writings, among them *The Gift of Death.* Derrida demonstrates how ethical reflection is prompted and driven by the vexation of eventually having to interrupt reflection and deliberation in order to act ethically. However, along with this moment of action and spontaneity, there is also a moment of undecidability and necessary irresponsibility introduced that is both the condition of possibility and impossibility of ethical action.

Adorno expands on a similar observation in his lecture course on *Problems of Moral Philosophy.* He suggests that it is both a necessary yet impossible aspiration for moral philosophy to reflect on that which evades it, namely the moment of action and spontaneity without which ethical action would degenerate into mere rule-following.[6]

In his discussion of Kantian moral philosophy, Adorno points to the detrimental and indeed unethical consequences if one were first to determine conscientiously whether an action's maxim would correspond with the categorical imperative in order to decide whether one should give shelter to a person who knocks on one's door while he is being chased at gunpoint.[7] Adorno insists that there is a crucial aspect of ethical practice that cannot be resolved by theoretical reflection. Yet he also guards against rendering the priority of spontaneity and practicality absolute; instead, in the name of a critical moral philosophy, he insists on the reflective wrestling with this moment of action that evades reflection.[8]

In addition to the break necessitated in the name of action to which Derrida and Adorno alert us, Butler's argument offers another kind of break as being crucial to ethical reflection: the demand that ethical reflection become critical as well as political. For Butler, the division between ethics and politics is consequently not one that simply maps onto reflection as opposed to action. Moreover, this break is what lends credence to the ethical practice of responding to others and rendering oneself accountable to others. So if we take up Butler's argument that critique emerges in relation to "the question of power," then in its questioning of power, critique makes for the political character of the ethical inquiry and at the same time addresses the question of the credibility of the ethical inquiry.

One could suggest that with critique's addressing questions of power and social norms, we are moving into the realm of politics and out of the realm of ethics. However, I would like to argue that these questions do not move us beyond the scope of ethics but instead importantly belong to ethics in the perspective of social ethics. Butler's more recent work seems to vary between these two approaches to the role of critique in casting the relation between ethical and political thought as a transition from ethics to politics or as an ethical perspective on politics. In particular in *Giving an Account of Oneself,* ethics for Butler seems to pertain to the question of the self, self-formation, and the individual in relation to concrete others. With the added dimension of social norms and relations of power, we enter the domain of political theorizing. Both *Undoing Gender* and *Precarious Life* allow for a different reading of this political theorizing with respect to ethics, so that ethics, as it is more generally understood, does not remain restricted to the individual dimension of formulating an ethos or to the individual response to an other. In particular, recognition and vulnerability are sites in Butler's work for thinking through the interrelation of ethics and politics with respect to social change and questions of justice. In the final chapter, I return to the question of justice as social justice to elucidate our considerations about critique. In this chapter, I would like to focus on the problem of normativity at stake in critique, which renders critique the practice and endeavor of inquiring into this "ought."

To offer a critique also means to examine how we are to understand the particular address and demands that this "ought" seems to deliver. This "ought" seems to imply that beyond figuring out the possibilities for alternative actions that can be taken, another question is at stake, namely, how to know and how to decide among these alternatives. Reflecting on alternatives to decide with which one ought to side becomes an explicitly moral issue, insofar as this question of what to do is posed in relation to what is good and just—with all the incongruencies that might open up between the question of the good and the question of the just. The labor of critique is to make explicit the implied and underlying sets of norms and criteria and to establish the conditions for asking what criteria and what aims one ought to follow. In what follows, I examine the problematic that results from reformulating this question in terms of normative criteria and principles of what ought to be done.

The problematic is one of two conflicting aims of critique, namely to undo as well as to ground normative criteria, which seems to me a problematic that is impossible to settle and at the same time crucial to retain. I consider this problematic in conversation with the Foucault-Habermas debate, which serves as an important backdrop to Butler's own critical work. To ask the question of what criteria can and ought to guide reflections on moral conduct neither settles nor evades the difficulty that aspirations of moralities are coupled with the ambivalent histories of these aspirations, which have often also fostered their own violent and repressive implementations.

If the question of how things ought to be and what ought to be done is not a question that can be settled by unearthing a set of absolute standards and their application, then neither moral philosophy nor critique can be the endeavor to conclusively ground normative standards. Rather, insofar as the criteria and categories through which we approach the question "What ought I to do?" are not by necessity up for interrogation and reinterpretation, critique becomes the endeavor of opening up these criteria and categories for reexamination. Here, then, might lie a difference between two understandings of what the primary tasks of critique are, namely, whether critique must first and foremost ground those criteria for us or whether its purpose is to help us ask these questions.

While this alternative might sound as if one had to decide between one or the other, I would like to suggest that the importance of critique lies precisely in settling too easily neither with the impossibility of grounding criteria for moral norms nor with the costs of deciding for an even preliminary elaboration of sets of criteria. In what follows in this chapter, I examine this problematic that opens up between the rejection of absolute grounds—immanent or transcendent alike—and the rejection of pure contingency; even so, this means that the problem of grounding and justification keeps returning and producing unwelcome effects and questions.

The Aporetic Foundations of Critique between Knowledge and Power

So what does it mean to sustain a critical understanding of morality? This question arises particularly keenly when absolute grounds for morality are no longer recoverable. Absolute grounds appear no longer as retrievable for philosophy, since those grounds that once seemed to provide a firm foundation for moral knowledge and a perspective for evaluation and criticism have effectively been called into question. Among those lost grounds are the moral subject, the good will, conscience, codes of conduct, religion, God, and truth as such, all of which once seemed to be able to guarantee a source of certainty and objective knowledge about good and evil, right and wrong, just and unjust.

In attempting to address the difficulties that the loss of absolute grounds poses, one of the several different turns that philosophy has taken is the turn to language and discourse. While Habermas uses discourse and language to articulate an ideal of communicative reason as the key to rethinking moral philosophy under postmetaphysical conditions, Foucault critically examines discourses that become invested by social norms with moral worth. Foucault—and poststructuralist scholarship more generally—performs a radical turn to language that exceeds the examination of moral judgments as merely a particular kind of speech act. Poststructuralist scholarship calls into question not only the nonlinguistic referents of moral discourse but also the traditional understanding of language as representing a material reality outside language itself. Foucault, Derrida, and Butler, among others, demonstrate how discourses produce and not merely represent the realities to which they relate. They show that language is always prescriptive as well as descriptive and that all linguistic claims and our realities are always culturally and historically specific and mired in power relations and social norms. Their work reveals that at the core of discourses and everyday practices there are instabilities and undecidabilities regarding their meanings, their worth, their grounds, and their legitimacy.

These turns to language, discourse, and communication consequently bring forth extremely productive sites for critique. They do so, in particular in poststructuralist thought, because language, discourse, and communication are not appropriated to salvage an ideal point of reference that can establish norms and ideals against which realities and conflicting visions and projects can be measured and adjudicated. These questions of criteria remain open, and the impasse is that there seem to be two alternatives: either accepting that critiques of existing and emergent norms and criteria can always only be belated, or conversely, positively elaborating sets of criteria for adjudicating normative claims. The question is how to get beyond this impasse by thinking differently about the problematic that any set of criteria on the one hand claims to critically assess socially and politically contingent frameworks of norms and on the other hand is conditioned itself.

There may not be a conclusive answer to this problematic, and to an extent it seems that the critical edge of critique lies in its interminable nature, which stems from this aporia of normativity between knowledge and power. First, the aporia of normativity becomes an issue for critique or a reflection on critique in two ways. Critique is committed to call into question and uncover the ways in which claims to validity always emerge greater in scope than can possibly be warranted. At the same time, the question of normativity catches up with critique also from within, insofar as critique itself and its claims must be critically examined. Second, insofar as there is no ideal point of reference that would guarantee a ground, the conditions for critique become thoroughly aporetic, although no less urgent.

One of the key debates dealing with these problematics is the Foucault-Habermas debate. It seems to me that this debate allows us, even in its schematic rendition, to grasp the particularly epistemologically aporetic situation that conditions the problematic of moral normativity with which critique continuously has to wrestle. The Benhabib-Butler exchange in *Feminist Contentions*, in which Nancy Fraser and Drucilla Cornell participate as well, echoes in some ways the Foucault-Habermas debate and works along some of the same lines of conflicting commitments. The exchange between Benhabib and Butler in *Feminist Contentions* differs from the Foucault-Habermas debate in part because the Benhabib-Butler debate actually took place as direct encounters, while the Foucault-Habermas debate is one that had been successively postponed until finally an actual encounter was no longer possible because of Foucault's untimely death. Nonetheless, by the time of Foucault's death, the debate between the two men had been underway for some time, taking place mostly in some fairly brief and otherwise rather indirect comments by Foucault and then in two critical essays by Habermas in *The Philosophical Discourse of Modernity* that explicitly engage Foucault's work.[9] One staging or "restaging" of that debate takes place in the volume *Critique and Power: Recasting the Foucault/Habermas Debate*, edited by Michael Kelly.[10] This volume not only gathers together several essays by Foucault and Habermas but also offers several critical essays by theorists who engage both thinkers but who eventually align themselves more or less strongly with one or the other.

One of the key issues of the debate between Habermas and Foucault is the relation between power and reason and how a critical social theory is to proceed. Both Foucault and Habermas engage in radicalizing the critique of metaphysical thought and elaborate on the project of postmetaphysical critical thought. To this end, Habermas argues that through a reconstructive process of self-reflection on reason, reason can and has to be rethought as intersubjective and communicative. Through establishing an ideal of communicative rationality, Habermas retrieves rational consensus achieved by deliberative procedures as normative criterion. Norms are justified if, under ideal conditions, all persons affected by the norms in question would freely consent.[11] Foucault's approach runs counter to such an approach that reconstructs, even if only preliminarily, an ideal of reason. Instead, Foucault is committed to a genealogical inquiry that queries reason and rationality as historical categories and asks how they were discursively produced through constellations of power and through which social institutions they became invested with the power to determine what counts as knowledge. While for Habermas critique leads to communicative ethics and deliberative rationality that can legitimately counter the claims of power, for Foucault critique analyzes power and discourses to expose how they delimit what claims can appear at all in the name of knowledge and reason.

In the debate between Benhabib and Butler, Benhabib aligns herself with a Habermasian perspective of communicative ethics, while Butler argues in a Foucauldian vein. Similarly to the Foucault-Habermas debate, one of the key issues is the philosophical resource for critical social theory and action. Unlike the Foucault-Habermas debate, however, which does not touch on these issues with regard to feminist theory, the Benhabib-Butler debate examines the differences of the respective positions and debates in feminist theory and practice in addition to differences in their accounts of subjectivity and agency. Of late Butler returns in her writings to the issues that first emerge in this exchange and engages with the Habermasian position on several occasions. In her essays "What Is Critique? An Essay on Foucault's Virtue" and "The Question of Social Transformation" in *Undoing Gender*, she deals with the subject and agency in terms of these as a question of critique and of the normative evaluative criteria for critique.[12] Most recently, Butler takes up the connection between questions of legitimacy and critique in her lecture "What Is a Discipline?"[13] *Precarious Life* and *Undoing Gender* also engage with critique in relation to what and who count as human, as well as more specifically with issues of self-determination, freedom, and collective action.

In "What Is Critique?" Butler offers a brief summary of Habermas's assessment of the Foucauldian approach to critique:

> The perspective of critique, in [Habermas's] view, is able to call foundations into question, denaturalize social and political hierarchy, and even establish perspectives by which a certain distance on the naturalized world can be had. But none of these activities can tell us in what direction we ought to move, nor can they tell us whether the activities in which we engage are realizing certain kinds of normatively justified goals.[14]

From a Habermasian perspective, Butler explains, the limitations and possibilities of critique are tied to critique's remaining at odds with norms and normative frameworks. The potential of critique lies in its allowing us to emerge at a distance from the normative and normalizing practices and institutions in which we are enmeshed and participate in our everyday lives. These practices and institutions and the norms that are embodied through them can be questioned because, in the moment that these institutions and practices become available as objects for critical scrutiny, the validity of these normative frameworks is no longer taken for granted. As their validity is suspended, the underlying norms become contingent formations that can be not only questioned but also possibly changed.

That said, this Foucauldian critique that unearths and calls into question normative frameworks of our social and political practices is limited. This method of critique itself does not provide normative principles for ranking different projects of social change in a way that would help in deciding which kinds of projects one should support and which one should oppose. Foucauldian critique does not elaborate normative principles because its task is to interrogate the formation of norms and normalizing practices and not to institute positive normative criteria and goals. This raises the question, then, of in what way critique is able to orient moral conduct and political action. It seems to me that this intractable remaining at odds with normative aspirations and practices is what, from the Habermasian perspective, is the defect—and from the Foucauldian perspective, the virtue—of critique.

However, the question of whether critique can offer orientation regarding what action we ought to take might be a too-hasty characterization of what is at stake in the Foucault-Habermas debate. There is still another aspect of the Habermasian reservations regarding the Foucauldian position that Butler highlights. Not only is critique taken to be unable to tell us what to do next, but it also fails to tell us "whether the activities in which we engage are realizing certain kinds of normatively justified goals."[15] The problem with Foucauldian critique, in other words, is that it seems to be unable to orient action or normatively evaluate actions.

While critique in a Foucauldian vein does not provide or prescribe criteria or procedures for justification, this does not mean that there are no normative implications of this mode of critique. Habermas identifies an unwitting normativity as a "cryptonormativism" that is implicit but not accounted for in Foucault's approach to critique.[16] Habermas calls these normative implications cryptic and surreptitious because the normative commitments and aspirations emerging from and propelling Foucauldian critical scholarship are not rendered explicit and are not justified as norms subtending this notion and practice of critique.

In a similar vein, without naming the phenomenon "cryptonormativism," Richard Bernstein refers to these implications as an implicit valorization of undermining and calling into question certain normative and normalizing practices and institutions rather than others.[17] Not only do Foucauldian arguments value the practice of critique as a commitment to an openness to questioning norms, but this questioning and commitment to openness are substantiated in particular ways. Bernstein argues that through the particular institutional practices that Foucauldian scholarship interrogates and the particular examples that are used, differences and distinctions are being made between those norms that should be questioned and those that should be upheld.[18] In other words, the opposition of these two lists seems to suggest that there are substantive distinctions that are implicitly being made even by Foucault and by arguments aligned with his work. The Habermasian argument concerning the Foucauldian concept of critique is not that these normative evaluative distinctions should not be made but that there needs to be an account of the normative commitments as they are performed and mobilized through the Foucauldian paradigm of critique.

With regard to Butler's work, demands that follow this line of criticism have been articulated by Amy Allen and Amanda Anderson, among others. Allen proposes that "[Butler] needs some normative concepts . . . and to spend more time and energy defending the ones that are already working in her text."[19] Similarly, Anderson acknowledges that there are normative commitments at work in Butler's texts, but, she argues, these commitments remain unsubstantiated: "Not only does this account fail to elaborate any basis for its normative commitments, but there is an unexamined assumption that intrapsychic maneuvers translate directly into political claims."[20] Leaving aside the debatable assessment of the role of the intrapsychic account in Butler that Anderson offers, her demand of Butler lines up with Allen's insofar as both find the implicit normative commitments remaining inadequately accounted for.

Arising from such a demand for accounting or arguing for normative commitments is the question of which standards would determine when normative commitments count as adequately argued for and what conditions render arguments legible as grounding or justifying normative commitments. Allen and Anderson express a version of the Habermasian demand that Butler's texts meet with a skepticism and refusal to remove the criteria for justification from becoming subject to critique. Rejecting the idea that these criteria can possibly be settled formally, Butler's texts insist upon asking the question of how criteria for the validity of arguments are contingently produced in relation to social and political circumstances.[21]

In the following few pages, I would like to attend to this refusal to settle norms and criteria and lay out how neither a refusal of norms and criteria nor an always preliminary account of norms and criteria leads us to the aporia of normativity with which moral philosophy must grapple. The refusal to settle normative criteria rejects deriving normative criteria from a formal characteristic of critique, such as its calling into question any status quo or critique's commitment to a constitutive openness. To affirm the openness and open-endedness that critique requires as normative criteria does not solve the questions of how this openness would yield substantive criteria and where and how one would reflect critically on this openness as a criterion again.[22]

The force of Butler's argument lies, in my opinion, in her insistence that criteria and norms cannot be settled in advance or apart from understanding all criteria, norms, and normative aspirations as politically and historically conditioned. If this situation presents a theoretical impasse, it is one because on the one hand we have a limited perspective, while on the other hand there is the aspiration not to settle for a thorough relativism. In other words, we have nothing but contingent grounds, historically and socially conditioned knowledge, and so there is nothing that can function as criteria in a way that could adjudicate between different claims of what ought to be done. The question then is whether this insight does not lead into a relativist stance that forms the bottom line of all claims so that it becomes impossible to say more than that all claims are equal contenders for validity. By making such a comprehensive claim about the equal validity of all claims, a thoroughly relativist stance itself knows too much and no longer conceives itself as only one contender among many. So only if one refuses the retreat into relativism does it become possible to take seriously how positions conflict with each other and deny each other's validity.

In order not to be paralyzed by the impasse in the debate over critique, it seems important to return to the concern at the heart of it, which is the relation between critical reflection and moral conduct and action. We need to understand precisely how the reflections of critique can and cannot orient our actions and how a critical inquiry into normative frameworks and social practices allows us to discern between competing interpretations and evaluations of a situation in which action becomes necessary. I would like to take up Butler's more recent considerations on these questions and come at an angle to the debate that I have laid out so far. In what follows, I ask what the differences might be between postulating norms, accounting for them, and justifying and interrogating them, in order to examine what is at stake in the insistence on justifications for projects and norms and in the concerns about continuously receding horizons of universality.

Asking why one set of normative principles and convictions is to be preferred over another is different from asking how and where claims to the validity of a source of criteria and convictions emerge and attain their persuasiveness. Both of these are questions of critical reflection; the latter, however, is primarily an epistemological question, while the former is more directly practical—even if the two dimensions of an epistemological and a practical inquiry cannot ultimately be considered as absolutely separate inquiries.

If we approach critique from the epistemological angle of asking how to discern among different and competing claims to criteria, projects, and courses of action, then it seems to me that the debate over critique, contingent foundations, and ethical and political action goes beyond making Foucauldian arguments admit to their own normative impulses. The normative implications of critique are not solely a question of laying open the sources of one's own normative commitments and rendering them plausible. At stake is, rather, the problem that these commitments lay claim to a validity that is more than preference or personal predilection if these normative commitments express what is taken to be right and relevant in an ethical sense. This ethical validity should owe itself neither merely to customs that would make us receptive to agreeing with the commitments put forth nor merely to a position of power that would coerce us to accept the commitments as right. Despite these claims to a correctness or validity beyond persuasiveness and power, though, any validity invoked by normative commitments is conditioned by social and historical contexts as well as power relations. If the discussion becomes one of whether or not normative commitments are laid open, this problem of normativity is effaced rather than resolved.[23] What I would like to hold onto for our discussion is what I take to be the Habermasian dissatisfaction with settling for fully contingent foundations and normative commitments that emerge performatively and thus can only belatedly become objects for critical reflection.

Settling for belated reflection as the only possibility is not satisfactory if one wants to hold that we cannot simply accept history as the ultimate judge but that history is what needs to be judged. As a consequence, the question of criteria, their sources, and their legitimacy remains at issue. Even if it is practically impossible fully to attain a position apart from history, it remains important not to succumb to the view that eventually power and history determine what counts as right and just. The backdrop to such a refusal remains the outrage over existing violence and violation of lives. Nonetheless, there is no position that could attain a perspective that lies beyond either might or time, beyond either power or history. Any position depends on its being argued and being actively held by individuals within history, so in that limited sense, history does indeed judge and determine which perspectives and convictions become, remain, and are available at all. The task, then, is to refuse to allow power and history exclusively to determine what is right, while taking into account that power and history condition any such judgment that is made in the name of life, justice, or freedom. To understand that convictions, criteria, and norms are conditioned by relations of power and their historical situatedness is different from claiming that relations of power and historical circumstances fully determine normative stances. The question that becomes part of the task of critique is to ascertain how this conditioning works and what its effects are.

This demand to theorize critically the ways in which relations of power and cultural specificity condition categories, procedures, and criteria of explanation, deliberation, and judgment is addressed by Foucauldians to Habermasian articulations of an ideal of communicative reason. In response to this concern and the concerns raised by postcolonialist and cultural studies scholars more broadly, Habermasians have acknowledged that in practice there must be a constant renegotiation of the normative ideals derived from an ideal of communicative reason.[24] Yet these responses are still criticized from the Foucauldian perspective for effacing rather than making theorizable the problem of power and history as the conditions for knowledge and normative ideals that we could possibly come to know.[25] The problem with the Habermasian concession is that it considers only the practical applications but not the formulation of the ideal itself, conditioned by historically and socially contingent frameworks and by relations of power that delimit the criteria and categories of knowledge.[26] The question of how power conditions us, our actions, and our principles is relegated to an empirical problem that can be adjudicated theoretically with recourse to an ideal that can provide a reliable criterion for judgment.

The Foucauldian side refuses to put the problem of normativity to rest with the recovery of an ideal of communicative reason that despite being malleable and renegotiable, maintains the claim of resolving the "justificatory deficit." While the Habermasian solution seems to short-circuit the problematic of power and knowledge and the relation between social and moral normativity, the Foucauldian solution, by settling for contingency and belated reflection, seems to short-circuit the problematic with respect to the stakes in the disarticulation of social and moral validity. The Habermasian suspicion regarding the "problem of validity" remains important for keeping critique from settling too quickly for the impasse. Between these two suspicions—the Foucauldian one and the Habermasian one—we encounter the intractable relation between social and moral norms and the possibility of critique, not only with respect to moral conduct but also for claims to justice and legitimacy. It must be possible to address and elaborate this epistemological aporia without putting it to rest and without falling into practical nihilism.

Such nihilism or the charge thereof can occur in various ways; in part it can be an accusation that one draws upon for attending to the epistemological dimension and for elaborating an epistemologically aporetic situation that seems to remove us from the realm of action and leave us without firm grounds from which to act. Attention to the epistemologically aporetic can also give rise to nihilism when moral and political issues are subsequently reduced to a wrestling with and decision about the epistemologically undecidable. At stake in our considerations here is the relation between theoretical and practical reason and how the epistemological aporia conditions our practical reflections. Or, stated in different terms, at stake is how the way in which one formulates the relation between power and knowledge conditions what perspective on the limits, possibilities, and requirements for critique and moral and political deliberation ensues.

This question of how to formulate and attend to the relation between power and knowledge is one of the issues at the core of the Foucault-Habermas debate. As Michael Kelly sums it up, for Habermas the question is "How is the discourse of truth able to set limits to the rights of power?" and for Foucault the question is "What rules of right are implemented by the relations of power in the production of discourses of truth?"[27] In this formulation, it is clear that for Foucault power and knowledge are neither indistinguishable from each other nor opposed to each other as mutually exclusive domains. Rather, at issue are the ways in which power conditions the criteria for truth and its production.

Butler herself stands within the Foucauldian tradition that asks how relations of power and social norms determine what will be intelligible and count as true and right. In *Undoing Gender* she reflects on how we might arrive at criteria for distinguishing among different regimes of truth and she turns for assistance to Foucault's understanding of critique: "According to Foucault, one of the first tasks of critique is to discern the relation 'between mechanisms of coercion and elements of knowledge'" (*UG* 215, quoting Foucault). Following Foucault, Butler argues that prior to articulating normative grounds and principles, the task of critique is to inquire into the relation between "mechanisms of coercion" and "elements of knowledge."

This relation between coercion and knowledge is not already known, and this relation is posed as a question. Critique begins by interrupting any figurations of this relation and asks us to find out what kind of relation exists between coercive practices and institutions and the way knowledge is produced. By removing the fiction of a clear separation between truth and power, we are no longer thinking about truth by beginning with the notion that knowledge is true only insofar as it is different from coercion. Equally, power is not then solely conceived as a means of coercion. At the same time, the argument here is also not that truth is nothing but a mechanism of coercion or a set of insights reducible to social conventions and norms.

If critique sees as its task an examination of how the production of knowledge is bound up with discursive regimes of power, the question eventually is how to reflect on criteria to distinguish between different regimes of knowledge while taking into account that these criteria are themselves conditioned by discursive regimes of power. It seems to me that we can use Butler's writings to take us another step in this direction, as her work examines how the relation between power and knowledge constitutes subjects and bodies and potentially exerts violence by making certain bodies and lives unlivable. In these reflections, violence, human bodies, and lives are not taken as absolute in their meaning, but they emerge as criteria as well as sites of contestation for what ought to be done.

In this light, the question that Kelly offered as Habermas's—namely, how truth can set limits to the rights of power—has not been abolished but stands in a transfigured form. How truth can limit power must be rethought if we accept that the discourses of truth are implicated with power and may therefore not be able to set limits to power or at least legitimately lay claim to this limiting. Nonetheless, while this question of a critical perspective on the rights and workings of power is still standing, we can now take into account that no such position is beyond power. Any position is always entangled with relations of power and owes its terms and perspectives to culturally and historically specific contexts. In the absence of absolute criteria, critique must rely on the specificity of material conditions and histories of bodies and lives to examine how relations of power and social practices and institutions condition those lives and bodies.

Critique and the Limits of Moral Philosophy

The epistemologically aporetic situation addressed by the Foucault-Habermas debate raises the question whether moral philosophy is indeed still conceivable as a philosophical endeavor, especially if moral philosophy is seen to be more than an elaboration of an ethical dimension of encounters with others in terms of our constitutive relationality. The normative and generalizing aspirations as well as the structural social and political dimension of critique cannot be reduced to the ethics of moral conduct. Rather than ceding the impossibility of moral philosophy, I would like instead to rethink the relation between ethics and politics through the aporia of critique that ensues from the understanding of all knowledge as socially conditioned.

Moral philosophy in the strict sense might, as Adorno suggests, rely on the possibility of thoroughly grounding morality in the possibility of establishing with certainty criteria for distinguishing good from bad, right from wrong, and just from unjust. This need for certainty forced Kant to seek recourse in morality that lies in the "good will" alone at the expense of consequentialist considerations, because consequences of actions are uncertain and are never fully controllable by the agent. Butler, with Adorno, rejects Kantian purism for ethical and moral reasons and insists on taking consequences as well as their uncertainty into consideration. To a more radical extent than Adorno, Butler's considerations in this direction are marked by her reconceiving the subject as formed only in and through relations with others and society. Insofar as the need for critique arises out of these very concrete social and political situations, the problematic for an inquiry into critique entails an epistemological as well as an ethical and political dimension.

If social criticism—the ethical and political side of critique—excludes, short-circuits, or ignores this epistemological conundrum of being historically and socially conditioned, then critique runs the danger of becoming uncritical. Yet to address that epistemological conundrum and hold it in play does not yet guarantee that critique will be properly critical; it continuously needs to work on becoming critical. Critique in this regard is critical precisely insofar as it is this unfinished and interminable project. The differences between various approaches to critique and manifestations of it as social criticism need to be assessed with regard to how they attend in different ways to this interminability and how this epistemological openness is repeatedly closed and opened again with respect to concrete social and political circumstances. Critique's commitment to its own openness and interminability gives rise to a normative dimension that is always negative in the sense that it will refuse to settle for any reality and ground that lays claim to being unquestionable. What is normative about critique is also always bound to concrete situations and therefore is not possible to guarantee outside or beyond the particular instantiations and manifestations of critique.

This negative dimension of critique's normative commitment is not purely negative, insofar as one cannot question the legitimacy of a particular set of norms, laws, institutions, or practices without laying claim to a right both to question and implicitly to offer another understanding of what would make for more legitimate norms, laws, institutions, or practices. Butler lays out this right to question as being central to the operation of critique by engaging Foucault's short essay entitled "What Is Critique?" In her argument, she revises the Enlightenment understanding of critique with regard to the universal rights that the Enlightenment began to claim:

> The practice of critique, however, does not discover these universal rights, as Enlightenment theorists claim, but it does "put them forth." However, it does not put them forth as positive rights. The "putting forth" is an act which limits the power of the law, an act which counters and rivals the workings of power, power at the moment of renewal. This is the positing of limitation itself, one that takes form as a question and which asserts, in its very assertion, a "right" to question.[28]

Critique here is not a positing of rights in the name of renewing power. Rather, critique always works in the name of undoing and questioning—but this questioning is not unqualified. The qualification that characterizes the particular questioning of critique is the limitation and hesitation that it imposes on the power of law. Despite this questioning power of critique, this does not mean that whatever position emerges in its wake is by virtue of its opposition to the status quo necessarily superior or more legitimate than those laws and practices that are being called into question. It is not settled whether that in whose name positive law and existing normative frameworks are called into question is by necessity "better" or "more right" or "more just." Any qualification cannot be drawn from the purely formal criterion of calling into question or reworking of the existing conditions but has to allow for more substantive articulations. I argue in the final chapter for considerations that address more specifically the dimensions of universality, justice, and recognition.

So while these insights imply that critique is an ethical practice and a practical virtue, this aspect of critique has been of lesser concern in my argument than have the implications of critique for thinking about power and social and moral norms. It is important to mark, however, the practical and subject-formative side of critique. From this perspective, critique implies a continuous self-formation through critical questioning of social norms, practices, and institutions, because one comes into question for oneself insofar as one is sustained by those norms, practices, and institutions.[29] Even though critique relies on this practice, the normative claims of critique, as well as the conundrum of normativity, cannot be relegated to the personal in terms of a practice. Instead, I would like to consider the relation between ethics and politics through the interminability of critique and its status as being reducible to neither epistemological critique nor social criticism.

By understanding critique as encompassing both epistemological and social concerns, we are still well within the tradition of the Enlightenment and even in the tradition of Kantian critique. The latter is characterized by the fact that the criticism of absolutist rule becomes important and possible precisely as the subject of reason becomes the institution that is able to call into question traditional authorities of knowledge. Kant's elaborations do not take social injustices as their starting point and aim, but Kantian epistemological critique has a social dimension in that it was formulated against social and political authorities in the name of universal reason and the right to question authoritarian rule. Social criticism hence is not unrelated to epistemological critique; instead, these two concepts mutually condition each other.

But in this formulation of critique as key to moral philosophy, the opposition between freedom and nature is no longer as clear-cut for us as it was for Kant. For Kant reason was unified, universal, and unconditional and could guarantee a critical distinction between freedom and nature.[30] In *Problems of Moral Philosophy* Adorno argued that Kant may be considered one of the few true moral philosophers, if not the last, because of his strict separation between freedom and nature:

> [W]e might say that Kant's moral philosophy is moral philosophy *par excellence*, moral philosophy as such. Because it rules out empirical reality from consideration, . . . this extreme segregation of the realms of nature and morality, is what makes possible something like a fully articulated and logically consistent philosophy of morality. (*PMP* 106/158)

Without the strict opposition and separation of freedom as the realm of the unconditioned from the realm of the contingent, it is impossible to find a stringent and unconditional vantage point in relation to which to ground criteria and principles for a critical consideration of what is against what ought to be. Today asking the question of the possibility of moral philosophy might no longer revolve around the separation between nature and freedom, but a contemporary formulation of the problem of moral philosophy's grounds and limits may very well be centered on the relation between power and knowledge or power and truth.

If the relation between power and truth as a problematic of critique is inherent in moral philosophy, then the relation between ethics and politics can no longer be figured through aligning politics with power and ethics with truth. Rather, power is an issue for both ethics and politics. Moreover, insofar as there are no longer any absolute grounds or principles to which we might seek recourse, the question of how critique can orient action becomes a quandary of the relation between ethics and politics. In *Giving an Account of Oneself* Butler draws on Adorno to argue that moral conduct cannot be a question of a purely individual good will under exclusion of social conditions that pose the need for ethical deliberation. Social conditions and the consequences of our actions have to enter into our deliberations of what would be the right actions to take.

The larger context of Butler's argument in that work is that the subject needs to be considered as a question rather than as a precondition of moral philosophy. The subject, especially as the subject of ethical and political action, is not thinkable apart from its formation, and for moral philosophy two consequences follow. On the one hand, moral philosophy has to take into account the self-reflexive self-formation of the ethical subject that occurs insofar as we find ourselves in need of considering and determining how to conduct ourselves, which actions to take, which causes to oppose, and which to advance. On the other hand, this formation and these deliberations never take place independently of social conditions, normalizing practices, and institutions, as well as of the unconscious and irrecoverable past of the subject that is always marked by personal relationships and social and cultural contexts. This issue of the formation of the ethical subject becomes important for critique not only as subjective practice; instead, the subject and its formation are one site through which we can further inquire into the relation between ethics and politics. Precisely because subject formation carries in it the index of power and politics, considering the relation between ethics and politics through critique becomes central for moral philosophy.

Subject formation in this regard is important because it provides us with an analytic of power and social normalization by clarifying the material effects of schemes of intelligibility. Critique is concerned with and emerges in part along with the question of asking how subjects are formed and how schemes of social and political intelligibility determine who counts as a subject, as an individual, and as a human being. Articulated in conversation with Butler but also as a key category for moral philosophy, critique, to the extent that it begins as a question of intelligibility, has a dimension that is perhaps primarily epistemological. But crucially this question has ethical and political import not because critique is to provide grounds for a truth beyond power; the problematic of critical inquiry arises over the predicament that knowledge and truth are not simply opposed to power. That knowledge and truth are conditioned by power matters as an epistemological issue for critique because the delimitation of knowledge and truth determines in return who and what counts as human and inhuman and which conditions count as inhuman enough to warrant different kinds of interventions.

In his 1963 lecture course *Problems of Moral Philosophy*, Adorno insists that the predicaments that haunt moral-philosophical endeavors continue to matter for theoretical reflections at least insofar as they prompt the question of whether it is still possible to have something that we may call moral philosophy. Despite his skepticism, he wants to hold on to the critical potential that terms like "morality" or "moral philosophy" have for theoretical reflection, because as terms that give rise to a certain discomfort, they dispose us critically toward them. Nonetheless, in his final lecture, on July 25, 1963, Adorno hesitates to affirm straightforwardly the possibility of moral philosophy for the present while having just spent an entire semester repeatedly emphasizing the importance of being able to grasp the predicaments that lie at the core of moral philosophy. It seems that if there is still anything for Adorno that may be called moral philosophy, then it is an endeavor concerned with orienting individual and institutional practices.

Now, more than forty years on, in the absence of reference points beyond contingent relations in an empirical historically and socially conditioned world, moral philosophy turns into a political account. Moral philosophy raises and insists on the question of the morally good, but it has to engage this question equally as one of the "right form of politics." Butler quotes Adorno to make this point: "In his [Adorno's] words, 'anything that we can call morality today merges into the question of the organization of the world. We might even say that the quest for the good life is the quest for the right form of politics, if indeed such a right form of politics lay within the realm of what can be achieved today' (*PMP*, 176/262)" (*GA* 133).[31] Adorno and Butler seem to say here that morality, if there can still be such a thing today, is not other to politics but becomes a question of politics insofar as politics is the mode of action through which the social conditions for moral conduct are effectively created. With this understanding of politics, political action is not relegated to action taken by or in relation to the state and its institutions, but politics is found wherever the conditions for human life are created.

Not just any politics can be considered as an instantiation of morality, but, as Adorno indicates, only the right form of politics can possibly qualify. With the dimension of morality, the question of criteria of right and wrong continues to matter; however, it seems that Adorno implies in the final lectures of his course that moral conduct can no longer—if it ever could—be regarded as a sphere of action and standards beyond or prior to politics. Moral conduct, living in a way that could be called "good," according to Adorno, has to be in the first place a question of "organizing the world" so that the good life can be possible at all. Or, to put it another way, insofar as the possibility of the good life cannot be guaranteed, the quest for transforming our world has to make possible a situation so that the question "What is the best life to strive for?" can be posed meaningfully at all. With this question of organizing the conditions of our lives, social justice emerges as a horizon for critique and the question of moral conduct is reformulated as a question of social ethics and political ethics.

As Adorno formulates moral conduct as a question of the politics of social organization, he continues to invoke an understanding of the good as a reference point for both moral and political life. Precisely insofar as we continue to consider the good life an important question to ask, we are with these considerations in the realm of moral philosophy. Moral philosophy must pose the question of the good life in the form of the question of the right politics, one that takes into account both the social and the institutional conditions and consequences of ethical action. I would argue that the reverse formulation is equally important, namely, that moral philosophy provides a genuine perspective on the question of the right politics insofar as the question of the good life remains a horizon that frames the inquiry into political and social realities and their possible transformation.

Insofar as the consequences of actions and social conditions continue to matter for what can possibly count as good, the distinction between better and worse forms of organizing collective life is not given up. In his famous dictum in *Minima Moralia* "Wrong life cannot be lived rightly,"[32] Adorno seems resigned to give up altogether the possibility of a right life and with it the relevance of distinguishing between right and wrong and between better and worse. But only if the conditions of this world are unchangeably wrong could Adorno's claim imply that making distinctions between better and worse no longer counts. Instead, we live in a time when the improving means of producing new and more refined knowledge have made it very clear that the conditions of our bodies, our lives, and our societies have expanded exponentially in complexity as well as scope. This expanding complexity fuels on the one hand the urge to create more accurate and scientific ways of knowing and on the other hand an unprecedented clarity with which we see that none of us can control the complex ways in which our societies function on a local and global level. Adorno argued that it was hard enough in his day to know what actions to take to respond to the social and political situation in a manner that would qualify as decent, let alone as morally good (see *PMP* 116/173). It seems that this assessment has lost nothing in its timeliness over the past four decades—and might have become only more true.

In the face of these challenges, Adorno's response seems to oppose Kant, who acknowledges that it is impossible to know the consequences of our actions and argues consequently that the only criterion that could possibly serve to determine moral goodness is the goodness of the will. For Adorno—as much as he acknowledges the stringency of Kant's argumentation—Kant's conclusion abets a retreat to the personal or the oft-cited moral rigor of Kantian morality. Instead, Adorno insists that retreating to the personal is to be resisted, precisely because he refuses all forms of accepting and arranging oneself within existing social circumstances. Adorno argues against acting in absolute and rigorous accord with moral principles at all costs and without regard for the specific consequences of one's actions.[33] This is not a relativist stance that gives up the possibility of moral conduct in its entirety, but in this reformulation, morality becomes a question of tarrying with the realizable and with the question of how we can and ought to organize the world today. The critical labor of moral philosophy, in that sense, is precisely not an endeavor to reach absolute grounds from which we could set out to strive for moral goodness. Rather, the critical work of moral philosophy is a political engagement with questions of justice, insofar as justice is precisely the question of the good life posed in a generalized manner beyond the particular perspective of a given individual's good life.

So far what we have formulated with Butler and Adorno and with reference to the Foucault-Habermas debate is that critique is central for moral philosophy as a mode of inquiry situated at the juncture of ethics and politics. Critique assesses the workings of power while refusing to settle the question of normative demands in any easy way. Yet the problematic of criteria and their normative underpinnings that we have taken up from the Foucault-Habermas debate remains relevant. We return now to this problematic within the changed formulation of asking how the "right form of politics" may be discerned among other possible, even if only imaginable, forms of politics. By addressing the problematic this way, we have also added to our considerations the question of how "the realm of what can be achieved today" is delimited. Within this framework, we might, with Butler and Foucault, revise Adorno to ask how norms and institutions delimit what can appear as achievable as well as what kinds of criteria for right and wrong might ensue. While Adorno appears to be doubtful about the chances for finding and realizing the right politics—"if indeed such a right form of politics lay within the realm of what can be achieved today" (*PMP* 176)—it seems that with Butler we might insist that the political relevance of critique as a theoretical, epistemological inquiry and as social criticism is not yet to be surrendered to the realm of the unachievable.

Moral philosophy in these terms is not about formulating principles for moral conduct. Instead we might follow Adorno, who holds that moral philosophy in the present would be possible only through a critique of its problematic categories: "On the question of whether moral philosophy is possible today, the only thing I would be able to say is that essentially it would consist in the attempt to make conscious the critique of moral philosophy, the critique of its options [possibilities, *Möglichkeiten*] and an awareness of its antinomies" (*PMP* 167/248). While I concur with the emphasis on this epistemologically critical endeavor as being crucial to moral philosophy, it seems that in the end Adorno's approach remains perhaps too much on the side of this epistemological critique of the antinomies without substantially moving into elaborating more specifically what kinds of categories can guide critical inquiry and political action. The reflection on such categories does not mean that one needs to offer a normative utopia or a system of normative aspirations, but it might be possible not to confine ourselves fully to the reflective practice that Adorno puts forth as the ambivalent limit of what philosophy can eventually offer.

Adorno rehearses the crucial realization that one can never avoid being implicated in the very structures that one wants to oppose, but the small glimpse of hope that Adorno wants to hold on to—even if he takes it back two sentences later—is that:

> Perhaps the situation is that if we start to reflect on what is involved in joining in, and if we are conscious of its consequences, then everything that we do—everything that goes on in our minds to contribute to what is wrong—will be just a little different from what it otherwise would have been. (*PMP* 168/230)

While crucial to his argument, Adorno's suggestion that accompanying every act with a critical reflection is the only possible response to the question "What ought we to do?" seems eventually to turn away from the collective, social, and political dimension of the question of morality.

Drawing on Butler's critical inquiries into social norms, I would like to open a perspective on critique that differs from Adorno's and that counters his individualizing and aestheticizing move. Butler's work has been committed to the political dimension of theory through drawing on Foucault's work on power and normalization as well as on Kristeva's and Derrida's work in order to analyze how social norms and social power work through abjection to produce a constitutive outside to social life.[34] Butler takes us into a political direction without relying on a universalism of communicative reason, as Habermas seems to do, partly in response to Adorno. Holding in play both the aporia of normativity and the aspiration to articulate the social and political dimension of critique, I would like to take up Butler's reflections on the relation between social and moral normativity and on questions of recognition as matters of social justice.

With this dimension of critique that relates to questions of social justice, we are moving into considerations of what can be called political ethics. The concerns of social justice and political ethics are in my view profoundly within the scope of moral philosophy. As a theoretical reflection on the possibility of ethics, moral philosophy is not only a theory of moral conduct and a critical assessment of the conditions and principles of moral conduct. Since the question of justice has been a central question of moral philosophy, the scope of moral-philosophical inquiry goes beyond the ethics of personal conduct and takes up structural, social, institutional, and political questions. At the same time, however, moral philosophy cannot settle these questions in a realm of pure philosophical speculation. Moral philosophy has continuously to become other than itself, as this question of justice takes it into the realm of social and political theory as well as into sociological, anthropological, economic, and scientific inquiries.

These encounters are complicated and varied, and this book does not claim to stage them, nor can all the questions that the perspective of justice raises be exhaustively answered in the context of putting Butler and moral philosophy into conversation. Even so, Butler's work allows us to open philosophical avenues for further elaborating such a turn to justice at the crossroads of ethics and politics. In the next chapter I therefore attempt to outline this question of justice more precisely by considering social recognition as a heuristic, critical tool to ask how social, legal, economic, and political practices work to delimit what and who will count as human and humane life and what normative—ethical and political—implications our understandings of "the human," "life," and "social justice" will have.

SIX

Critique and Political Ethics: Justice as a Question

None of us live as fully self-sufficient, autonomous beings; we are implicated in the lives of others not only at the beginning and end of our lives, but all throughout them. We live with others, proximate to others whom we encounter personally, whom we might wish to encounter, or whom we might wish that we would need not encounter, and with others whom we might never meet directly, but whose lives and plights are nonetheless enmeshed with ours, and not always for the better. A few of us live in relatively great wealth and comfort, consume more of the earth's natural resources than the rest of the world combined, and contribute to the destruction of the environment at an unprecedented speed, while much of the world's population lives in abject poverty, exploited to sustain and increase the wealth of the rich. However, even within so-called rich nations, wealth is far from distributed evenly, and the ways in which individuals and social groups are marginalized across the globe are not limited to economic sustainability. Whether we like it or not, whether we want it or not, we are part of this interconnected global relationship.

Since we cannot shed this collective social condition of living in this world, it would seem that considerations of ethics cannot limit themselves to the individually good life. Instead, the conditions of life as social and global issues, as well as their negotiation in politics, economics, and civil society, cannot fall beyond the scope of moral philosophy.

Because questions of power and of concrete social and political situations are at stake, considering critique in the context of moral philosophy cannot be reducible to merely theorizing the problem of morally normative claims. As I try to show in the previous chapter, the problem of normativity remains crucial for a critical moral philosophy. Normativity remains crucial as precisely that—a problem. Moral philosophy has to reflect on the aporia of having to formulate evaluative criteria to assess social and historical realities, while at the same time such formulations cannot but emerge from very particular social and historical positions themselves. On the one hand, it is impossible to arrive at normative criteria that are not tethered in cultural and political specificities, which means that these criteria might be blind toward the injustices and privileges on which they rely for their formulation. On the other hand, if one does not want to give in to a defeatist relativism or to uncritical advancements of particular normative programs, then it is necessary to argue for a critical normative dimension that is not reducible to the cultural and historical horizon of politics and power relations from which it emerges.

To consider this aporetic situation might seem mainly an epistemological pursuit; in a practical sense, this aporia is constantly suspended by actual affirmations of criteria in concrete criticisms and by articulations of specific political programs. One could assert—and many do—that there is not much more that moral philosophy could offer within this context other than explicating the ensuing irresolvable movement between asserting and critically undoing of whatever comes to be asserted.[1] Such a retreat into the undecidable, however, would mean an eschewing of the social problematics and the ways in which ethics is already bound up with questions of power and politics.

Against this background, I would like to suggest that we consider how critique as a key concept for moral philosophy is characterized by the double dimension of epistemological critique and social criticism. Both of these dimensions are necessary: critique only in the form of social criticism runs the danger of turning uncritical and possibly dogmatic; critique only in the form of an epistemological critique runs the danger of turning irresponsive, if not irresponsible, to social and historical conditions. That said, to take up social justice as a question for critical inquiry does not mean that a theoretical inquiry based in moral philosophy would begin from answers—not even in a reconstructive manner that assumes certain answers that are then reflectively ascertained and refined. But to start with a question means to begin by not knowing with certainty what ought to be and by discovering what ought not to be. In other words, to begin with social justice as a question means asking where and how suffering is happening unnecessarily, where lives are made impossible, whose lives are made unlivable by which social, economic, military, and political frameworks. In order to inquire into these frameworks, we can find a particular heuristics in Butler's work that insists on questioning how power and social norms work to enable and to constrain lives, to protect lives, and to expose them to violence.

By beginning with finding out about injustices, violence, and suffering first rather than beginning from elaborating normative standards of justice, concrete situations are not the field to which theoretical moral principles are applied, but these situations are the very starting point for moral inquiry. With the concern for social justice, such inquiries are directed to structural or systemic dimensions and are not reducible to individual investments in particular situations. With respect to political and social action, the question of what to do becomes especially difficult in a different way from how it has been in responding to concrete others. While in relation to others, passionate attachments—avowed and disavowed histories and desires—complicate the scenes of address and response, these complications are somewhat different from those of the social, economic, and political institutions and practices that structure our daily lives. The difficulties with these institutions and practices are that their efficacies eschew the possibility of conceiving of them as quasi-subjects to make sense of their "behaviors."

Social power is diffused and circulated through institutions and structures that are political, economic, social, and cultural. Consequently, the logics structuring events in these spheres cannot be grasped adequately by models of intentional action that order and explain the field of events by attributing actions to subjects who then pursue interests, make decisions, act on them, and react to other subjects' actions. Butler's work can aid us in taking these institutional and structural social dimensions into view, since her work comes at an angle to the question of subjectivity but does not abolish the question of what kind of agencies and subjectivities certain institutions—such as states in relation to their sovereignty—might attain. Butler performs analyses of power that seek to expose how subjects are formed and how practices and institutions acquire and proliferate their formative powers. The subject is not given up as a philosophical category but is turned into a critical category by pursuing the question of how subject formation occurs through specific social and political constellations.

In the first part of this chapter, I develop how we can understand the question of justice to mark a juncture between politics and ethics from which we can think further about a political ethics. In the final part of this chapter, I would like to elaborate on the critical perspective for moral inquiries that Butler's persistent return to recognition offers by asking how social normalization works. This approach, however, does not imply that normative claims are eclipsed. Instead, the normative dimension on which moral philosophy insists expresses and invigorates aspirations for making our world more livable, more just, and less violent for all. That said, the foundations of norms, both social and moral, are historically and culturally contingent and not compelling in an absolute way. The difficulty with the normative dimension of moral principles is that despite their contingency, their validity should exceed contingent and arbitrary decisions. In other words, if held to as a normative demand, the validity of, for example, the demand for respect and recognition for human life is expected not to be contingent on whether or not we might collectively decide that this is for now, at this point in history, a good principle to stand by. Instead, this demand is attributed a validity that exceeds the historical origins and manifestations of the demand, even if in practice the demand that life be respected and recognized depends on its being held, aspired to, and worked for, also against its own selective and exclusionary history.[2]

While in the previous chapter I consider the unavoidable, aporetic situation that ensues from understanding moral normativity as socially conditioned, in this chapter I would like to address how the universality at stake in ethics implicates ethics in politics and how this aspiration to universality then poses the question of a translation between contexts, which is a translation without an original set of true answers.

The stakes in universality and normativity in moral philosophy are not simply problems of establishing principles and criteria, as if such principles and criteria were a precious and prized possession to be found at the end of some rainbow of reason. The problem of moral philosophy is not so much one of finding and guarding a truth or truths but arises from the fact that we live and act within history and within a world where people can and do suffer unnecessarily. Political and social actions and decisions both are necessary and necessitate that we deliberate on possible and past consequences, even though it is impossible conclusively to know such consequences in advance or even conclusively to account for them after the fact.

When we ask what is the best course of action to take to make our world a less violent place, we quickly reach moral and political quandaries in such deliberations. For example, a rigorous pacifism and denunciation of all use of violence pose the problems of nonintervention, considering how refusing to intervene might aid the exacerbation of violence. At the same time, settling firm principles by which to determine what counts as justified violence and what is a "just war" is equally problematic, because such an endeavor presupposes that different kinds of violence can be compared and that some can be justified, so that certain violent effects can be considered morally acceptable. Moreover, such an approach assumes that there can and must be abstract principles that could be settled apart from and prior to considering the differences between concrete instances of violence. Instead, to hold all moral possibilities in play, one would have to inquire what frameworks of differentiating violence from coercion are in place, under which conditions certain forms of violence can and cannot appear as legitimate, and which kinds of suffering come to be acceptable in the name of which hopes.

These questions cannot be solved theoretically by reducing historically concrete situations to a set of hypothetical examples that would afford formulating a taxonomy of relevant principles. While for moral philosophy it is key to begin its investigation by discovering and opposing instances of injustice and inhumanity, it is problematic if these instances are taken up in theoretical reflections with a goal of deriving and justifying general principles. At this point, once again the aporetic situation of critique and normativity demands giving up on neither the need for and aspiration to a principled denunciation of injustice nor the need to call into question the very presuppositions that already prefigure the field of what can be recognizable as an injustice. Taking injustice and justice as horizons for critique directs us to examine social, economic, legal, and political institutions and practices, and this examination becomes a matter of political ethics whenever it turns into a deliberation over how we can change these structures so that life might become more sustainable not just for a few but for all.

The Question of Justice as a Hinge between Ethics and Politics

The understanding of political ethics that I am trying to elaborate here will not take power or the state and its institutions as exclusive characteristics of politics that then set politics apart from ethics.[3] Politics is also not a means for implementing ethical principles that must be found to be independent from politics. Instead, I will consider politics as what we engage in when we contest the manners in which our lives are communally organized. Seen in this light, we might say that politics takes place wherever the shared conditions of our lives are created, sustained, and transformed. This means that politics is not a prerogative of state institutions or of citizens in relation to a nation-state but can just as well take place through social movements, economic entities, or legal struggles.

Politics considered this way is the negotiation of institutional and practical frameworks that in return produce and regulate the concrete conditions of our lives, such as, for example, labor practices and laws, the organization of transnational capital, legal systems, health care, or education. None of these aspects exhausts the sphere of politics, but they can become a matter for politics when their negotiation is at stake. Political action is thus not confined to the sites of state institutions and state-sanctioned procedures; rather, politics happens wherever governance becomes a question in terms of organizing our communities and the shared conditions of life.

It is when we consider these issues in relation to justice that we introduce an ethical horizon for these political debates. This horizon is, I argue, not necessarily implied in politics; one could think of other horizons, such as profitability or imperial interests, that could easily dominate as horizons for political deliberations. But the perspective of morality cannot evade the question of justice because of the implied universalizing dimension of moral considerations. The question of moral conduct—"What ought to be done? How to respond well to this situation?"—demands that we turn to the larger question of how we ought to arrange social conditions so that they make life possible not only for a few but for all. Along with the question of arranging society and the conditions of life, however, moral-philosophical considerations also of necessity have a political dimension. This does not mean, however, that all moral questions are always political in a strong sense, if, for the dimension of politics to play a role, there must be this larger social perspective at stake. For these social issues to become specifically a matter of political ethics, they must first appear in the form of social criticism with respect to justice claiming the need for a more just arrangement of our conditions of life.

There are three aspects that I would like to argue as key to political ethics. First, to think about political ethics, we have to understand how ethics itself becomes political. In any bid for how we ought to organize social life, any particular concept of ethics enters into contestation with other bids. Ethics and normative visions cannot be seen as a set of principles or norms found elsewhere that need only the proper politics to mobilize an apparatus of institutions for their implementation and realization. Instead, ethical deliberations are themselves an issue of politics, despite or precisely because of their aspirations to put forth a bid for how things ought to be. Second, if political ethics is committed to act critically, not only will it have to reflect on the social and political issues that give rise to the ethical deliberations but equally it will have to interrogate its own categories continuously. Third, political ethics must be characterized by taking social justice as the central perspective for its interrogations and considerations.

In making this move to political ethics, the conjunction between politics and ethics raises two fundamental questions. One question can be circumscribed by the concern Wendy Brown raises in *Politics out of History*[4] as the crucial problem that political theory has with moral philosophy, which is that moral philosophy has a tendency to depoliticize the issues it considers. While Brown's critique poses the challenge of theorizing the political dimension in political ethics, the second, accompanying question is: What characterizes political ethics such that it might be considered a part of moral philosophy? To address both these aspects, I consider here why, if moral philosophy has this depoliticizing tendency, one would not simply give up moral philosophy in favor of political theory. The brief response, which I tackle at length in the rest of this chapter, is that the question of justice is at its heart a question of moral philosophy, alongside the critical reflection on normativity and its aporetic aspirations.

Turning to the challenge of politics in political ethics, we have to consider Brown's diagnosis of the tendency in moral philosophy to dispense with the very politics that it already mobilizes in how it represents the moral issues and reflections. Moral philosophy frequently sets up its inquiries by introducing questions that, as Brown argues:

> formulate a moral problem abstracted from the specific context in which such questions arise, and disavow as well the discursive framing through which they are proffered. Precisely for this reason morality often has been regarded by critical political thinkers as not simply naive but a depoliticizing form of political discourse.[5]

Brown identifies two aspects as key to the political dimension of a critical reflection: the specifics of the context out of which the moral quandary arises, and the discourses through which the quandary is negotiated. By eschewing the particulars of the contexts and the discursive and rhetorical structures of the moral-philosophical inquiry itself, the ensuing reflections operate in a depoliticizing manner. As the contexts and histories that prompted moral inquiries vanish into hypotheticals and stylized examples that allow for a taxonomy of criteria and moral principles, politics becomes reduced to an application of these principles and the politics inherent to moral deliberation can no longer be reflected on critically.[6]

At the same time as it has these depoliticizing effects, morality does not become irrelevant or exterior to political discourse. Rather, Brown suggests, morality is itself a kind of political discourse. The problem that she addresses is not that moral discourse is inherently lacking in being political itself, but that moral discourse in this move seems both to withdraw the issues it deals with from political contestation while still monopolizing the field of politics by turning concrete, specific, and real social problems into abstract and often hypothetical quandaries framed in terms of good and bad, right and wrong. Brown's assessment thus allows us to reformulate the notion of what it means to become critical from that of a more general epistemological critical turn to that of a critical approach to moral philosophy with respect to its role in politics and its relation to social and historical contexts. For moral philosophy to become critical requires that it avow and reflect on its own entanglements in politics.

With this problematic, as Brown formulates it for us, we can now distinguish political ethics from other endeavors that offer ethics as a philosophical solution to politics, such as Plato imagined it in *The Republic*.[7] Instead of regarding historical and cultural contexts as secondary to moral-philosophical considerations, these considerations need to mark how moral inquiries originate from concrete situations, which cannot be distilled into abstract principles. Butler's work is helpful here, because Butler frequently takes current social and political questions as an occasion for critical inquiry not only into the social and political situations but also into the philosophical tools with which we approach these situations. These concrete situations are issues to which a critical response needs to be formulated, and critique, as Butler's work performs it, brings a philosophical framework for inquiring into these problematics as well as letting the concrete issues call into question the philosophical framework itself. If we approach moral philosophy with this method of critique, then the theoretical reflections that arise are not self-contained questions abstracted from social realities. Rather, theoretical concerns such as subject formation, agency, responsibility, and accountability emerge out of and in response to social, historical, and political issues and debates as they arrange our present and become a question for future action.

Social, historical, and political issues become questions for moral and political inquiry insofar as they are not self-evident for us in what they mean and what responses they might require from us. As Butler points out in *Giving an Account of Oneself*, the loss of self-evidence is crucial to Adorno's approach to moral philosophy: "Adorno makes the claim that moral questions arise only when the collective ethos has ceased to hold sway . . . indeed, there seems to be a tension between ethos and morality, such that a waning of the former is the condition for the waxing of the latter" (*GA* 4). For Adorno, morality begins precisely when the unquestioned codes and rules for conduct are no longer self-evident. In this understanding, morality is a practice of reflection and deliberation, whereas ethos describes habituated frameworks and rationales for action. This distinction and the tension between ethos and morality imply neither that one is superior to the other nor that one but not the other ensures ethical action. Instead, for moral questions to become an issue for inquiry and reflection, a critical distance from both collective ethos and habitualized responses is necessary.

Yet even though posing these questions requires an interruption of the collective ethos, we are returning here neither to the individual of contractarian theories who chooses rationally to enter into select relations with others nor to an ideal of moral subjectivity that stands in opposition to the collective. The aim is not to privilege morality over ethos but to understand how the collective ethos frames our moral inquiries. Morality as a matter of not knowing what to do animates critical reflection in the sense of distinguishing and negotiating between the alternatives of what course of action to follow. It is because of this productive moment of not knowing that, contrary to common expectations, morality—or at least what is critical about it—has to do more with questions than with answers.

When the occasions for such questioning are social and political, we need to examine the status quo, but when we move to take political action, we also end up attempting to realize normative visions. These visions are both political and ethical when they articulate how better to organize the social conditions of our lives and the ways in which laws, conditions of labor, and social and political institutions structure and provide for what we and our living together are and can be. In this light, politics refers both to questions of power and realization and to questions of the collective conditions of life. It would be problematic to identify too readily this political ethics with a democratic politics, where to be "properly" democratic would in turn define what it means to be "properly" political. Ethics can be political in various ways; among them are becoming moralistic, democratic, or authoritarian. By presupposing that to be political means engaging in democratic contestation, one would introduce a normative version of what it means to be political on a descriptive, definitional level rather than as an avowed normative aspiration. With a definition that limits politics as democratic, one puts forth a prescription without acknowledging it as such or examining its origins, while at the same time one also loses the possibility of grasping the specifically political nature of nondemocratic forms of discourse and governance. Both seem to me highly problematic for a critical political theory as well as a critical moral philosophy.

To introduce prescriptive content by defining a concept, such as defining politics as democratic, is different from moralism. A prescriptive definition purports neutrality where there are already in play substantive choices about what one ought to think and do. Conversely, moralism presents an openly moralizing discourse that mobilizes the prescriptive choice by an emotional appeal, such as by shaming dissenters. By acknowledging moralism as a form of how ethics can perform and intervene politically, we gain the possibility of distinguishing between different constellations into which ethics and politics can enter. In *Politics out of History* Brown suggests that we read moralism as a political phenomenon that ensues from staunch attachments to moral ideals that have become politically unreachable: "The consequence of living these attachments as ungrievable losses—ungrievable because they are not fully avowed as attachments and hence are unable to be claimed as losses—is theoretical as well as political impotence and rage, which is often expressed as a reproachful political moralism."[8] Moralism, Brown suggests, is not a necessary consequence of ethics becoming political, but it haunts moral deliberations at the very time when their realizability is at stake. If the attachments to moral ideals and their supposed superiority are met with political unrealizability, then the ensuing experience of political powerlessness can lead in turn to moralistic politics.

This moralistic turn can happen anywhere on the political spectrum. Addressing in particular the Left's disavowed attachments to the liberal state, Brown argues that when a loved object is no longer available, whether or not it ever truly was, the loss cannot be mourned and then let go, because (in this example) one never avowed one's investments in the state in the first place. Instead, disavowed losses and heightened attachments to lost objects and visions can translate into moralistic political discourse. Moralism seen in this light is a particular form of becoming political and of dealing with the perceived gap between how society is arranged and how one believes it should be. Moralism responds to fill the gap between one's normative vision for social change and the available possibilities for change by refusing to engage with the latter. Moralism thus allows one to maintain the purity of one's ideals and one's moral rightness without having to strike political compromises and without having to call one's own position into question.

To enter into contestation, however, does not mean that one has to give up one's position, commitments, and ideals but simply that one can no longer claim them with the same certainty and absoluteness. This contestation provides perspective. In other words, on the most general level, moralism is moral convictions directly translated into a political program where the rightness and righteousness of this program are not available for critical questioning. While being disempowered might make groups more prone to moralistic political discourse, a particular group's wielding power and being able to realize its vision of social change does not by necessity mean that they will be immune to moralism. If a normative political project is realized, it is no longer tied to the sentiment of resentment; it simply becomes dominating. But insofar as a group presumptuously cites the reality of its own hegemony as endorsement of the rightness of its political vision, this political program might nonetheless carry moralistic features. The fact that a particular political program with specific normative commitments is hegemonic and able to manage power effectively does not render it right.

Equally, being politically disempowered is not an index of the ethical quality of a particular normative vision. So how can we avoid moralism but still find a place for moral arguments and deliberations in politics?

It seems to me that we have already introduced a different way of becoming political by the reference to contestation, which I understand to be a key feature of democratic politics. Democratic politics requires that each position strives for its own realization while being willing to encounter other positions and undergo changes as a result of these encounters. At stake is becoming political in a way that remains critical and resists becoming dogmatic, which means remaining open to reformulating one's goals and commitments while at the same time being committed to a position and its principles. Contestation and critique presuppose that we find ourselves in situations where social and political issues raise difficult questions of what to do and provide various positions for consideration. For engaging critically in politics and ethics, it is necessary that we acknowledge the provisional status of our solutions as well as the categories, norms, and guidelines that we deploy to make sense of and determine what to do.

It is precisely in this "not quite knowing" how best to act that critical philosophical engagement becomes possible—and vital. Philosophical reflection can then go in at least two directions. One would be to collect the various possible responses available and attempt to adjudicate between them while reflecting on the normative evaluative criteria that might serve to make distinctions and decisions. Another direction—and I understand Butler's work to proceed along these lines—would be to remain skeptical of beginning with a philosophical reflection that aims to ground the discussion in a set of normative criteria. This second approach would proceed analytically and critically in the sense of an "archaeology" in Foucault's sense in order to uncover the frameworks and categories that condition how we perceive and interpret the issues at stake.[9] This archaeological inquiry asks how and through which terms and constellations of institutions, practices, agents, and norms political issues come to us as such and through which norms and terms possible alternatives become thinkable at all. That the primary aim in this approach is not to excavate and shape normative principles argumentatively does not mean that it has no normative implications. The normative aspect enters through the kinds of questions that this approach draws on to guide the inquiries. This mode of critique specifies normative demands as a matter of posing particular questions rather than applying particular principles.

Attending to this rhetorical dimension of normativity by framing it as a question allows a critical perspective on the conditions of social codes and power relations that delimit the ways in which discourses come to have normative consequences. In her introduction to *Gender Trouble*, Butler explains that with respect to gender, a simple description becomes performatively prescriptive: "The question . . . of what qualifies as 'gender' is already a question that attests to a pervasively normative operation of power. . . . Thus, the very description of the field of gender is [in] no sense prior to, or separable from, the question of its normative operation" (*GT* xxi). Hence we can understand the "normative" as a rhetorical category that emerges performatively, even at the back of a discourse that aims to be merely descriptive but that has normalizing and normative effects insofar as it delimits who and what fall under the auspices of what is being described. We find ourselves at the intersection of critique, ethics, and politics when we examine where, how, and in what ways discourses, inquiries, and claims come to deliver normative claims and appeal to values and inscribe them.

Effective political as well as ethical discourses rely on their rhetorical effects to become persuasive. Insofar as persuasion, power, and rhetoric are at work in any form of communication, moral argumentation cannot function as a mode of inquiry or communication untouched by power. But by taking an approach that makes it a normative demand to pose questions, such as examining the social and historical conditions of issues and interrogating them in terms of justice, a space for an encounter between conflicting interpretations is opened up.

So the particular normative dimension of critique for which I am arguing here enters through a demand to examine how power and social norms and practices delimit and shape our lives and political projects. The primary question is no longer what makes political ethics specifically political but how political ethics is a particular formulation of moral philosophy because it attends critically to normativity and justice. Butler's work is helpful in thinking about critique in the context of political ethics because of the political focus for critique that it offers through its examinations of power relations and the norms that negotiate social intelligibility.

Turning to intelligibility as a key category for thinking about exclusion and normalization is particular to Butler's understanding of a critique that interrogates how social norms bring about subjects. The social norms at work in social institutions and practices delimit how we become recognizable as subjects, as bodies, as members of particular groups. They delimit the ways not only in which one is recognized and understood by others but in how one's own perspective is equally conditioned by these frameworks. Posing the question of intelligibility allows us in turn to interrogate social norms with respect to how they make possible and impossible lives by making them and their needs recognizable and contenders for being legitimate demands.

Critique is therefore not simply social criticism, in the sense of raising complaints about social wrongs; rather, critique also takes an epistemological critical turn by considering how social norms condition social ontologies and enable or foreclose certain lives and subjects. This mode of inquiry makes available for critical evaluation the underlying, disavowed, and often naturalized frameworks that delimit what kinds of lives and subjects become possible at all. But critique does not stop there. In her essay "Explanation and Exoneration, or What We Can Hear" in *Precarious Life*, Butler extends her understanding of frameworks of intelligibility to consider how historical and political events are allowed to enter into our discussions, which ones become audible, and which ones never reach our attention. Taking Butler's approach, we can ask how social frameworks already delimit a range of possible interpretations of these events and possible responses and exclude certain other interpretations and responses. As we examine our discourses and categories, we need to query what kinds of power relations subtend them, what exclusions they perform, in which ways they might lead to intensifications of violence, and how we might change them.

This approach to philosophical reflection through archeological and critical inquiry does not primarily focus on offering and backing up normative visions of how we ought to organize society. The aim is not to articulate abstract universal principles or criteria with which one could adequately evaluate the existing conditions in any given place. That said, this method does not simply amount to a repudiation in the name of an—unwittingly universalizing—particularism that deems any normative and context-traversing horizon impossible in the name of honoring cultural specificity. Instead, the aim is to work out analytical categories through which normative aspirations can be examined, formed, tested, and contested. Beginning by asking what discourses and norms condition social and political issues, political ethics focuses on interrogating the different histories and contexts of the debated issues.

As an ethical and political inquiry, this "archaeological" approach cannot resolve the pending quandary of the normative questions. It is the challenge of political ethics to reflect on how to pose these questions in terms of how we ought to respond to them, what stance we ought to take, and for what reasons. Theorizing the conjunction of these two moves—the "archaeological" starting point and the reflection on normative aspirations and their reasons—results in a commitment to a practical philosophy that approaches issues of moral conduct through their political dimension and that insists in the context of political deliberations that we reflect on the ethical dimension. Political ethics, as we can articulate it in conversation with Butler's work, examines what makes life livable with regard to the various contexts and situations and issues that we might find ourselves wrestling with.

In what follows I would like to take up Butler's suggestion that ethical inquiry is a perspective that comprises both the personal and a wider collective scope. Butler suggests in *Undoing Gender* that the question of the social conditions of life:

> becomes a question for ethics, I think not only when we ask the personal question, what makes my own life bearable, but when we ask, from a position of power, and from the point of view of distributive justice, what makes, or ought to make, the lives of others bearable? (*UG* 17)

Butler herself does not explore further the implications of this way of thinking for ethical deliberations that transcend the personal by theorizing the aspiration to a position of power within ethics. Her approach nevertheless opens a way to understand how ethics goes beyond the question of the individual good life in two ways: first, by extending this concern for the good life to others and, second, by taking up and aspiring to a position of power from which this question is examined. Moral discourse mobilizes aspirations of power, and not in ways that necessarily discredit moral deliberations. Instead, the pursuit of power itself has to be rendered open to critical analysis, including the forms that such critique might take, such as using institutional power, mobilizing social power by taking to the streets, or influencing and shaping the various forms of economic power through a variety of means. That said, from the perspective of justice, to aspire to power in the name of a particular version of justice and resultant social change does not justify the political program itself and put an end to the debate. Instead, this is the point where political debate begins.

The perspective of justice at stake, which Butler mentions specifically, is one of distributive justice, although this is not elaborated further. I would like to argue for a revision of this defaulting to distributive justice by turning instead to social justice. Social justice does not exclude issues of just distribution; rather, social justice seems to me to comprise more than fair distribution of goods and a just principle for making these decisions of allocation and distribution. In focusing solely on issues of distribution, other nonmaterial dimensions of the collective conditions of life cannot be addressed. In particular, questions of recognition tend to remain outside considerations of justice and are treated as less crucial aspects than the material conditions of life.[10] Butler's work makes it possible to rethink social justice through her critiques of social intelligibility. Her approach allows us to address material conditions together with the need for recognition and the difficulties of articulating a generalized normative framework because of the concomitant normalizing power.[11]

If we take Butler's theorizing of subject formation as a heuristic that emphasizes intelligibility and recognition as crucial, the perspective of justice as a guide for critical inquiries cannot be limited to distributive justice. By our examining how recognition works through cultural and social practices and institutions to condition material lives, relations of power become available for critical inquiry in ways that a framework of a just distribution of goods cannot address. Posing the question of justice as a critical inquiry and keeping the aspiration to and for power as well as to and for universalizing claims alive are crucial to the work of political ethics. Keeping these perspectives in mind allows moral philosophy to avoid being centered exclusively on the individual as well as to avoid dissolving the individual simply into a collective. Rather, the concept of justice at stake with respect to the issue of universality is that of the dignity of all as each individual one in his or her particularity. With respect to the issue of social justice, this concept of justice and universality then becomes a question of the conditions for sustainable life, as life is constituted in sociality and relationality.

Asking what makes lives livable allows for a political ethics rather than guiding and ensuring an ethical politics. In other words, the question is not in the first place how power can be held in check and be guided by justice and thus formulated as an ethically qualified politics. Political ethics is not a blueprint for an ethical politics, because we cannot determine principles of justice without already being embroiled in politics. Instead, political ethics begins with insisting on ethical reflection becoming political precisely insofar as the question of justice is introduced as a political question and is thus entangled with concerns over power and social norms. Justice is not the question that secures ethical reflection a vantage point fully other to politics, but justice as a question is what opens ethics toward political action. The question of justice works as a hinge in two ways for theorizing political ethics. First, the theoretical reflection that emerges in and out of political debates over what is to be done is ethical insofar as the question of justice is at stake. Second, ethical theory is political insofar as the question of justice is one of social change that never arises outside relations of power; thus moral philosophy and justice in particular are always also questions of power.

I have argued so far that there is not a normative framework in the sense of a set of abstract principles and their justification that a project of elaborating a political-ethical theory produces, but that the normative aspect emerges through an insistence upon posing the question of justice as a question of social justice, as one of making lives more rather than less sustainable and of reducing rather than increasing violence. Nevertheless, these questions remain—and, it seems to me, importantly so—committed to an openness and a certain fragility against which they cannot quite make themselves immune in advance to entering into concrete debates. Owing to the importance of this openness, I have argued for understanding the normative dimension through the demand that we pose to these questions pertaining to justice and to the conditions that render lives livable, that we unearth which particular visions of a livable life emerge in our debates, and that we struggle over which solutions to embrace within particular debates.

Moral philosophy and ethical reflection can move beyond the question of the care of oneself and that of a self-reflective ethos only when the question of justice is introduced that pertains to more than one person.[12] Justice cannot exist in a solipsistic world; justice presumes sociality and plurality, that there can be a justice in difference, which is precisely the difficulty and task that give rise to political ethics. Political ethics as a theoretical project arises in response to the question of justice and insists in return upon posing the question of social justice, of how social change is to be effected such that living together in a more just world becomes more rather than less possible. This perspective of social justice is also precisely the particular qualification that moral philosophy adds as an analytic framework in its discussions of the bid for power. Social justice as a category for inquiry and deliberation is, however, not an insurance policy for a better use of power. Because of this uncertainty, our critical inquiries must remain suspicious and committed to examining carefully how justice and social justice function as rallying points in political debates. We have to ask time and again: Whose justice, for whom, in what ways, and at what cost?

In order to pose these questions, the uneasy relationship between social norms and moral norms can offer us a heuristic to guide critical inquiries into injustices. The evaluative aspect of morality and its insistence on the bid for justice need to be considered together with the always also normalizing bid of morality. In particular, a critical inquiry has to evaluate where and how universalizing claims to justice function in exclusionary ways, awarding justice and respect only to some while revoking the humanity of others. Critique as an "archaeology" of power and normalization has to pose these problems of recognition and universality as ones that inhere in the dimension of morality and justice. Taking up the aspect of recognition further in relation to social and moral normativity can, as I argue in the next section, aid us as a heuristic for posing the question of justice and deepening our understanding of critique as oscillating between the aporia of normativity and the political and ethical aspiration of social criticism.

Critical Recognition and Social Criticism as Questions of Justice

This final section concludes this book by pointing beyond its limits, insofar as it only briefly takes up social criticism and social justice, acknowledging that these aspects cannot be dealt with exhaustively within a few pages. If this brief final section succeeds, it will do so only insofar as it does not close down but rather opens up the field for a more fully fledged inquiry into how we might formulate the relation between critique and social justice. To that end, I would like to point to some lines of inquiry that Butler's work provides in rethinking social justice and social criticism as horizons for critique by mobilizing rather than quelling the political and ethical potentials that lie in the open-endedness of critique.

It seems to me that we can formulate a heuristic for social criticism derived from the method of Butler's trenchant inquiries into how norms produce subjects through normalization and by administering and withholding recognition. One might even say that recognition is one of the central questions that runs through Butler's works, from her published dissertation *Subjects of Desire* to, most recently, *Giving an Account of Oneself* and *Undoing Gender*. The approach taken by Butler's works is never to categorize recognition and formulate principles or criteria for gauging when due and proper recognition has been offered, but to work on and from the margins. So instead of beginning or ending by envisioning what it would look like when the critical work has all been done, I would like to suggest that we can, with Butler, work toward a critical political ethics by finding inroads into social criticism through querying from the margins without at the same time absolutizing those margins.

Butler's work is always located at the margins of recognizable and unrecognizable lives, with abject bodies that must be contained, regulated, and kept from public view. From these margins we can inquire how social and political mechanisms make lives unlivable, not only when recognition is withheld but also when it is extended in ways that sustain lives but make them less rather than more livable. For example, as Butler argues in *Excitable Speech*, the United States military's "don't ask, don't tell" policy extends recognition to its members only on the condition that homoerotic desires are disavowed and that a public heterosexual facade is maintained. Recognition is thus administered as a fragile construct of probationary recognition that can be withdrawn at any moment should the individual slip up. This policy does not mean that the military recognizes that there are gay, lesbian, and bisexual personnel in its ranks but that it recognizes them only insofar as they keep their desires and their families from public view.

It would be problematic, however, to conclude from this debate that there is some "truth" of a gay, lesbian, or bisexual identity that the military fails to acknowledge and recognize affirmatively. Indeed, such assumptions of general identity characteristics lie at the very heart of the problem at the core of identity politics, because they end up categorizing and normalizing individuals into identities to which they then have to be and remain true in order to continue to be recognized. The question of how to offer and receive recognition is precisely the question of how recognition can avoid being turned into a static program of identity politics that mistakes desires and what individuals are as truths of identities that could be ascertained and used as benchmarks for measuring the success of institutions and individuals in offering proper recognition. The ethical concern about norms and practices by which we are socially recognized is not simply that recognition may be denied but also how it is made available in ways that require undergoing a silencing and disavowal on whatever terms of lovers, friends, and family members.

In conjunction with a critical perspective on social norms, recognition not only appears as a personal need or desire but becomes legible in a social regulatory dimension that exerts violence as a mechanism for marginalization. Individuals and groups are marginalized when the social recognition that is available implies and demands the denial of attachments, taking on positions of inferiority or pathologization. The struggles of the transgender community are an example of how deviant bodies and desires can be made recognizable only when they are contained within the discourse of medical cure.

Butler offers a striking examination of such a requirement to pathologize oneself in her essay "Undiagnosing Gender" in *Undoing Gender*, in which she discusses how the diagnosis of gender identity disorder (GID) provides a way to become recognized as transgendered. The lives and desires of transgendered individuals become recognized, supported, and publicly acceptable to a certain extent only when the individuals subject themselves to the diagnosis of GID. Recourse to a medical diagnosis means that recognition is made available through a therapeutic medical discourse that considers the current state of the individual's body and desires as pathological. The desire to change one's gender becomes acknowledged as a legitimate desire that is eligible for medical and social support only on the condition that one undergoes a pathologization of one's body and one's desires.

Under such conditions, being transgendered is not socially recognizable as a normal—rather than a pathological—way of living one's gender. Consequently, recognition and support are not available for living one's gender as a project of transformation, for living at an angle to the binary, static, gender norms. While transgendered bodies and desires are not utterly denied recognition, they are recognized only through the available schemes of normality, as a medical condition to be cured. To push this point beyond the particular, instead of idealizing social recognition, the critical potential of thinking about recognition lies in examining how recognition is administered and what social, institutional, and psychic formations sustain which kinds of lives as normal and recognizable and which other lives as marginal and exposed to violence.

Recognition as a normalizing and pathologizing discourse works not only in the literal sense of a medical regime, as in the case of the transgendered, but also metaphorically, when we consider questions of post- and neocoloniality with respect, for instance, to migration politics. Discourses of recognition in this debate are aimed at mitigating and controlling the volatile situation of immigrants, but these discourses also reproduce these individuals as liminal subjects in the societies to which they immigrate. Recognition turns out to be an ambivalent possibility when immigrants are cast as potential foreign bodies that threaten the health of the nation if they become too many. While recognizing the realities of immigration and immigrants, the state and social practices through which recognition are extended, such as visas, work permits, and community centers, also function to contain and control immigration and immigrants. Metaphors of hygiene return in discussions over sanitized immigration policies that allow for distinguishing the useful, benign immigrants from the ones that will grow like a cancer within the country.

The remarks of France's former minister of the interior, President Nicolas Sarkozy, blatantly demonstrate such views on immigration when in October 2005 he invoked the need for a Kärcher device to clean up France's illegal immigrant population.[13] With less inflammatory polemics but greater structural efficacy, the new immigration laws enacted in July 2006 in France work to make immigrants, legal and illegal, officially recognizable as subjects with a liminal existence. Beginning in 2007, immigrants are required to register to allow the government to assess their situation and to discern who should be allowed to stay because their skills are deemed useful to the state and because they are considered properly integrated and assimilated into French society.[14]

Through this kind of recognition, although the situation of particular individuals is ameliorated, changes in policy reinforce the regulatory power structures by propagating a certain racial, socioeconomic, and cultural ideal of the population and propagating its integration into this particular version of the people. This kind of recognition works in favor of consolidating the power of the state by extending its official recognition and demanding that potential recipients come forward to make themselves recognizable. In his book *Bound by Recognition*, Patchen Markell elaborates this exchange of recognition between individuals and the state in which state power is strengthened, even when individuals or groups ask the state to recognize them: "That mode of address [of groups asking the state to recognize their identities] . . . furthers the state's project of rendering the social world 'legible' and governable; to appeal to the state *for* the recognition of one's own identity—to present oneself as knowable—is already to offer the state reciprocal recognition of its sovereignty that it demands."[15]

Making oneself knowable means exposing oneself to the other, in this case the state, and, as Markell argues, this knowability of citizen-subjects also aids the state in governing the social sphere. Moreover, in demanding to be recognized by an other, one not only asserts oneself in relation to this other but also affirms the other and this other's power to offer recognition. With respect to the state, this means concretely that in demanding to be recognized by the state, individuals and groups also recognize this state and present themselves as governable, as subjects of and to this state. There is thus an unavoidable complicity in the status quo when one seeks and receives recognition, because through this very action one is compelled to seize on those norms, practices, and institutions that are available. Even in attempts to change these available structures, one cannot avoid acknowledging to a certain extent the authority of these structures and the institutions through which they are legitimized.

The regulatory dimension of social recognition through state institutions points us toward examining the ambivalence in claims to recognition and the different frameworks through which recognition becomes possible socially, politically, legally, and personally. We might ask whether every aspect of our lives and every claim need to be recognized. Such an endeavor of all-encompassing recognition would result in an unsustainable identity politics and finally translate into a demand to make everything about ourselves recognizable, namable, and assessable; such an embrace of uncritical recognition would also amount to a version of relativism that occults the political struggles between different positions that conflict with each other. As Markell explains, multiculturalism works precisely by encouraging claims of justice to be formulated in terms of recognition of cultural identities. With such a move, the egalitarian claims of social justice are discharged into claims of cultural difference, thus displacing the political question of how to reorganize unjust economic wealth and labor conditions onto a question of civic ethos of mutual acknowledgment and tolerance.[16] The issues that the horizon of justice comprises are neither reducible to questions of recognition nor resolvable through considerations of social, interpersonal, and institutional recognition. It seems to me, however, that within the dimension of recognition, it becomes possible to direct a critical inquiry into different elaborations of what both justice and recognition mean as ethical and political projects and how they are realized individually and institutionally.

What recognition means as an ethical principle is delimited by concrete material conditions as much as by our relations to others, by our needs and desires, and by social, legal, and political terms, norms, and institutions. Recognition is an ambivalent project, since in our relations to others we do not always seek the same kind of recognition from all. We might even want to remain unrecognizable to some, or from others we might want to be recognized differently from the kind of recognition that we already receive. In our relations to others as well as to impersonal institutions, recognition not only makes us into certain kinds of subjects but also is a conduit through which social norms and histories of power differentials are administered, negotiated, and renegotiated.

Hence recognition is not simply a critical tool with which one can assess value and normative good and in whose name injustices can be denounced; instead, the demand for recognition points to a situation with critical potential where recognition emerges as a demand that either is not met or is becoming impossible to meet. To discover and unravel these conflicts in recognition as sites for ethical and political debate, it is necessary to begin by working from the limits where recognition becomes a question as it is practiced and as it is demanded. Butler argues that the experience of the limits and breaking points in our ways of knowing and dialoguing provides occasions in which ethics can appear as a question:

> [T]he question of ethics emerges precisely at the limits of our schemes of intelligibility, the site where we ask ourselves what it might mean to continue in a dialogue where no common ground can be assumed, where one is, at it were, at the limits of what one knows yet still under the demand to offer and receive acknowledgment. (*GA* 21–22)

Ethics for Butler is a question that is contingent upon a situation in which we do not know what to do and so come to ask how we should and can act, while the situation equally demands action. Ethics, in other words, emerges in the form of a practical question at the limits of our knowledge, certainties, and habits, when we are at our wits' end. Moreover, ethics becomes a question in relation to an other or others, especially when these others are both elsewhere and yet somehow affecting this "we" and so the limit encountered is in particular characterized by a breakdown of any common ground that as a shared basis could continue to ensure the possibility of dialogue.

With this loss of anything in common, equally one's categories and terms that "we" use to understand, make sense, navigate, and negotiate situations and relations with others come into crisis. At the same time, the question of ethics emerges under precisely these conditions, as Butler suggests, but only insofar as this "we" is still beholden to the situation and in particular insofar as we are "still under the demand to offer and receive acknowledgment" (*GA* 22). For Butler the question of ethics arises as a question of how to continue dialogue, how to offer and receive recognition when the very conditions of the possibility for recognition and communication seem to have been eroded or are acknowledged to have never been there in the first place. Yet the question of ethics could not emerge were there not the demand for recognition in play. If we apply this insight to asking what recognition is and how it ought to be implemented in social, legal, and personal relations, then we have to begin from thinking about how recognition fails and ask about the ethical significance of different kinds of failures.

The question of how recognition fails can prompt us to ask how in some ways recognition perhaps *has* to fail, because that which it aims to recognize cannot be recognized without being transformed in the process. Instead of seeking recognition for every aspect of our lives, the critical question for an ethics of recognition might be how to distinguish between instances in which recognition and the possibilities and protection that it offers are indispensable and other instances in which discourses of recognition are more constraining than enabling. Instead of insisting on recognition as the measure and criterion for injustices suffered and as the antidote to all social wrongs, moral questioning might take as its starting point deciphering where and how in our societies human beings are being marginalized. As an ethical demand, recognition has to make room for not knowing what it means to offer and receive social recognition, in order to rework institutions as well as our personal interactions through which we relate to and recognize each other.

The demand for recognition in Butler's work is tied to a desire to live, but—as Butler elaborates it—neither this desire nor this life are unambivalent; this desire is ambivalent because living as a desiring being means to be vulnerable, implicated in the lives of others, dependent on its relations to others, and to some extent always undone by others. One key aspect of Butler's work is to make us consider how the desire to be is not just an individual question but is a matter of what it means to live with others, how lives are valued, and how expansive our versions of living together are. The desire to live is, as Butler demonstrates, not to be taken for granted, and the ways in which recognition is available can in fact undo the desire to be. Lives can be undone by the possibilities available to them and by the choices demanded, so that one might eventually rather not be than have to be like that, in that world, under these conditions.

It seems to me that this predicament is what is at stake, for example, for Antigone, when she chooses not to be and hence to risk her life rather than be in a world where the body of the dead brother is left in the fields to rot. Antigone and her claim, as Butler argues in *Antigone's Claim*,[17] cannot be recognized in a way that would sustain the bonds and actions that are crucial for Antigone. In Butler's interpretation, what is at stake in the play are claims about how to organize communal life, and Antigone's way of approaching the question of recognition is not reducible to identity politics. We might say that there is a self-understanding to which Antigone adheres and which makes her act as she does, but I would argue that we need to understand that this self-understanding is not an identity that is the starting point for her claims. Rather, her self-understanding emerges only implicitly, performatively through her commitments to a conflicting vision about how to live together, how to organize the community, and how to honor communal bonds. Hence the recognition that Antigone seeks both for her mourning and for the value of her brother as a life lost is not a demand for public recognition of a private claim; rather her claim challenges how communal and political life is organized, whose lives are valued, and whose lives are considered dispensable.

To consider how to discern between different forms of recognition and different claims to it, we might return the perspective of recognition as both an ethical demand and a form of social normalization. Butler revisits this double aspect of norms as social and moral norms in her essay "The Question of Social Transformation" in *Undoing Gender*. The crucial aspect of social norms, as she explains with respect to gender norms, is that they govern "the process of normalization, the way in which certain norms, ideas and ideals hold sway over embodied life, provide coercive criteria for normal 'men' and 'women'" (*UG* 206). Considering social norms in this light means to understand and address the processes of normalization and the productive rather than the critical and restrictive aspect of norms and the way in which they operate surreptitiously to produce subjects. Normalization works through social practices and institutions that delimit the bodies and persons we can possibly become. There is no vantage point fully beyond social power and the practices that animate, produce, and reproduce social norms. So the aim of critique is not to find life beyond norms or beyond power but to examine and distinguish between the different ways in which social norms "make" us all; how they form subjects, desires, and aspirations; and in which ways their normative stipulations shape lives.

Instead of seeking answers to the question of what makes life more livable by distinguishing moral from social normativity, I would like to suggest that we can use this problematic relation as a method of critique. The intertwinement of social and moral normativity can provide a lens through which to discover what kinds of lives are made livable and recognizable by which kinds of practices and norms before we move to ask what more just conditions would look like. In these endeavors we must keep in mind that to practice critique itself implies we accept a normative dimension, since normative commitments and aspirations emerge at the back of concrete criticism. Thus the problematic of social and moral normativity returns within the critical inquiry itself, and we need to ask what role moral criteria and aspirations play in critique.

In "The Question of Social Transformation," Butler cautions against asserting morally normative criteria as the basis and grounds for critique. In particular, she argues that nonviolence or social justice need not be considered as a norm in order to oppose violence. She distinguishes her own position from those who "will say that the opposition to violence must take place *in the name of the norm*, a norm of nonviolence, a norm of respect, a norm that governs and compels the respect for life" (*UG* 206). Butler's concern seems to be about a position that would hold that only a norm can validate or legitimate one's opposition to the violence that normative practices and institutions might exert. The articulation of that other norm in whose name one resists is often not recognizable within the dominant discursive frame. Butler makes legible this problematic that follows from the inseparability of the normative and normalizing dimension and insists that action cannot require that first normative justification has to be provided. Moreover, she seems to argue against another normative precept, namely, "that the opposition to violence *must* take place in the name of the norm" (*UG* 206; emphasis added) as a guarantee and binding principle that grounds the actions to be taken. Since frequently or perhaps for the most part we do not ascertain conclusively the normative principles on whose grounds and in whose names we take action, Butler's argument is an important interruption of the overprivileging of normative foundations and a caution against considering clarity about them as a prerequisite for action.

However, it seems to me that insofar as moral philosophy attempts to reflect on and articulate a notion of critique in relation to the question of norms and normative criteria, the problematic presents itself in a slightly different form. The concern at this juncture is not to stipulate or refute a demand that action must take place in the name of a norm. Rather, the concern emerges insofar as we consider how opposing violence does not require a normative grounding but how such opposition produces a normative vision and performatively lays claim to the validity of another normative perspective, a perspective that becomes recognizable only belatedly. In that way, it seems to me, one cannot help but invoke another norm, even if this other norm is neither available for full articulation nor yet affirmed in its validity.

It is not as if one finds or even needs to find an appropriate norm first in whose name one then opposes a given situation, but insofar as one comes to oppose a given situation, it seems to me that this opposition performatively establishes a counternormative perspective. If we oppose certain forms in which norms operate and if we oppose them "for reasons of social justice" (*UG* 206), then social justice and the particular manifestation that it takes, at least in a determinate negation, are emerging at the back of this action of opposition as normative concepts. The claim that "if one objects to normalization, it is in the name of a different norm that one objects" (*UG* 206) then can be read to offer a different description of what happens in the act of objecting, insofar as this "different norm" is something that one cannot help but invoke. The question for moral-philosophical reflection then arises differently, namely by moving to a critical reflection that unearths and undoes rather than establishes the normative commitments that are invoked. Under these circumstances we might indeed query this different norm and ask what kind of normative formulation has now emerged, with what claim to legitimacy, and which frameworks are assumed to delimit what can appear as "legitimate" and persuasive. Importantly, however, these questions are more than anything else a problem for moral philosophy and not a question to which moral philosophy has a conclusive answer.

Butler's intervention points us to how the problem of norms raises the question of what the task and limits of moral philosophy are. There are differing understandings of what is and should be the task of moral philosophy; with respect to normative commitments this difference might be formulated as whether moral-philosophical reflection is to ground and establish normative principles and criteria for their validity or whether it is to offer means and perspective by which to call existing and emerging norms into question. As I am arguing in conversation with Butler in this chapter and the previous one, it seems important to me that the problematic of norms does not become the exclusive or predominant concern of moral philosophy. Otherwise its reflections become restricted to worrying over normative foundations for moral conduct. As a consequence, the distinctly practical problem with which these worries begin—how to discern how to respond best to situations in which we do not know what to do—end up diffused into a primarily epistemological problem of principles and their validity, and the practical aspect becomes reduced to the question of applying the principles in order to derive morally valid stances.

As one aspect that moral philosophy queries we might, then, frame the problem of norms in moral philosophy not in terms of an opposition between one position that demands action on the grounds of normative principles and another position that demands action in absence of normative principles. Instead, the problem that I would like to foreground is that these normative principles are always performatively emerging and in that way, too, are present in one's actions, as there is no possibility of getting fully outside of them, even while it is equally impossible fully to grasp them and reflectively ascertain their validity outside of social conventions, norms, and practices.

A shift in our perspective on moral normativity might become possible, however, when we consider "moral norms" as moral guidelines that are not practical recipes for action in that they do not straightforwardly produce a calculus to determine what we should do. As guidelines or ideals, they are not immune to turning into unquestioned social ideals when their claims are accepted as self-evident and fixed in their content. These ideals, as moral or as social, can become violent and produce a moral quandary when an insistence on them intensifies the violence. Yet there is an aspiration in moral ideals, especially in the universality of the desire to make the world more just for all, that seems important to me for critical politics. This aspiration, however, is also the problem of moral ideals that inscribe a tendency to become narrow-minded, unabiding, and intolerant against differences. The critique of moral ideals and their relation to violence has to be equally open-ended, since social criticism depends not only on convictions about what is just and unjust but also on substantive criteria that explicate those convictions. Even though we might attribute to these criteria a validity that is not reducible to the contingent approval of others—just because someone disagrees with us, this does not already convince us that our criteria are faulty—those normative convictions are also never available to us beyond our historical and cultural contexts. The possibility of critical evaluation of normative commitments emerges not in a monologic endeavor but in encounters with others and other contexts that compel us to translate these commitments across cultural and social contexts and to enter into political contestation to negotiate conflicting commitments and translations.

These convictions become explicit only with regard to particular situations and never in a purely abstract way and—in that sense—never absolutely but very concretely, and they become available for critical reflection only in that belated and conditioned way. For critical reflection, this means that when "How to respond? What ought to be done?" becomes a question, we need to launch an inquiry in two directions. First, we need to debate what ought to be, which responses, visions, and criteria to hold to, and what that would mean concretely in that situation. Second, we need to inquire into how our normative commitments arise out of concretely contingent situations and how they do and do not surpass these contexts as they claim to aid us in addressing questions of justice—which begin with the discovery and denunciation of concrete injustices.

The labor of social criticism starts, not stops, with the denunciation of injustices, and it further compels political contestation and a move to action in order to rework the conditions which cause unnecessary suffering. In these last few pages, I would like to formulate in conversation with Butler's work how the political-ethical considerations of justice and recognition might proffer an orientation that is critical but neither nihilistic nor moralistic. The question of social change is not only—and not even primarily—a question of normative principles, although, as I lay out above, I argue for respect and social justice in their ethical as well as critical dimensions. It seems to me, however, that we get further with the question of social change and critique when we take into consideration the kind of shared labor that is necessary to change social norms. Instead of developing normative visions of how recognition should be conferred and how sexuality and gender should be recognized in politics, Butler's work allows us examine the preconditions for taking a critical stance toward social norms, for making the question of what ought to be done differently available at all.

In *Undoing Gender* Butler argues, "Indeed, the capacity to develop a critical relation to these norms presupposes a distance from them, an ability to suspend or defer the need for them, even as there is a desire for norms that might let one live" (*UG* 3). Butler calls into question the assumption that if we truly wanted to and only thought about it a bit, we could attain sufficient distance from the norms and values and their workings that let us live and by which we function in our everyday lives. As long as the norms that are in play allow us to live somewhat well, at least for the most part, we do not realize how much we depend on these norms and how not falling into the norm renders one open to unwanted forms of violence. As long as one has the "right" skin color, the "right" gender, the "right" body, the "right" demeanor, it is hard to see how vulnerable one is outside the norm and how much the inclusion within the norm can be an issue of survival, not at all simply an issue of desiring acceptance of one's "extravagant life-style." There is a need and desire for those norms and for being normal that comes from wanting and needing to evade violence and discrimination and that makes it difficult to emerge at a distance from those norms in order to rework them.

This reworking and one's participation in it are not contingent on an identity that one might or might not possess and that then grants some of us privileged access to critical relations to norms. Apart from the problems of identity politics, being subject and vulnerable to violence is not really a privileged position; it is one of privation. Solidarity and participation are not based on identity categories but they bring about a kind of exposure that one might or might not have experienced in the same way otherwise. Social change can be achieved neither alone nor from a position that remains at a distance from involvement in collective efforts. As Butler argues, "The critical relation [to norms] depends as well on a capacity, invariably collective, to articulate an alternative, minority version of sustaining norms or ideals that enable me to act" (*UG* 3). Because suspending and reworking norms are not something that one can do individually, on one's own, this need for collectivity and collective efforts results from the fact that we are dependent on relations with others and on being sustained in some way in our relation to norms and ideals and in the ways by which they confer recognition. As for Antigone, this recognition and sustainable living are not reducible to a "private" realm and "private" issues but implicate us in the lives of collectives and the practical everyday life in which ethical and political quandaries arise and are negotiated.

Understanding our lives and the lives of others, individually and communally, as a starting point for ethical and political questions is a reminder that moral philosophy as practical philosophy has as its aim enabling rather than impeding a living appropriation of its insights. The subject as an ethical agent has become the problem, rather than a self-evident presupposition, for moral philosophy, because we can no longer assume that conscience is the voice of good within us, nor that we could be in full control over our own desires, thoughts, and actions, nor that we could ever attain full critical distance from the social norms and ideals that form us. As the notions of absolute knowledge and moral certainty are rapidly vanishing and the complexity of our world is rapidly increasing, the question of what ought to be done has lost nothing in its openness or in its actuality. This openness and the loss of absolutes do not make practical philosophy impossible but can rather enable a redirecting and reinvigorating of the questions of moral philosophy and the conceptual tools that it offers us to pose them.

Critique can aid us in this endeavor, as it allows us to examine the categories and discourses that condition our encounters with others and the world around us and through which we also develop a sense of how we understand ourselves. These categories and discourses exist neither statically nor homogeneously but only as lived and inhabited, as everyday practices. With this understanding of categories as modes of living in the world, it becomes possible to consider how these categories themselves can be called into question for us when we deliberate what to do, what stances to take, and how best to shape our future. Among these categories fall very concrete conceptions, such as what "human" means, what delineates "humane treatment," what count as conditions that work toward a more just world that one must strive for. Insofar as we need to query our categories and their normative concretizations with regard to the cultural contexts and the histories of these categories, critique can know no end. There is no "truth" about any category, no conclusive and all-inclusive rendition that is possible from a human perspective. At the same time, we have to use categories and normative criteria, as there is no future absolutely free of norms with their normative and normalizing implications. There is no absolute ground that a theoretical inquiry could settle, because philosophy itself is a historically and culturally bounded endeavor. Nonetheless, the horizon of justice and morality introduces a critical aspiration to universality, and between this aspiration to universality and cultural specificity, the need for cultural translation returns.

What justice might look like will be a matter of ethical and political debates about concrete situations where injustices need to be opposed. The challenge is a difficult one. Neither conscience nor moral principles can guarantee us certainty in knowing what we ought to do and how to live well together. Responsibility as responding to others and critique as a critical perspective on the claims of power and a refusal to settle with injustices can invigorate and aid, but not guarantee, an ethical life. At the end of the day, how to live, especially how to live well, can be negotiated only in concrete encounters with others. Moral philosophy might have a part in enabling us in these negotiations, in which we become more rather than less aware of our shared humanity. Ethics might in the end be a task of refusing to settle for injustices and unnecessary suffering while understanding that lasting, big, social changes might be the fruit of persistent collective labor through which we embrace rather than eschew sociality and imagine anew what a more humane world and a more decent society might look like.

NOTES

INTRODUCTION

1. For some examples of this turn to ethics, see Garber, Hanssen, and Walkowitz, *Turn to Ethics*; Eskin, "Introduction"; Couzens Hoy, *Critical Resistance*; Wood, *Step Back*; Attridge, "Singularities, Responsibilities"; Critchley, *Ethics of Deconstruction*; Derrida, "Afterword"; Eaglestone, *Ethical Criticism*; Diprose, *Corporeal Generosity*; Madison and Fairbairn, *Ethics of Postmodernity*; Hillis Miller, *Ethics of Reading*; Wyschogrod and McKenny, *The Ethical*.

2. I am taking my cue from Theodor W. Adorno, who explains in the first of his 1963 lectures in *Problems of Moral Philosophy:* "I once suggested that the concept of ethics was actually the bad conscience of morality, or that ethics is a sort of morality that is ashamed of its own moralizing with the consequence that it behaves as if it were morality, but at the same time it is not a moralizing morality. . . . [I]t seems to me that the dishonesty implicit in this is worse and more problematic than the blunt incompatibility of our experience with the term 'morality.' . . . [T]o reduce the problem of morality to ethics is to perform a sort of conjuring trick by means of which the decisive problem of moral philosophy, namely the relation of the individual to the general, is made to disappear." See Adorno, *Problems of Moral Philosophy*, 10. Hereafter abbreviated in citations as *PMP*.

3. For an incisive and thoughtful critique of moral philosophy's centering on laws and norms and an argument for approaching moral philosophy through its problematics, see Waldenfels, *Schattenrisse der Moral*.

4. This framing of responsibility as a matter of imputability and freedom of will, which is then cast as a matter of choice and rationality, can be found as early as Aristotle's *Nicomachean Ethics* (bk. III, 1–7). The recent discussions of ethical theory in the so-called analytic debate have generally tied the question of responsibility to matters of judgment and punishment. In Rawls, *Theory of Justice*, for example, responsibility emerges as a principle in the section on duty and obligation; in Gert, *Morality*, "responsibility" is discussed in the chapter

"Moral Judgments," and Gert concludes the section on responsibility by explaining, "Which responsibility standards are adopted has significant consequences, because judging how much a person is to be blamed affects how much he is to be punished" (Gert, 322–23). Christine Korsgaard's intervention in this discussion is interesting, since it enters at an angle, as she begins by explicitly explaining responsibility in terms of being "held *answerable*": "When we hold a person responsible, we regard her as answerable for her actions, reactions, and attitudes" (Korsgaard, *Creating*, 188). Furthermore, according to this view, holding someone responsible is an attitude we *unavoidably* take on with regard to another person, and according to Korsgaard, this holding someone responsible is that which performs as subject formative, because "to hold someone responsible is to regard her as a *person*—that is to say, as a free and equal person, capable of acting both rationally and morally" (Korsgaard, *Creating*, 189). Korsgaard emphasizes here that responsibility as address to another implies a mode of subject formation by "regard[ing] her as a *person*." But although her account of responsibility thus moves us to the question of subject formation, she seems not to move away from responsibility as imputability as the basis of her account. This hasty gesture to the analytic discussion in ethical theory by no means does this debate justice but it might at least show the intensity in most theories of the tie between responsibility and judgment.

5. There are several essays that deal with Butler and ethics in her work, such as Salih, "Judith Butler and the Ethics of Difficulty," which argues for understanding Butler's work as performing a particular ethics of difficulty; Diprose, "Responsibility in a Place"; Jenkins, "Plurality, Dialogue and Response" and "Toward a Nonviolent Ethics"; McRobbie, "Vulnerability, Violence and (Cosmopolitan) Ethics"; Mills, "Normative Violence, Vulnerability, and Responsibility"; and Haker, "Fragility of the Moral Self." There are several recent books that explore Butler's contribution to political theory, such as Lloyd, *Judith Butler*; and Loizidou, *Judith Butler*. Among studies that engage with politics and ethics in Butler more specifically through a feminist perspective are Alcoff, *Visible Identities*; and Zirelli, *Feminism and the Abyss of Freedom*.

6. Over the last few years a number of books have come out that introduce and parse key questions in Butler's thinking, among them Kirby, *Judith Butler*; Salih, *Judith Butler*; Bublitz, *Judith Butler zur Einführung*; and Villa, *Judith Butler*.

7. Butler, *Precarious Life*. Hereafter abbreviated in citations as *PL*.

8. Butler, *Undoing Gender*. Hereafter abbreviated in citations as *UG*.

9. Butler, *Giving an Account*. Hereafter abbreviated in citations as *GA*.

10. Butler, *Psychic Life of Power*. Hereafter abbreviated in citations as *PLP*.

11. On understanding the political as irreducible to a concern with power and power relations and on keeping the concern about governance as a characteristic, see Brown, "At the Edge."

1: SUBJECTS IN SUBJECTION: BODIES, DESIRES, AND THE PSYCHIC LIFE OF NORMS

1. Many scholars have written on this aspect of Butler's work. See, e.g., in the German debate, the contribution, among others, by Duden "Frau ohne Unterleib," who argues with reference to *Gender Trouble* that Butler's theorizing institutes a new subjectivity, namely, that of the disembodied woman. Maihofer, *Geschlecht als Existenzweise*, offers the criticism that the reality of the bodily materiality is lost and dissolved into being nothing but a "surface" or "fiction." Hauskeller, *Das paradoxe Subjekt*, 112, contends that Butler's concept leaves no room for referring to "violence, exploitation or repression, which are experienced at least also as bodily alienation and overpowering," allowing Hauskeller then to argue for the necessity for changing an actual situation of oppression. On the question of thinking the relation between nature and culture and between matter and language, see also Kirby, "When All That Is Solid"; Kirby, *Judith Butler*; Hollywood, "Performativity."

2. See List, *Grenzen der Verfügbarkeit*. In particular, in the chapter "Das lebendige Selbst," List argues for a prediscursive self that she calls the bodily self *(Körperselbst)*. Similar arguments for a prediscursive facticity of the bodily self appear in Wendel, *Affektiv und inkarniert*.

3. Butler, "How Can I Deny?" 256, emphasis in the original.

4. Butler, *Bodies That Matter*, 66. Hereafter abbreviated in citations as *BTM*.

5. See, e.g., Derrida, *Of Grammatology*. Derrida argues against understanding language and matter as ontologically radically distinct and against language as a representational ideality that is transparent toward the material reality it represents. Instead, he proposes a chiastic understanding that insists on the paradox of referentiality that poses itself when we attempt to sort out the relation between language and material reality. On the one hand, language itself is not immaterial since it depends on muscles or machines producing signs that are material themselves. On the other hand, things are texts in a narrow sense because when one grasps and experiences material reality, one can never conceive of it outside of signs. Even more radically, Derrida subjects to deconstructive attention this "one" that seems to be the reason why things would be texts in themselves. The textuality of things is, consequently, more radically that things are as concrete and distinct entities only through their differentiation from each other, which is a process of signification. Derrida explains that it is the deferral and differentiation, as temporization and spatialization, which makes material reality as well as knowledge about it possible (and also impossible, in the sense that it can never fully be present to itself), that are the effect of *différance*. See also Derrida, "Différance."

6. "Language" and "discourse" in this discussion are not to be understood in a narrow way as merely the practices of speaking and writing. Against the background of Derrida's argument about writing in the general sense as a movement of difference that conditions material reality, we can understand language

more generally as the ways through which signifying differences work to make available distinct phenomenality.

7. Butler, *Gender Trouble*. Hereafter abbreviated in citations as *GT*.

8. See also the original discussion in Foucault, *Discipline and Punish*.

9. Karen Barad takes up Butler's critique and joins her in understanding the work of culture and society as a subsequent shaping and imprinting on a preexisting material existence. Barad, a feminist scholar in science studies, takes up Butler's work in the context of elaborating an "agential realism," which engages performativity to argue for a generalized understanding of performative constitution of bodies, human as well as inhuman, animate as well as inanimate. As she explains, agential realism strives to take into account "materiality [as] an active factor in [the] process of materialization." Barad, "Posthumanist Performativity," 827.

10. See Foucault, "Nietzsche, Genealogy, History."

11. In the first chapter, entitled "An Account of Oneself," in *Giving an Account of Oneself*, Butler lays out how when one attempts to elaborate on one's past to explain who one is, one necessarily gives a fictional account of oneself, because there is no stable, preexisting, original referent that then is captured in the narration. The self is constituted through the narration, and in that way the self is also always a fictional rendition of that person. Hence narratives as biographies and equally as autobiographies cannot be taken as the truth of a person—or at least not as a different truth from the truth of any other work of fiction. But it seems to me that Butler's arguments imply an even stronger case regarding understanding the self through the conceptual tools of narrativity. Narrativity and its theoretical frameworks might not be sufficient to theorize the temporal and historical dimension of individual and collective experiences. We might in fact have to think at an angle to the ways in which the narrative dimension inscribes itself so easily and forcefully when we think about autobiographies, biographies, stories, and histories.

12. Hauskeller, *Das paradoxe Subjekt*, 111, argues "Butlers Text zeigt, daß sie Materie als diskursives Produkt und damit auch als passive denkt, daß sie keine eigene Aktivität des Körpers oder anderer *Referenten* konzipiert." Here it seems that Hauskeller misreads Butler insofar as she does not acknowledge that Butler's contribution is not to assert passivity on the one side and activity on the other or to allocate separate aspects of these to entities; rather, Butler's point is to show the interrelation between passivity and activity and to raise the question how it works when one turns into the other.

13. Butler, Laclau, and Žižek, *Contingency, Hegemony, Universality*. Hereafter abbreviated in citations as *CHU*.

14. On this point Butler's engagement with Levinas is particularly interesting, since the role of desire is a distinctive difference between Butler and Levinas. Butler's affirmation of desire as a constitutive dimension does not mean, however, that desire is pure positivity for her; rather, she emphasizes the importance of negativity. See, in *Undoing Gender*, "Longing for Recognition," 131–

51, in which she argues against Jessica Benjamin's notion of "intersubjective recognition," and in particular "The End of Sexual Difference?" 192–93, 198, in which, commenting on Rosi Braidotti's *Metamorphoses*, Butler explicitly argues against Deleuzian positivity.

15. Attempts to find a "soft" normativity in thinking about social pathologies and to understand practical philosophy as a therapeutic kind of theorizing seem highly problematic in light of the normalizing effects of therapeutic discourses and the violent histories of pathologizations. Foucault's work on madness and sexuality is only one example pointing to the problems with pathologization regarding lives that became categorized as madness and sexualities that became subsumed as medical cases.

16. Foucault, *History of Sexuality*. Hereafter abbreviated in citations as *HS*.

2: MORAL SUBJECTS AND AGENCIES OF MORALITY

1. In Arendt, *Responsibility and Judgment*.

2. There are several convergences between Nietzsche's scathing review of morality and the arguments Freud put forth in the register of psychoanalysis. I will deal here in particular with Nietzsche's *On the Genealogy of Morals* and his method of genealogy as a philosophical critique of culture insofar as he fabricates a counteraccount for how certain philosophical concepts, such as conscience, humility, or retributive justice, became instituted as culturally or civilizationally necessary. See Nietzsche, *On the Genealogy of Morals*. The German version cited is Nietzsche, *Jenseits von Gut and Böse*.

3. Kant, *Critique of Practical Reason*.

4. See the opening to Kant, *Groundwork of the Metaphysics of Morals*, 7: "It is impossible to think of anything at all in the world, or indeed even beyond it, that could be considered good without limitation except a good will."

5. Mahmood, *Politics of Piety*.

6. Adorno, *Problems of Moral Philosophy*.

7. Nietzsche's notion of internalization seems to come very close to Adam Smith's "man within," the internalized gaze of others that leads to a split within a person's psyche and sets up an "agent-I" and a "spectator-I." The spectator is the one assuming the Humean "common point of view" and evaluating the agent; this leads to an assessment that has not only praise or blame at its end, but praiseworthiness or blameworthiness. To find oneself praiseworthy is to find that others ought to praise one for the quality of question that led to a certain action. The Smithian account for how, on the basis of emotivism, one can come to action-guiding conclusions is intriguingly similar to that presented by Nietzsche, who then, of course, continues to critique this internalization since it shows the failure and arbitrariness of all morality and moralizing. The relationship of the tradition of Smith and Hume to the accounts of psychoanalysis would be interesting to pursue at some other time. See Smith, *Theory of Moral Sentiments*; Hume, *Enquiry Concerning the Principles of Morals*.

8. Butler characterizes Nietzsche's project of genealogy as "seeking to find out how the very notion of the origin became instituted" in "What Is Critique?" 223.

9. Rather than assuming conscience is a universal feature of human development, Nietzsche's critique is made possible by his suspending that assumption of universality and by understanding the concept of the "universal fact" of conscience as owing its own origins to a particular time and cultural horizon. To argue that the faculty of conscience emerged contingently and not as an anthropological necessity means that what conscience is understood to be and the ways in which it is taken to work are structured by the history of its emergence. To the extent that conscience continues to hold an important place in moral deliberation, it is impossible simply to opt out of having a conscience solely by pointing to the fact of the contingency of the formation of this faculty and institution in moral discourse. However, the fact that we cannot by a single gesture deny and renounce this history and our being implicated in it does not also mean that we are fully determined by it.

10. Nietzsche's texts persistently raise the question of how anti-Judaism and anti-Semitism figure in them and the part these stances play in his arguments. It seems to me that we have to discern between critiques of particular positions, policies, or values and attacks on groups and individuals solely on the basis of their being different. Racist ideologies—in the broadest sense—can be understood as proceeding primarily by rendering a particular group—for example, the adherents of a religion—homogenous by naturalizing certain characteristics that are then taken as grounds for ascribing to this group a natural inferiority (and in return affirming the superiority of another group). Without being overtly racist, texts can to variable extents be suggestive of or give rise to racist interpretations. That they inspire such interpretations neither simply acquits nor simply condemns the texts in question; instead, the possibility of such interpretations highlights even more strongly the importance of reading and interpreting texts responsibly, of knowing where to follow and where to break with the texts.

11. Butler makes an interesting and important move when she offers a constitutive limitation, here the limitation of one's self-understanding, not as predicament of a human "condition," but rather as predicament of the human *community:* "Indeed, to take responsibility for oneself is to avow the limits of any self-understanding, and to establish these limits not only as a condition for the subject, but as the predicament of the human community itself" (*GA* 83). By situating the predicament as a question of life in community with others, it becomes clear that the limitation attains its status as a predicament precisely not by virtue of an ontological horizon but by virtue of its consequences for social and political life.

12. In the German original, the chapter is entitled "'*Schuld*,' '*schlechtes Gewissen' und Verwandtes*."

13. Especially interesting is that in the German original, the phrase "passive inability to rid oneself of an impression" reads "passivisches Nicht-wieder-los-werden-können des einmal *eingeritzten* Eindrucks" (emphasis added); the *eingeritzt* is dropped in the English translation, although it becomes important for Nietzsche, and for Butler in her discussion of Nietzsche, that the impression is made with such force that it carves its image into the will and thus also entails a notion of injuring or penetrating. The notion of imprinting, inscribing, carving in of that which is then remembered is also discussed in Ricoeur, *Das Rätsel*.

14. Stegmaier, *Nietzsches "Genealogie der Moral,"* 132, characterizes this quality of conscience this way: "Gewissen ist, noch bevor es ein gutes oder schlechtes Gewissen ist, Wissen von der Bedeutung des eigenen Handlens für andere, *vor* dem Handeln, vor allem aber auch *nach* dem Handeln" ("Even before conscience is good or bad conscience, it is a knowledge about the meaning of one's own actions for others, *before* one acts, but especially also *after* one has acted" [my translation]).

15. Butler mentions the following in *Giving an Account of Oneself* regarding Nietzsche's account of the emergence of the subject through punishment and bad conscience: "In *The Psychic Life of Power*, I perhaps too quickly accepted this punitive scene of inauguration for the subject" (*GA* 15). In the discussion that follows, Butler holds present the Nietzschean scene but she also suggests that there might be a different subject of ethics in view, at least partly emerging not solely through internalized punishment and moralized debt rendered into guilt: "Indeed, whereas Nietzsche considers the force of punishment to be instrumental to the internalization of rage and the consequent production of bad conscience (and other moral precepts), Foucault turns increasingly to codes of morality, understood as codes of conduct—and *not* primarily to codes of punishment—to consider how subjects are constituted in relation to such codes, which do not always rely on the violence of prohibition and its internalizing effects" (*GA* 16).

16. See Barvosa-Carter, "Strange Tempest"; Benhabib, "Feminism and Postmodernism"; Benhabib, "Subjectivity, Historiography, and Politics"; Campbell, "Plague of the Subject"; Cheah, "Mattering"; Disch, "Judith Butler"; Hollywood, "Performativity, Citationality, Ritualization"; Magnus, "Unaccountable Subject"; McNay, *Gender and Agency*; Nelson, "Bodies (and Spaces) Do Matter"; Schwartzman, "Hate Speech, Illocution"; Vasterling, "Butler's Sophisticated Constructivism."

17. Among other works by Derrida, see *Gift of Death*; *Acts of Religion*; *Politics of Friendship*; "Force of Law"; and *Specters of Marx*.

18. Compare with this Butler's arguing in "For a Careful Reading" (*Feminist Contentions*, 127–144) against agency as a transcendental condition of subjectivity: "What notion of 'agency' will that be which always and already knows its transcendental ground, and speaks only and always from that ground? To be so grounded is nearly to be buried: it is to refuse alterity, to reject contestation, to

decline that risk of self-transformation perpetually posed by democratic life" (131–132).

19. Austin, *How to Do Things*.

20. Derrida, "Signature Event Context."

21. See Butler, "Explanation and Exoneration."

22. Allen, *Power of Feminist Theory*; and Mahmood, *Politics of Piety*, both comment on these three sources as key to Butler's understanding of agency.

23. For a more complete argument on Butler's use of psychoanalysis, see Chaps. 1 and 3.

24. Butler, *Gender Trouble*, clarifies that not "every new possibility *qua* possibility" is to be heralded (189). Theorizing subject formation cannot predict or determine in advance what the outcome and effects will be. Rather, theorizing figures as a critique, as an interruption of the hope of opening a horizon for imagining how it could be different. The outcome of the norms and addresses at work in subject formation is not predeterminable with regard to the individual action nor with regard to the signifying rules that are the underlying grammar of the action. In *Excitable Speech* (hereafter abbreviated in citations as *ES*), 147, Butler explains explicitly that the outcome of resignification is open: "By understanding the false or wrong invocations as *reiterations*, we see how the form of social institutions undergoes change and alteration and how an invocation that has no prior legitimacy can have the effect of challenging existing forms of legitimacy, breaking open the possibility of future forms." The act of reappropriation can bring about actions that might be applauded, condoned—or condemned. The point here is merely to show the openness to the possibility of reappropriation that is ensured by the inevitable slippage that takes place due to the character of iterability, no matter what judgments we might make concerning the utterance or the act. This openness does not yet mean that all actions are rendered indistinguishable and that we will not and cannot evaluate actions, but this openness is characterized precisely by the impossibility to ensure and predetermine the outcome. Most recently, in *Undoing Gender*, Butler argues that resignification cannot provide evaluative norms out of itself to distinguish between different forms of change, a claim she demonstrates by offering different examples of resignification. The criteria are those she suggests emerge in relation to the question of violence and the radical democratic project.

25. Lloyd, "Radical Democratic Activism" takes up Butler's argument for approaching radical democratic practice through the politics of resignification and argues for considering how the specific historical, social, and political circumstances condition the activism that becomes possible.

26. Mahmood, *Politics of Piety*, 14.

27. Ibid., 14–15.

28. Another aspect that Butler engages more thoroughly in *Giving an Account of Oneself* is on issues about a sense of their own past and future that in her

earlier work her subjects do not seem to be capable of. Her subjects seem to have a history that is only perceivable from a theoretical point of view; they themselves appear unable to perceive themselves as historical beings. Michael Levenson raised this issue in his review of *The Psychic Life of Power* and *Excitable Speech* (Levenson, "Speaking to Power," 62), in which he argues that there seems to be no "sense that we live and change through time" and that Butler's "subjects never really grow: They are always only being founded, caught in the nest where they were first hatched." McNay, *Gender and Agency*, 46, presents the idea that acting for a subject has a subjectively futural dimension and we might understand agency as "an act of temporalization where the subject transcends the present through actions that have an inherently anticipatory structure." Cavarero, *Relating Narratives*, raises similar issues regarding the question of having a story and a sense of oneself over time.

29. My argument works in a different register from Mahmood's; however, her point that moral deliberation and moral principles cannot be understood apart from the practices of self-formation is important to keep in mind within the context of our discussion here. Mahmood understands these formative practices as ethical practices in a Aristotelian-Foucauldian tradition that draws in particular on the work of Asad, *Formation of the Secular* and *Genealogies of Religion*. By insisting on critique and deliberation, my argument—viewed through the critical lens of Mahmood's argument—might be construed as returning us into the hands of what figures as the "liberal tradition" criticized in Mahmood, *Politics of Piety*. However, neither critique nor deliberation are reducible to what figures in Mahmood as the version of freedom and autonomy of liberalism. Rather, it seems to me that with deliberation and critique as the conceptual frameworks that my argumentation tries to elaborate and consequently insists on, we would reach one of the points where moral philosophical work has to enter into dialogue with other fields and other studies to inquire into how in various traditions practices of critique and deliberation are delimited, circumscribed, and put to work. We would then have to undertake the hard labor of translation and communication across traditions, cultures, and fields. It seems to me that liberalism has the tendency in Mahmood's text to become too homogenous and too much of the grounds for motivating her theoretical argument—almost unwittingly entangling it in the very conceit that it wants to undo; namely, her argument aspires to resist and subvert the powerful, dominant tradition of liberal thought, while the agency and persuasiveness of this argument could, one hopes, have been recognizable and effective outside this paradigm of repression and resistance. The argument in itself functions more complexly than her opposition of liberal rational morality and Foucauldian ethics as politically relevant self-formation seems to suggest, because Mahmood mobilizes the ambivalences that emerge when we consider the specificity of practices and their political, historical, and religious contexts in relation to the kinds of subjects that are formed and presupposed in them. With this intervention that brings into the open disavowed presuppositions in feminist theory

and political convictions, Mahmood's study is enormously productive in making possible and necessary a reconsideration of the relationships among religion, ethics, and politics.

30. In Benhabib, et al., *Feminist Contentions: A Philosophical Exchange*, 45.

31. Butler, "What Is Critique?" 225.

32. Purtschert, "Judith Butler: Macht der Kontingenz."

33. Butler, "Contingent Foundations," 45.

34. The problem of conceptualizing *conscious* agency and *deliberate intentional* action in Butler has been criticized explicitly by Nelson, "Bodies (and Spaces) Do Matter," 340, who sees the reason for this difficulty that Butler "conceives of conscious agency as stemming from an *autonomous* (pre-discursive) subject." Another critic pointing to this aspect is Vasterling, "Butler's Sophisticated Constructivism."

3: RESPONSIBILITY AS RESPONSE: LEVINAS AND RESPONSIBILITY FOR OTHERS

1. Levinas, *Otherwise Than Being*. Hereafter abbreviated in citations as *OTB*.

2. Prior to *Giving an Account of Oneself*, Butler engaged with Levinas only in much briefer fashion: in the essay "Precarious Life" in the book by the same name; in the essay "Ethical Ambivalence," in *The Turn to Ethics;* and in the German *Kritik der ethischen Gewalt*, Butler's 2002 Adorno Lectures that were subsequently revised and significantly expanded to be published in English as *Giving an Account of Oneself*.

3. Levinas, *Entre Nous*, 99, (hereafter abbreviated in citations as *EN*), emphatically asserts that instantiations of the primary responsibility for the other "can only be discreetly. It cannot give itself out as an example, or be narrated in an edifying discourse. It cannot, without becoming perverted, be made into a preachment."

4. Levinas rejected psychoanalysis because he considered it to function in the service of the antihumanism of the human sciences, which he saw as running the risk of annihilating the sanctity of the human ("*la sainteté de l'humain*"). Nevertheless, casting the subject as being wounded by an irrecuperable past that emerges incessantly as a conscious subject only in attempting to respond to this wounding has strong resonances with psychoanalytic accounts that cast a trauma of separation that remains forever irrecoverable as the key to the individuation of the subject. For a sustained and careful interrogation of the proximity between Levinas and Freudian and Lacanian psychoanalysis and possibilities of relating them, see Critchley, *Ethics—Politics—Subjectivity*. In *Giving an Account of Oneself*, Butler notes the incompatibilities between the Levinasian and psychoanalytic position and explains that her aim is not to claim that in the end they could be rendered compatible, but instead her interest lies in certain convergences that emerge with regard to attending to a decentering of the subject through the other that carries ethical valences and has important

consequences for theorizing responsibility and moral and political philosophy more generally.

Further differences between Levinas and psychoanalysis could be traced with regard to the role of desire, the unconscious, and trauma. Referring to Jean Laplanche's criticism of Levinas, Butler points to Levinas's writing infancy out of his account of the subject. See Laplanche, "Responsabilité et réponse," where Laplanche argues that the Levinasian subject is always already an adult; infancy and subject formation as implicated in and complicated by the developmental dimension seem to remain a peculiar zone of silence in Levinas.

5. Butler repeatedly argues for the importance of understanding the unconscious and its formation as implicated in social relations. On this issue, see especially *Bodies That Matter* and *Contingency, Hegemony, Universality*, in which Butler insists on the social formation of the unconscious, particularly in response to Slavoj Žižek.

6. See Haker, "Fragility of the Moral Self."

7. On the ethical valence of figurative language and in particular the "face" in Levinas, see Perpich, "Figurative Language and the 'Face.'"

8. Levinas, "Substitution," 80.

9. See Levinas, "Ethics as First Philosophy."

10. As Butler suggests in *Giving an Account of Oneself*, as we read Levinas and find ourselves addressed by his works, we become responsible for Levinas in wrestling with how to read and how to respond to his words: "Indeed, Levinas' words here carry wounds and outrages, and they pose an ethical dilemma for those who read them. Although he would circumscribe a given religious tradition as the precondition for ethical responsibility, thereby casting other traditions as threats to ethicality, it makes sense for us to insist, as it were, on a face-to-face encounter precisely here where Levinas claims it cannot be done. Moreover, although he wounds us here or, perhaps precisely because he wounds us here, we are responsible for him, even as the relation proves painful in its non-reciprocity" (*GA* 95). Butler makes this remark with respect to how persecution and Judaism function as terms in which historical, cultural, and philosophical events and interpretations are collapsed, often not unproblematically so. The context and occasion for these critical, difficult reflections are in particular Levinas's writings in *Difficult Freedom: Essays on Judaism*, but it seems to me that Butler's conclusions are useful and important with respect to reading Levinas's work in general.

11. On the question of Levinas's discourse as extraphilosophical as well as on ethical language and violence in Levinas, see also Derrida, "Violence and Metaphysics."

12. Butler comments further on this rhetorical dimension of ethics in a recent interview in Murray, "Scenes of Address."

13. The role of the commandment as key to subject formation and ethics raises the question of what relation is inscribed between religion and philosophy. This question emerges not only with respect to Levinas in particular but

in general whenever an absolute command is introduced. In Levinas specifically, the commandment figures ambiguously and is not solely or explicitly identified as divine voice, even though Levinas draws on biblical terms and examples in his writings. Asking what underlying connections between religious and philosophical thought are performed and mobilized does not necessarily invalidate the philosophical argument. The issue is not that apodictically moral philosophy cannot have any relation to religious thought and is not even that religious aspects cannot ground moral philosophy. If we take seriously that all argumentation is culturally and historically indexed, then there cannot be an absolute foundation in any case. But this would mean that, first, it would be necessary to account for the particularity of religion as the source or the foundation of philosophical arguments. Second, it would be important to examine whether and how these arguments become translatable across contexts. So if the commandment "Thou shalt not kill" is introduced and if it comes from one or more specific religious traditions, this introduction of religious figures does not disqualify the philosophical account, but the question is whether the philosophical argument can still be plausible when the particular religious tradition as a reference framework is no longer in place. It would seem that in Levinas's case, the face and the commandment figure as an imperative expression of basic regard and respect that the encounter with another life commands. It is interesting to note, however, that the moment of the commandment is also the moment when an imperative enters as a commanding force not because of an argument but simply as a function attributed to the face.

14. Responsibility here is thus quite different from the Kantian paradigm in which my obligation, *Sollen*, implies and presupposes my capacity to fulfill the obligation, *Können*. In Levinas, responsibility as my obligation to the other is radically constituted through my *Nicht-Können*, my irremediable capacity fully to assume and fulfill this obligation.

15. See Freud, "Economic Problem of Masochism."

16. Levinas, *On Escape*.

17. Temporality and (perhaps even more so) history are intricate issues in Levinas, especially because history interestingly does not figure at all as a category in his phenomenological inquiry. History seems to be absent from his conceptual framework both in its social dimension as well as its individual dimension. With respect to the latter, Laplanche criticizes Levinas for having missed decentering the subject as an adult subject by its constitutive relation to the irrecoverable past of infancy. See Laplanche, "Responsabilité et réponse."

18. Derrida, "Hostipitality," 362, argues that hospitality exists only when the other is not expected, when not only is the expected welcomed but also the unexpected, the one not invited: "If I welcome only what I welcome, what I am ready to welcome, and that I recognize in advance because I expect the coming of the hôte as invited, there is no hospitality."

19. This does not mean that one does not have to engage with and attempt to understand, trace, and perhaps even make sense of sufferings past and present

in the name of opening a future when these sufferings will not have to be repeated. But it will be necessary to ask how such attempts are to attend to the necessary betrayal that they themselves perform. One could suggest that the primary locus of Butler's inquiry into ethics in her texts is her wrestling with an ethics of writing. In that sense, her engagement with ethics is performative, performing a certain kind of ethics of critique in order to open the horizon concerning which we might come to ask the question of ethics, of how ethics might come to figure, of what violence and nonviolence might mean and how they operate. Butler's texts demand these questions, as they refuse to offer quick answers and instead challenge readers. See also Salih, "Judith Butler and the Ethics of 'Difficulty.' "

20. Butler argues for understanding "conditions" and their relations to actions of individuals, rather than beginning with a language that seeks unilateral causes: "A condition of terrorism can be necessary or sufficient. If it is necessary, it is a state of affairs without which terrorism cannot take place. If it is sufficient, its presence is enough for terrorism to take place. Conditions do not 'act' in the way that individual agents do, but no agent acts without them. They are presupposed in what we do, but it would be a mistake to personify them as if they had acted in the place of us" (*PL* 11).

21. Perhaps there is room for the subject and for thinking the subject opening up by putting into play the "I" awakening in a state of being terrified, panting, and shivering, and the "I" awakening in a state of being brokenhearted. For a version that grants priority to the other in understanding subject formation through brokenheartedness, see Nancy, "Shattered Love." Another question pertaining to the death of the other is how mourning the death of an other would look in the Levinasian account. It seems that Levinas's philosophy is a cry for life. What does the reality of the loss of an other mean with regard to the dyadic relationship? In *God, Death, and Time*, 12, Levinas does not address the question of loss and mourning but offers an intriguing gesture where the regular syntax breaks down: "Someone who dies: a face that becomes a masque." If death means the transition from appearing as a face into the stillness of a masque, then one could think about how an other might be sentenced to "death within life" by petrifying and arresting the face of another into a masque. In *Precarious Life* Butler offers considerations about the arrest of the face and of loss and mourning as questions that circumscribe political and ethical conundrums. Butler offers other interesting inroads into the problematics of death, loss, and mourning by engaging with Walter Benjamin in "Afterword: After Loss, What Then?" On mourning and Levinas, see also Derrida, *Adieu to Emmanuel Levinas*.

22. This response is for Levinas to be bound up with the biblical tradition of *hineni* as a response to a divine call. The Hebrew *hineni* is usually rendered "Here I am" or "I am ready" in English translations, and some of the best-known biblical references to the term are the binding of Isaac when Abraham is

addressed and responds "*hineni*" and is then told to sacrifice his son (Genesis 22:1); a voice from within the burning bush that calls Moses and to which he responds "*hineni*" (Exodus 3:4); Isaiah being asked to offer the name of a person to be sent to prophesy to Israel and responding "*hineni*" (Isaiah 6:8–9).

23. What does it mean that still Levinas *speaks* this breakdown of the subject, consciousness, logic, and principle to us? What does it mean that he delivers this breakdown, especially while this breakdown in the face of the other seems to be the point where all attempts to interpret or even make an argument for or against reach a limit? This limit is that posited by the suffering of the other and its unjustifiable character. What does it then mean if one asks the question, "Why *substitution?* What is *this* substitution?" Does that mean one can ask the question, that it is a logically possible question, but then what? Is it already engaged in making sense of suffering? Are there ways to conceive of this responsibility other than in these terms of substitution and expiation?

24. On Levinas and psychoanalysis, especially on traumatizing of the subject, see Critchley, *Ethics—Politics—Subjectivity*. On trauma and a notion of the unconscious with regard to phenomenology, see Bergo, "What Is Levinas Doing?"

25. The good in Levinas is capitalized as "Good," and with the terminology of the Good choosing the subject, there are distinct resonances in Levinas of an identification of the Good with a divine transcendence. However, Levinas also argues that "From the Good to me, there is an assignation: a relation that survives the 'death of God' " (*OTB* 123).

26. In *Giving an Account of Oneself,* Butler explains that the problem with the fusion or confusion of preontological and ontological categories lies in that a social specificity is inscribed at a level that is not open to social and historical criticism and reworking, precisely because it is claimed as preontological: "If Jews are considered 'elect' precisely because they carry a message of universality, and what is 'universal' in Levinas's view is the inaugurative structuring of the subject through persecution and ethical demand, then the Jew becomes the model and instance for preontological persecution. The problem, of course, is that 'the Jew' is a category that belongs to a culturally constituted ontology (unless it is the name for access to the infinite itself), and so if the Jew maintains an 'elective' status in relation to ethical responsiveness, then Levinas fully confuses the preontological and the ontological. The Jew is not part of ontology or history, and yet this exemption becomes the way in which Levinas makes claims about the role of Israel, historically considered, as forever and exclusively persecuted. The same confusion between the two domains is made clear in other contexts where, with blatant racism, Levinas claims that Judaism and Christianity are the cultural and religious preconditions of ethical relationality itself and warns against the 'rise of the countless masses of Asiatic [*des masses innombrables de peuples asiatiques*] and underdeveloped peoples [who] threaten[] the newfound authenticity' (*DF*, 165) of Jewish universalism. This, in turn, resonates

with his warning that ethics cannot be based on 'exotic cultures' " (*GA* 94, quoting from Levinas, *Difficult Freedom*).

27. In a response to Mills and Jenkins, Butler, "Reply," 185, elaborates that considering the possibility of a nonviolent ethics does not mean that one seeks to eliminate violence from ethics, but instead, Butler explains, "my view is that nonviolence, when and where it exists, involves an aggressive vigilance in relation to aggression's tendency to emerge as violence." As a consequence, she suggests that the ambivalence and struggle characterizing responsibility cannot be resolved into a harmonizing recognition of a universally shared vulnerability: "If nonviolence has the opportunity to emerge here, it would take its departure not from a recognition of the injurability of all peoples (however true that might be), but from an understanding of the possibilities of one's own violent actions in relation to those lives to whom one is bound" (194). On violence and nonviolence and critique on the crossroads of ethics and politics, see also Butler "Critique, Coercion, and Sacred Life" and "Violence, Non-Violence: Sartre on Fanon."

28. With regard to the question of what practical philosophy Levinas's approach to subject formation yields, it might be important to consider the precise ways in which this obligation to compare that remains bound to the ultimate responsibility for the other is different from the consequentialist accounts of ethical and moral deliberation.

29. As Levinas comments: "Consciousness is born as the presence of a third party. It is in the measure that it proceeds from it that it is still disinterestedness" (*OTB* 160).

30. In opening by introducing the question of moral conduct as that of "moral conduct in a social frame," *Giving an Account of Oneself* frames ethics as an enterprise that cannot be examined apart from a critical appraisal of its social and political preconditions and consequences. However, the book does not pursue these deliberations explicitly as a matter of reformulating how practical judgment is theorized. Butler argues for rethinking ethics by demonstrating the critical importance of giving an account of the emergence of the moral subject and of the norms that condition the subject and the situations in which it acts. While the aim of Butler's argument, at least in my reading of it, is to rethink ethics through critical social and political theoretical insights, it seems to me that the term "judgment" tends to be understood predominantly in its evaluative connotation that pertains to past actions. In *Giving an Account of Oneself*, this past-oriented connotation tends to overshadow the second connotation of judgment in practical philosophy, toward future action. As we rethink moral philosophy through responsibility and critique as key categories and as this endeavor also implies a rethinking of normative ethics, the aim in the work here is not to do away with judgment—which is also not what Butler's work argues for. But in rethinking moral judgment, it appears to me important to mobilize the double dimension of moral judgment and understand the consequences of its dual temporal orientation.

31. Although beyond the scope of this book, it would be interesting to examine how considering this question of "What ought I to do?" produces a convergence between Aristotle and Kant in terms of the practical syllogism or practical judgment. In the *Nicomachean Ethics*, Aristotle regarded a syllogism as practical when the conclusion is an action, and as Kant argues in the *Critique of the Power of Judgment*, practical judgment is one that compels and brings about a particular action. The orientation toward action as a peculiarity and key feature that characterizes practical judgment seems to me to raise some questions with regard to Arendt's suggestion for reading aesthetic judgment as political judgment in Kant; see Arendt, *Lectures on Kant's Political Philosophy*. Arendt makes Kant's aesthetic judgment fruitful for thinking about political judgment by focusing especially on how aesthetic judgment works by wooing, not proscribing, consent. But the problem with reformulating political judgment through aesthetic judgment is, in my view, that political judgment is also about what ought to be done and that aesthetic judgment for Kant is crucially completely severed from practical judgment and rather is akin to theoretical judgment. Pursuing these issues further might be an occasion to probe again the relation among knowledge and practice and practical knowledge through understanding how a deferral of judgment is necessary for critical inquiry, more precisely as a deferral of prescriptive judgment. But this deferral of prescriptive judgment in favor of critical inquiry will nonetheless return us to the need for practical judgment in order to respond to the question of "What ought to be done." So it would seem that theoretical knowledge and the inquiry into it would attain their dignity—and practical value—precisely through their impracticality, because they can dislodge what might seem to be settled knowledges of what ought to be done.

32. The situation is peculiar, because there is no one who could absolve the subject; there is no primary goodness of the subject that could be restored and, moreover, for what one needs to be forgiven that then remains as that which is unforgivable. We are always already in need of forgiveness, the being remains unforgivable, but, as the radically unforgivable, it is that which enables forgiving. If forgiveness is a giving of that which is undeserved, then one cannot forgive that which is forgivable but only the unforgivable. See Derrida, *On Cosmopolitanism and Forgiveness*.

33. Butler, "Politics, Power, and Ethics," sec. 10. Butler inquires into the nexus between the limits of acknowledgment and ethics more extensively in *Kritik der ethischen Gewalt*.

4: AMBIVALENT DESIRES OF RESPONSIBILITY: LAPLANCHE AND PSYCHOANALYTIC TRANSLATIONS

1. In *Giving an Account of Oneself*, Butler elaborates this impossibility of full self-knowledge as the "opacity" of the subject and argues for the ethical valence of this opacity.

2. See Laplanche, "Aims of the Psychoanalytic Process."

3. Laplanche, "Time and the Other," 256.

4. Stanton, "Interview," 10.

5. To understand "seduction," as argued by Laplanche, as a fundamental human situation that initiates and orchestrates the emergence of the ego as well as the unconscious does not mean negating the possibility of sexual abuse in this encounter, nor does it negate the necessity to negotiate how to discern, to find criteria, to distinguish nonabusive situations from abusive situations. Laplanche is very clear that abuse is a concern, as he emphasizes in an interview in 2000; see Fletcher and Osborne, "Other Within." However, the "general seduction theory" insists on a disarticulation between seduction and abuse; not all seduction is abusive, just as seduction is neither celebrated nor heralded. The introduction of "seduction" as a category is, rather, an attempt to capture and take seriously the situation that as infants we enter and grow into this world through relations with those who take care of us and that these relations are radically asymmetrical, and not only in terms of the infant's dependency on being taken care of.

6. Laplanche, "Time and the Other," 254–55 n. 46, sums up his choice of the notion of enigma and its key characteristics as follows: "An enigma, like a riddle, is proposed to the subject by another subject. But the solution of a riddle in theory is completely in the conscious possession of the one who poses it, and thus it is entirely resolved by the answer. An enigma, on the contrary, can only be proposed by someone who does not master the answer, because his message is a compromise-formation in which his unconscious takes part." Laplanche terms this an enigma rather than a riddle, since the implication of the term "riddle" is that the one posing the riddle has the solution to it at his or her disposal, whereas in an enigma there is no solution available.

7. Laplanche, "Drive and Its Object-Source," 189.

8. Stanton, "Interview," 10.

9. Laplanche, "Responsabilité et réponse," 164, makes this point explicitly: "Ce primat nous reporte à une situation qui n'est pas d'autocentration, une situation qui n'est pas même de réciprocité ou comme on dit d'interaction, une situation qui n'est pas de communication réciproque, une situation par essence dissymétrique où je suis passif et désarmé par rapport au message de l'autre." ("This primacy takes us back to a situation which is not one of self-centering, a situation which is not even one of reciprocity or, as one says, of interaction, a situation which is not one of reciprocal communication, a situation which is by essence dissymmetrical where I am passive and disarmed in relation to the message of the other" [my translation].)

10. On silence as a response that refuses to engage the address and thereby calls into question the legitimacy of the address, see Butler, *Giving an Account of Oneself*, 12: "Silence in these instances either calls into question the legitimacy of the authority invoked by the question and the questioner or attempts to

circumscribe a domain of autonomy that cannot or should not be intruded upon by the questioner."

11. Laplanche, "Psychoanalysis, Time and Translation," hereafter abbreviated in citations as PTT.

12. Laplanche, "Transference." Hereafter abbreviated in citations as TPA.

13. It seems important to note that the one who meets the analyst, although mostly called an "analysand" by Laplanche, here becomes the "patient." The use of "patient" as not fully equivalent to "analysand" seems to emphasize the notion of patiently undergoing something, and in this context "patient" foregrounds the clinical dimension and might bring into play a notion of "pathology," raising the question of what counts as a cure and what kind of cure is sought.

14. This problem of recognition and relation in responsibility resonates with Susan Sontag's deliberations on the pain and suffering of others that are represented and looked at in images. She argues that in looking at images, the other is rendered into someone only seen and is eclipsed as someone who might be seeing herself. See Sontag, *Regarding the Pain of Others*. See also Butler's reference to Sontag in her essay "Precarious Life" in the book of the same title. Taking up Levinas's formulation of the face as delivering an ethical demand, Butler argues in this essay that there are always political frameworks in place that condition which faces and lives can be apprehended as human and which ones are dehumanized by means of their representation and in that way are deprived of their ethical force.

15. Caruth, "Interview with Jean Laplanche," sec. 140.

16. Laplanche, "Responsabilité et réponse," 162.

17. Graf, Review of *Kritik der ethischen Gewalt*.

18. I argue in the last two chapters that moral philosophy cannot give up the question of normativity, but this dimension does not necessarily make these moral philosophical considerations "strong." Rather, I argue that the problem of normativity and the question of justice compel moral philosophy to commit itself to critique as epistemological critique and as social criticism. With the perspective of critique and the question of justice, ethics becomes political, as it has a stake in the negotiations about how to organize society.

19. Foucault, *Fearless Speech*. Hereafter abbreviated in citations as *FS*.

20. On philosophical discussions of forgiveness in relation to its political, legal, and ethical dimensions, see, e.g., Arendt, *Human Condition*; Derrida, *On Cosmopolitanism and Forgiveness*; Jankélévitch, *Forgiveness*; Ricoeur, *Memory, History, Forgetting*.

21. Both Derrida and Ricoeur elaborate on the difficulties in forgiveness regarding the unconditionality of forgiveness and the aporia that in the strict sense only the unforgivable, which cannot be settled, requires forgiveness. See Derrida, *On Cosmopolitanism and Forgiveness*; and Ricoeur, *Memory, History, Forgetting*.

22. On the past being between history and memory, see, e.g., Ricoeur, *Memory, History, Forgetting*; LaCapra, *History in Transit*; Koselleck, *Vergangene Zukunft*.

23. Important contributions to the impossibilities and possibilities of thinking about memory and history through the conceptual and practical frameworks of narration and narrativity have been made in the field of trauma analysis as a theoretical question. See, among many others, Caruth, *Trauma*; Caruth, *Unclaimed Experience*; Felman, *Juridical Unconscious*; LaCapra, *Writing History, Writing Trauma*; Leys, *Trauma*; Ronell, *Finitude's Score*.

24. Stanton, "Interview," 17.

25. This indolent absent presence of the past in the present complicates how we approach the phenomena of memory and forgetting. See, e.g., Ricoeur, *Memory, History, Forgetting*.

26. Laplanche, "Wall and the Arcade," 204.

27. Ibid.

28. A more comprehensive inquiry into the problematic of accountability would have to take into consideration the complications that the political and collective dimensions present; see e.g., Derrida, *On Cosmopolitanism and Forgiveness*; Ricoeur, *Memory, History, Forgetting*; and Jankélévitch, *Forgiveness*.

29. Laplanche, "Interpretation between Determinism and Hermeneutics," 164.

5: THE APORIA OF CRITIQUE AND THE FUTURE OF MORAL PHILOSOPHY

1. Butler, "What Is Critique?" 212, comments on the problem of a self-reflexive inquiry into critique that emerges if one attempts a critical reflection on critique, which means that one has to "attempt to distinguish between a critique of this or that position and critique as a more generalized practice, one that might be described without reference to its specific objects."

2. My argument here is also one in favor of resisting the attempt to find a "superconcept" under which one could subsume all the critical work that is to be done. In resisting systematic unicity, another problem breaks open that has equal critical potential, namely the question of how the different aspects—in this case an inquiry into critical moral philosophy—fit together and how to hold them in play with each other without subsuming them under another higher unifying principle and without renouncing any relation between them.

3. Cavarero, *Relating Narratives*, elaborates emergent ontologies of the self in relations to others as narratable and traversed by a desire for a story and history that gives the self texture in an inevitably fragmented way. These emergent ontologies are in return taken to imply strong political demands. What is problematic in her argument is that she makes a move akin to a phenomenological reduction that establishes a constitutive condition, the self, which later becomes taken again as grounds for political claims. She articulates the

narratability of the self as a constitutive condition created from the fragmentary texts and narrations that is the self and that one cannot evade: "The ontological status of the narratable self becomes distinguished, therefore, from the text of her story; even if it is irremediably mixed up with it" (ibid., 35). This narratable self and its ontological foundations are dependent on a particular exposure and relationality to others. Through this relationality the constitutive conditions then become the grounds for her version of an ethics and politics of recognition: "The narratable self thus re-enters into what we could call a relational ethic of contingency; or, rather, an ethic founded on the *altruistic* ontology of the human existent as finite" (ibid., 87). This ethic is specified in that "she [the self] wants and gives, receives and offers, *here and now*, an unrepeatable story in the form of a tale" (ibid.). The conclusion Cavarero then draws is that "This ethic finds therefore a fundamental principle in the recognition that every human being, whatever her qualities, has her unjudgable splendor in a personal identity that *is* irrefutably her story" (ibid.).

4. For a further inquiry, it might be important to consider the differences that open up between ontological and anthropological accounts and their role in moral philosophy.

5. The question of an act of faith, religious or nonreligious, and which role it is to play in a philosophical account of moral philosophy might eventually be one of the formulations of the aporetic foundations of moral philosophy. As a set of rigorous arguments for a nonreligious faith that emerges from the philosophically aporetic situation of reason under the conditions of late modernity, one could consider Jacques Derrida's examinations of the undecidable and responsibility, the mystical foundations of law, the madness of reason, forgiveness and the gift, and aporias of the unconditionally conditioned. See, among other works, Derrida, "Force of Law"; *Eyes of the University*; *Rogues*; *Gift of Death*; and *Politics of Friendship*.

6. Adorno, *Problems of Moral Philosophy*, 34, argues that freedom and responsibility are precisely the capacity and problem of not following rules, which provides an interesting convergence with Derrida's reflections in *Gift of Death* and "Force of Law."

7. Philosophical reflection cannot fully grasp moral conduct because moral conduct is constitutively bound up with a requirement of spontaneous action and there are situations in which launching into elaborate ethical reflections would be the immoral rather than the moral thing to do. As an example of such a situation in which immediate action is required, Adorno offers the situation Kant uses for his famous (or infamous) inquiry into whether there is a human right to lie when a person being chased by the secret police knocks on one's door asking for refuge. Adorno's point about how the moment of action and decision cannot be dissolved into reflection or fully negotiated by reflection is crucial. The clarity the example produces is, however, misleading because its moral clarity relies on the fact that it involves someone who is "about to be

killed or handed over to some state police" (*PMP* 97), where Adorno's "Staatspolizei" has very unambiguous resonance with the secret state police, the Gestapo, under National Socialism in Germany. Although it is an important example, since too often refugees—those who are very clearly refugees—are not welcomed but sent back to their home to perish, nonetheless the status of the fugitive in the example seems clearer than it often is. One could draw on Derrida's argument in "Hostipitality" to understand how Adorno's openness here is already conditioned and reflectively determined. Derrida radicalizes the problematic by elaborating on how the knock on the door forces a radical openness because it is an openness without knowing the other and so is an openness precisely for the *un*invited. Taking these insights out of the context of Derrida's argument to the problematic that Adorno addresses, a more radical formulation becomes available, because the demand to act and decide attains its urgency before one is able to know enough about who is knocking and who is chasing the one who is knocking.

8. In *Problems of Moral Philosophy* Adorno comments at various points on the need to wrestle theoretically with the moment of action that escapes practical philosophy because it is a kind of spontaneity that action requires but which can no longer be reflectively fully captured. At the same time, in order for the practical not to become dominating and ideological, there needs to be this theoretical attempt to reflect on what escapes reflection (see, e.g., Lecture Nine in *PMP*).

9. Habermas, *Philosophical Discourse of Modernity* [*Der philosophische Diskurs der Moderne*].

10. Kelly, *Critique and Power*.

11. See, in particular, Habermas, *Between Facts and Norms*.

12. Fraser, "False Antitheses," and "Pragmatism, Feminism, and the Linguistic Turn," addresses the implicit normative distinctions that are at play in particular in Butler's work on resignification in *Gender Trouble* and *Bodies That Matter*. Fraser argues that resignification cannot provide a sufficient basis for normative criteria—a claim with which Butler explicitly agrees in later works—and that the normative evaluative criteria need first to be rendered explicit and then articulated further.

13. Judith Butler, "What Is a Discipline?" I am grateful to Judith Butler for providing me with the text of this lecture.

14. Butler, "What Is Critique?" 213.

15. Ibid.

16. Habermas elaborates this criticism in Lecture Ten, "Some Questions Concerning the Theory of Power: Foucault Again," in *Philosophical Discourse of Modernity*, 266–93/313–43. In the German version, this lecture is "Aporien einer Machttheorie" ("Aporias of a Theory of Power").

17. Bernstein, "Foucault," seems to assess Foucauldian critique along similar lines.

18. Bernstein argues: "Foucault can be read as always seeking to expose instabilities, points of resistance, places where counterdiscourses can arise and effect transgressions and change. . . . Nevertheless, even if we stick to the specific and local, to the *insurrection of subjected knowledges*, there is an implicit valorization here that never becomes fully explicit and yet is crucial for Foucault's genre of critique. . . . What is never quite clear in Foucault is why anyone should favor certain forms of resistance than others. Nor is it clear why one would 'choose' one side or the other in a localized resistance or revolt" (ibid., 229).

19. Allen, *Power of Feminist Theory*, 77.

20. Anderson, *Way We Argue Now*, 38.

21. Although not in direct response to Allen and Anderson, Butler, "Question of Social Transformation" acknowledges the need for substantive decisions and criteria and proposes "radical democratic theory and practice" as a resource from which to derive substantive criteria. She argues that evaluative norms cannot be deduced from resignification, that not any resignification is good by virtue of being a reappropriation: "[W]hich action is right to pursue, which innovation has value, and which does not? The norms that we would consult to answer this question cannot themselves be derived from resignification. They have to be derived from a radical democratic theory and practice" (*UG* 224). It is not resignification and the fact of change but instead radical democratic practice and theory that are posited as principles or sources of the normative criteria with which to distinguish between different actions and possibilities. The normative sources in this passage arrive on the scene only with the introduction that they cannot be grounded themselves in the way that the undermining of normative frameworks and their manifestations works. By this act of positing rather than deducing the sources of normative principles, Butler's argument performs a commitment to openness and the contingency of any foundation as substantive principle precisely insofar as the source of criteria is claimed and not deduced. It seems to me that the ways in which normative commitments and the frameworks through which we derive and articulate moral norms arise and come into effect are indeed contingent formations, contingent on our cultural and social backgrounds.

The lingering question here is whether there is any way to distinguish between different sets of norms and criteria in precisely the moment when more than one set becomes available and possible. The quandary of normative grounds is not put to rest by the response that the norms to adjudicate between various sets of criteria of right and wrong "have to be derived from a radical democratic theory and practice" (*UG* 224). It appears that if we were to stop with this answer, we would have only pushed back the question of criteria one more level. What is the status of this normative demand that the relevant norms *have to be* derived from this source? The question then is whether there is a way of deciding and adjudicating between different sources from which one might derive those evaluative norms. Would a "compassionate conservative theory and practice" count as an equally valid source of normative evaluative criteria? Are all sources equally valid in the moment of their positing so that whatever is posited has equal validity until further negotiation? It seems to me that if critical inquiry is to be retained as possibility, then it becomes impossible to put these questions to rest and answer them conclusively. The aim is not to quell disagreement preemptively but to refuse fully to settle for history deeming right those positions that end up prevailing. At stake is the refusal to settle for the impossibility of discerning theoretically between different sets of criteria for what will count as just and unjust, while at the same time acknowledging the impossibility of anything but contingent affirmations and the need for contestation beyond this refusal. What is at issue is the need to continue to examine normative commitments, how they are formed, to what ends, with what implications do we align ourselves with one position rather than another, and how to distinguish between and among them.

A shift in perspective might become possible by turning from the question of naming normative sources to the substantive implications, which nonetheless does not and cannot resolve the epistemological problematic. With respect to Butler's argument in *Undoing Gender*, what is key is not just that radical democratic theory and practice are the source of criteria but that the problems that need to be addressed are "a less violent future," "a more inclusive population," and social justice in cultural specificity. I will return to some of these points in the following chapter.

22. Heike Kämpf has suggested that this openness emerges as a normative criterion that Foucauldian critique has to offer; see Kämpf, "Politische Philosophie," 116: "So it is not in the first place a matter of distinguishing good from bad reworkings of the concept, . . . but the *reworkability* itself is the normative criterion with regard to which language and linguistic practice have to be measured" (emphasis in the original). Yet it seems to me to that with this move to openness as a normative criterion, if we left the considerations at that point, we would run into the problem either that this account remains too formalistic or that the ultimate normative criterion turns out to be settled with this openness (and thus no longer open for discussion), leaving the question theoretically settled but retaining the normative dimension only as a practical question of application and implementation.

23. Anderson's turn to ethos is problematic in this regard, because she undoes the underlying epistemological critical problem by filling the alleged formalism with a personal ethos. Yet the problem to be addressed was the question of validity, and by resolving an epistemological problem through reflections on authenticity, the critical dimension ends up being leveled out.

24. See Habermas, *Postnational Constellation*; Anderson, *Way We Argue Now*; Benhabib, *Claims of Culture*. Benhabib, "Liberal Imagination," 409, emphasizes that "[T]he interplay between the democratic politics of inclusion by marginalized groups and the ensuing expansion of the traditional liberal concept of

rights and entitlements, that is, the democratization of liberalism and the liberalization of democracy, is one of the most inspiring developments in our often dispiriting modern and postmodern experiences." Benhabib approvingly comments on an expansion of liberal concepts, but even though with this approval a certain renegotiation of these concepts is valorized, this renegotiation seems to have very clear limits in that the concepts as the baseline need to be fundamentally retained.

25. Butler, Laclau, and Žižek, *Contingency, Hegemony, Universality*, 3, in the introduction comment on their problem with attempts to settle a substantive universality theoretically through recourse to universal human features: "Along the way, we each consider different ideological deployments of universality, and caution against both substantial and procedural approaches to the question. We thus differentiate ourselves (already internally differentiated) from the Habermasian effort to discover or conjure a pre-established universality as the presupposition of the speech act, a universality which is said to pertain to a rational feature of 'man,' a substantive conception of universality which equates it with a knowable and predictable determination, and a procedural form which presumes that the political field is constituted by rational actors."

26. Mouffe, *Democratic Paradox*, 49, elaborates her understanding of agonistic democracy through her critique of deliberative theories of democracy: "Consensus in a liberal-democratic society is—and will always be—the expression of a hegemony and the crystallization of power relations. . . . To deny the existence of such a moment of closure, or to present the frontier as dictated by rationality or morality, is to naturalize what should be perceived as a contingent and temporary hegemonic articulation of 'the people' through a particular regime of inclusion-exclusion." What Mouffe finds problematic about deliberative theories such as Habermas's or Benhabib's formulations is that they justify principles of exclusion by establishing communicative rationality as a normative ideal. From this normative ground, deliberative democratic theories develop procedural principles in which to ground the legitimacy and authority of democratic institutions. It seems to me that the opposition between deliberative democracy and agonistic democracy is in some ways overstated, because Mouffe, especially in her more recent work, ends up equally working with a normative assumption about constitutive democratic institutions and practices. Mouffe, *On the Political*, 120–21, for example, in a section entitled "The Limits of Pluralism," writes: "The pluralism that I advocate requires discriminating between demands which are to be accepted as part of the agonistic debate and those which are to be excluded. A democratic society cannot treat those who put its basic institutions into question as legitimate adversaries. . . . Some demands are excluded, not because they are declared to be 'evil,' but because they challenge the institutions constitutive of the democratic political association." The question that remains open in this positing of democracy is from where the democratic association and its institutions attain their normative validity. A reflection

on this validity need not and—as both theorists of agonistic and of deliberative democracy have argued—cannot establish an absolute, metaphysical validity. But the reference to the facticity of that form of association and its being factually valued as a good abbreviates a critical reflection on how principles of legitimate institutions and of legitimate exclusion are formulated and negotiated.

27. Kelly, "Foucault, Habermas," 378.

28. Butler, "What Is Critique?" 219.

29. Butler, "What Is Critique?" 226, elaborates that the practice of critique means that one comes into question for oneself by calling into question norms that sustain also one's own existence. Critique as a virtue of ethical self-formation is practiced, as Butler argues, "if that self-forming is done in disobedience to the principles by which one is formed, then virtue becomes the practice by which the self forms itself in desubjugation, which is to say that it risks its deformation as a subject, occupying that ontologically insecure position which poses the question anew: who will be a subject here, and what will count as a life, a moment of ethical questioning which requires that we break the habits of judgement in favor of a riskier practice that seeks to yield artistry from constraint."

30. That said, things are not quite as uncomplicated for Kant as I might have implied here; for example, *Critique of the Power of Judgment* betrays Kant's struggles with the difficulties that open up when we consider we are subjects in both the realm of nature and the realm of freedom.

31. While the English translation renders morality and politics as a quest, the formulation in the German original is weaker, with Adorno offering morality and politics as questions, even if, as practical questions, these questions might or perhaps only hope to initiate a quest.

32. Adorno, *Minima Moralia*, 39/59, "Es gibt kein richtiges Leben im Falschen."

33. See Lecture Sixteen of Adorno, *Problems of Moral Philosophy*, 158–62, in which he demonstrates that Ibsen's plays offer a critique of moral rigor and its devastating effects.

34. On Butler's explanation of the abject, see the introduction Butler, *Bodies That Matter*, 3: "This exclusionary matrix by which subjects are formed thus requires the simultaneous production of a domain of abject beings, those who are not yet 'subjects,' but who form the constitutive outside to the domain of the subject. The abject designates here precisely those 'unlivable' and 'uninhabitable' zones of social life which are nevertheless densely populated by those who do not enjoy the status of the subject, but whose living under the sign of the 'unlivable' is required to circumscribe the domain of the subject."

6: CRITIQUE AND POLITICAL ETHICS: JUSTICE AS A QUESTION

1. I believe that one of Jacques Derrida's key contributions to thinking about ethics and politics is to have radicalized Adorno's negative dialectics, which

holds that whenever a position tends to turn into an ossified articulation of principles, it betrays the particulars it aims to grasp and thus has to be called into question and critically interrogated. Derrida demonstrates how there is always already such an undoing happening, how meanings and institutions are not as stable as they might appear, and how their undoing is not the effect of a conscious, intentional agent. Nonetheless, this undoing and the ethical and political potential that might lie in it are not a guarantee, but this undoing in return can always be and is even always overridden again. See Adorno, *Negative Dialectics*; and Derrida, "Force of Law." I believe we can find one of the most important divergences by Butler from deconstruction with respect to the role that the epistemological impossibility of guarantees plays in her work. While her inquiries are committed to thinking from the contingent and to exploring the ensuing epistemological quandaries, the political dimension of her work exceeds the epistemological as she begins and returns to the analytics of how power and violence operate in concrete social and political constellations through marginalization and abjection.

2. Butler, *Undoing Gender*, 3, points out: "The category of the 'human' retains within itself the workings of the power differential of race as part of its own historicity. But the history of the category is not over, and the 'human' is not captured once and for all." "The human" is a category through which access to rights and to legal recourse against violations is negotiated. It is one category and discourse through which legal claims can be mobilized that transcend the legal structure of the nation-state. This invocation of what is human or inhuman is attributed to this context-transcending validity not only because these discourses of human rights have now attained a certain status of customary, though contested, right. But human rights lay claim to a context-transcending quality only insofar as this category of the human is attributed to an ethical force. Yet, as Butler points out, the category of the human and its history of racial bias have to compel us to examine how the assumed universal is exclusionarily conditioned in ways that blind it to the particular as well as to unequal distributions of power that become inscribed within the category as universal. So we need continuously to question the disavowed assumptions—as happened, for example, in uncovering how the notion of "the human" was assumed to be a white male yet in the universal formulation this gendered and raced specificity of "the human" had become invisible. Further, among others, children's advocacy and disability awareness activists challenged how conceptions of "the human" carry the index of being an able-bodied middle-aged adult at the expense of allowing us to mobilize the category of the human to address the specific precariousness and violations that characterize the situations of those of us humans who are disabled or younger or older. These limitations are not just a matter of faulty or incomplete reflection; they inhere in any formulation of a universal category because of its historicity. We need continuously to examine what the limits of our conceptions of humanity are, what this being human

means, who is recognizable as human, and to what effect. Although invoking human rights and pointing to dehumanizing living conditions by no means guarantees recognition and even less that action will be taken to amend the situation, the categories of the human and of human rights remain important discourses as heuristics, not as solutions for addressing very concrete conditions of misrecognition and disenfranchisement that confine lives to poverty, violence, exploitation, and discrimination.

3. In this approach I am indebted especially to the work of Wendy Brown, but this turn away from the state as a specific criterion of politics and the political sphere is also an argument that has been made in various ways by many others in political theory, e.g., by Wolin, *Politics and Vision*; Laclau and Mouffe, *Hegemony and Socialist Strategy*; and Mouffe, *The Democratic Paradox* and *On the Political*. While they differ in their approaches, Hannah Arendt and Carl Schmitt both argue against considering the state as the constitutive characteristic of politics. Arendt, *Human Condition*, elaborates on the sphere of politics through her understanding of political action that differs from labor and work. Schmitt, *Concept of the Political*, argues that the political becomes discernible through the concept of the enemy when any difference becomes so heightened that it organizes a collective into groups of them versus us.

4. Brown, *Politics out of History*.

5. Ibid., 25.

6. The use of examples in moral philosophy is an extremely intriguing subject, since the examples do more than merely illustrate and elucidate the abstract argumentation. It would be very interesting, although beyond the scope of this book, to study the rhetorical function of these examples and how they produce a seeming clarity and a consensus. Famous examples evoking a common understanding of what is morally reprehensible are slave owners and fascists. Yet there are discussions in moral philosophy that inquire carefully into the role of historical, cultural, and scientifically empirical data for moral arguments. One field where these discussions take place is that of "applied ethics," where the name of this field already betrays a problematic, since this term "applied ethics" seems to offer these realities as objects to which principles that are worked out elsewhere are to be "applied." Several bioethicists and feminist scholars have insisted on the crucial importance of sociological and anthropological research in moral arguments. They argue that absolute arguments are impossible and that focusing exclusively, for example, on the moral status of the embryo at the expense of other social dimensions disregards how one cannot deduce normative arguments from empirical data. Instead, moral arguments need to examine critically how empirical data are interpreted, positioned, and attributed normative value through social, cultural, and political discourses. For an example of one such critical bioethical study, see Haker, *Ethik der genetischen Frühdiagnostik*.

7. Plato, *Republic*.

8. Brown, *Politics out of History*, 21.

9. On Foucault's understanding of archeology, see, e.g., Foucault, *Archaeology of Knowledge*; Foucault, *Order of Things*; Dreyfus and Rabinow, *Michel Foucault*. For an analysis of Foucault's understanding of archaeology and its ethical stakes, see the comprehensive study on the status of ethics in structuralism and subject philosophy by Wils, *Sittlichkeit und Subjektivität*.

10. For an elaboration of how we might concretely think about dignity and decency in order to substantiate reflections on distributive justice, see Margalit, *Decent Society*.

11. On the problematic of recognition and redistribution, see the exchange between Honneth and Fraser in *Redistribution or Recognition?* See also Young, *Justice and the Politics of Difference*; Young, "Unruly Categories"; Honneth, *Kampf um Anerkennung*; Honneth, *Das Andere der Gerechtigkeit*; Fraser, "Rethinking Recognition"; Fraser, "Recognition without Ethics?"; Markell, *Bound by Recognition*; Taylor, "Politics of Recognition"; Ricoeur, *Course of Recognition*.

12. For Levinas the question of ethics arises from the address by the other, while the question of justice arises because there are always multiple others. Arguing against Spinoza and the *conatus essendi*, Levinas excludes concerns with the self from the sphere of ethical concerns. Self-preservation is not unethical, but it only becomes a concern of ethics with respect to multiple others and thus does not have a foundational role for ethics. See Levinas, *Otherwise Than Being* and *Is It Righteous to Be?* Unlike Levinas although influenced by his work, Adi Ophir argues that opposition to the suffering of others and to the social, political, and economic sources of these sufferings is the genuine question of morality, while the care of the self falls outside the scope of moral questions. See Ophir, *Order of Evils*. It seems to me that questions of the self need not necessarily be excluded from the scope of ethical concerns as they are part of the overarching question of how to live well. I would argue, however, that this question of how to live well needs to be understood from within the horizon of a shared sociality.

13. Mouly, "War of Words in France."

14. For an evaluation of the new law, see Murphy, "France's New Law."

15. Markell, *Bound by Recognition*, 31.

16. See Markell, *Bound by Recognition*, chap. 5, 152–76. On the evacuation of political contestation through discourses of tolerance, see Brown, *Regulating Aversion*.

17. Butler, *Antigone's Claim*.

Works Cited

Adorno, Theodor W. *Minima Moralia: Reflections from Damaged Life.* Translated by E. F. N. Jephcott. London: Verso, 1974.

———. *Minima Moralia: Reflexionen aus dem beschädigten Leben.* Berlin: Suhrkamp, 1951.

———. *Negative Dialectics.* Translated by E. B. Ashton. New York: Seabury Press, 1973.

———. *Probleme der Moralphilosophie.* Edited by Thomas Schröder. Frankfurt am Main: Suhrkamp, 1996.

———. *Problems of Moral Philosophy.* Translated by Rodney Livingstone. Edited by Thomas Schröder. Stanford, Calif.: Stanford University Press, 2000.

Alcoff, Linda. *Visible Identities: Race, Gender, and the Self.* New York: Oxford University Press, 2006.

Allen, Amy. *The Power of Feminist Theory: Domination, Resistance, Solidarity.* Boulder, Colo.: Westview Press, 1999.

Anderson, Amanda. *The Way We Argue Now: A Study in the Cultures of Theory.* Princeton, N.J.: Princeton University Press, 2005.

Arendt, Hannah. *The Human Condition.* Chicago: University of Chicago Press, 1958.

———. *Lectures on Kant's Political Philosophy.* Chicago: University of Chicago Press, 1989.

———. *Responsibility and Judgment.* Edited by Jerome Kahn. New York: Schocken, 2003.

Aristotle. *The Nicomachean Ethics.* Translated by David Ross. Oxford: Oxford University Press, 1925.

Asad, Talal. *Formation of the Secular: Christianity, Islam, Modernity.* Stanford, Calif.: Stanford University Press, 2003.

———. *Genealogies of Religion: Discipline and Reasons of Power in Christianity and Islam.* Baltimore, Md.: Johns Hopkins University Press, 1993.

Attridge, Derek. "Singularities, Responsibilities: Derrida, Deconstruction, and Literary Criticism." In *Critical Encounters: Reference and Responsibility in Deconstructive Writing*, edited by Cathy Caruth and Deborah Esch. New Brunswick, N.J.: Rutgers University Press, 1995.

Austin, J. L. *How to Do Things with Words.* 2nd ed. Edited by J. O. Urmson and Marina Sbisà. Cambridge, Mass.: Harvard University Press, 1975.

Barad, Karen. "Posthumanist Performativity: Toward an Understanding of How Matter Comes to Matter." *Signs* 28 (2003): 801–31.

Barvosa-Carter, Edwina. "Strange Tempest: Agency, Poststructuralism, and the Shape of Feminist Politics to Come." *International Journal of Sexuality and Gender Studies* 6 (2001): 123–37.

Benhabib, Seyla. *The Claims of Culture: Equality and Diversity in the Global Era.* Princeton, N.J.: Princeton University Press, 2002.

———. "Feminism and Postmodernism." In *Feminist Contentions: A Philosophical Exchange,* by Seyla Benhabib, Judith Butler, Drucilla Cornell, and Nancy Fraser. New York: Routledge, 1995.

———. "The Liberal Imagination and the Four Dogmas of Multiculturalism." *Yale Journal of Criticism* 12 (1999): 401–13.

———. "Subjectivity, Historiography, and Politics." In *Feminist Contentions: A Philosophical Exchange,* by Seyla Benhabib, Judith Butler, Drucilla Cornell, and Nancy Fraser. New York: Routledge, 1995.

Benhabib, Seyla, Judith Butler, Drucilla Cornell, and Nancy Fraser. *Feminist Contentions: A Philosophical Exchange.* New York: Routledge, 1995.

Bergo, Bettina. "What Is Levinas Doing? Phenomenology and the Rhetoric of an Ethical Un-Conscious." *Philosophy and Rhetoric* 38 (2005): 122–44.

Bernstein, Richard. "Foucault: Critique as a Philosophical Ethos." In *Critique and Power: Recasting the Habermas/Foucault Debate,* edited by Michael Kelly. Cambridge, Mass.: MIT Press, 1994.

Brown, Wendy. "At the Edge: The Future of Political Theory." In *Edgework: Critical Essays on Knowledge and Politics.* Princeton, N.J.: Princeton University Press, 2006.

———. *Edgework: Critical Essays on Knowledge and Politics.* Princeton, N.J.: Princeton University Press, 2006.

———. *Politics out of History.* Princeton, N.J.: Princeton University Press, 2001.

———. *Regulating Aversion: Tolerance in the Age of Identity and Empire.* Princeton, N.J.: Princeton University Press, 2006.

Bublitz, Hannelore. *Judith Butler zur Einführung.* Hamburg: Junius, 2005.

Butler, Judith. "Afterword: After Loss, What Then?" In *Loss: The Politics of Mourning,* edited by David L. Eng and David Kazanjian. Berkeley: University of California Press, 2003.

———. *Antigone's Claim: Kinship between Life and Death.* New York: Columbia University Press, 2000.

———. *Bodies That Matter: On the Discursive Limits of "Sex."* New York: Routledge, 1993.

———. "Contingent Foundations." In *Feminist Contentions: A Philosophical Exchange,* by Seyla Benhabib, Judith Butler, Drucilla Cornell, and Nancy Fraser. New York: Routledge, 1995.

———. "Critique, Coercion, and Sacred Life in Benjamin's 'Critique of Violence.'" In *Political Theologies*, edited by Hent de Vries. New York: Fordham University Press, 2006.

———. "Ethical Ambivalence." In *The Turn to Ethics*, edited by Marjorie Garber, Beatrice Hanssen, and Rebecca L. Walkowitz. New York: Routledge, 2000.

———. *Excitable Speech: A Politics of the Performative*. New York: Routledge, 1997.

———. "Explanation and Exoneration, or What We Can Hear." In *Precarious Life: The Powers of Mourning and Violence*. London: Verso, 2004.

———. "For a Careful Reading." In *Feminist Contentions: A Philosophical Exchange*, by Seyla Benhabib, Judith Butler, Drucilla Cornell, and Nancy Fraser. New York: Routledge, 1995.

———. *Gender Trouble: Feminism and the Subversion of Identity*. Rev. ed. New York: Routledge, 1999.

———. *Giving an Account of Oneself*. New York: Fordham University Press, 2005.

———. "How Can I Deny That These Hands and This Body Are Mine?" In *Material Events: Paul de Man and the Afterlife of Theory*, edited by Tom Cohen, Barbara Cohen, J. Hillis Miller, and Andrzej Warminski. Minneapolis: University of Minnesota Press, 2001.

———. *Kritik der ethischen Gewalt*. Frankfurt am Main: Suhrkamp, 2003.

———. "Politics, Power, and Ethics: A Discussion between Judith Butler and William Connolly." *Theory and Event* 4, no. 2 (2000), http://muse.jhu.edu/journals/theory_and_event/v004/4.2butler.html.

———. *Precarious Life: The Powers of Mourning and Violence*. London: Verso, 2004.

———. *The Psychic Life of Power: Theories in Subjection*. Stanford, Calif.: Stanford University Press, 1997.

———. "The Question of Social Transformation." In *Undoing Gender*. New York: Routledge, 2004.

———. "Reply from Judith Butler to Mills and Jenkins." *differences: A Journal of Feminist Cultural Studies* 18, no. 2 (2007): 180–95.

———. *Undoing Gender*. New York: Routledge, 2004.

———. "Violence, Non-Violence: Sartre on Fanon." *Graduate Faculty Philosophy Journal* 27, no. 1 (2006): 3–24.

———. "What Is a Discipline?" Paper presented at "The Fate of Disciplines," annual meeting of the Consortium of Humanities Centers and Institutes, Swift Hall, University of Chicago, Chicago, April 28, 2006.

———. "What Is Critique? An Essay on Foucault's Virtue." In *The Political: Readings in Continental Philosophy*, edited by David Ingram. London: Basil Blackwell, 2002.

Butler, Judith, Ernesto Laclau, and Slavoj Žižek. *Contingency, Hegemony, Universality: Contemporary Dialogues on the Left*. London: Verso, 2000.

Campbell, Kirsten. "The Plague of the Subject: Psychoanalysis and Judith Butler's *Psychic Life of Power*." *International Journal of Sexuality and Gender Studies* 6 (2001): 35–48.

Caruth, Cathy. "An Interview with Jean Laplanche." *Postmodern Culture* 11, no. 2 (2001), http://www3.iath.virginia.edu/pmc/text-only/issue.101/11.2caruth.txt.

———. *Unclaimed Experience: Trauma, Narrative, and History*. Baltimore, Md.: Johns Hopkins University Press, 1996.

———, ed. *Trauma: Explorations in Memory*. Baltimore, Md.: Johns Hopkins University Press, 1995.

Cavarero, Adriana. *Relating Narratives: Storytelling and Selfhood*. New York: Routledge, 2000.

Cheah, Pheng. "Mattering." Review of *Bodies That Matter*, by Judith Butler. *Diacritics* 26 (1996): 108–39.

Couzens Hoy, David. *Critical Resistance: From Poststructuralism to Post-Critique*. Cambridge, Mass.: MIT Press, 2005.

Critchley, Simon. *The Ethics of Deconstruction: Derrida and Levinas*. Edinburgh: Edinburgh University Press, 1992.

———. *Ethics—Politics—Subjectivity: Essays on Derrida, Levinas, and Contemporary French Thought*. London: Verso, 1999.

Derrida, Jacques. *Acts of Religion*. Translated and edited by Gil Anidjar. New York: Routledge, 2002.

———. *Adieu to Emmanuel Levinas*. Translated by Pascale-Anne Brault and Michael Naas. Stanford, Calif.: Stanford University Press, 1999.

———. "Afterword: Toward an Ethic of Discussion." In *Limited Inc.*, translated by Samuel Weber and Jeffrey Mehlman, edited by Gerald Graff. Evanston, Ill.: Northwestern University Press, 1988.

———. "Différance." In *Margins of Philosophy*, translated by Alan Bass. Chicago: University of Chicago Press, 1985.

———. *Eyes of the University: Right to Philosophy*. 2nd ed. Translated by Jan Plug. Stanford, Calif.: Stanford University Press, 2004.

———. "Force of Law: The 'Mystical Foundation of Authority.'" In *Deconstruction and the Possibility of Justice*, edited by Drucilla Cornell, Michael Rosenfeld, and David Gray Carlson. New York: Routledge, 1992.

———. *The Gift of Death*. Translated by David Wills. Chicago: University of Chicago Press, 1995.

———. "Hostipitality." In *Acts of Religion*. Translated and edited by Gil Anidjar. 356–420. New York: Routledge, 2002.

———. *Limited Inc.* Translated by Samuel Weber and Jeffrey Mehlman. Edited by Gerald Graff. Evanston, Ill.: Northwestern University Press, 1988.

———. *Margins of Philosophy*. Translated by Alan Bass. Chicago: University of Chicago Press, 1985.

———. *Of Grammatology*. Translated by Gayatri Chakravorty Spivak. Baltimore, Md.: Johns Hopkins University Press, 1998.

———. *On Cosmopolitanism and Forgiveness.* Translated by Mark Douglas and Michael Hughes. London: Routledge, 2001.

———. *The Politics of Friendship.* Translated by George Collins. London: Verso, 1997.

———. *Rogues: Two Essays on Reason.* Stanford, Calif.: Stanford University Press, 2005.

———. "Signature Event Context." In *Limited Inc.*, translated by Samuel Weber and Jeffrey Mehlman, edited by Gerald Graff. Evanston, Ill.: Northwestern University Press, 1988.

———. *Specters of Marx: The State of the Debt, the Work of Mourning, and the New International.* Translated by Peggy Kamuf. New York: Routledge, 1994.

———. "Violence and Metaphysics: An Essay on the Thought of Emmanuel Levinas." In *Writing and Difference*, translated by Alan Bass. Chicago: University of Chicago Press, 1978.

———. *Writing and Difference.* Translated by Alan Bass. Chicago: University of Chicago Press, 1978.

Diprose, Rosalyn. *Corporeal Generosity: On Giving with Nietzsche, Merleau-Ponty, and Levinas.* Albany, N.Y.: State University of New York Press, 2002.

———. "Responsibility in a Place and Time of Terror." *Borderlands* 3, no. 1 (2004), http://www.borderlandsejournal.adelaide.edu.au/vol3no1_2004/diprose_terror.htm.

Disch, Lisa. "Judith Butler and the Politics of the Performative." *Political Theory* 27 (1999): 545–59.

Dreyfus, Hubert, and Paul Rabinow. *Michel Foucault: Beyond Structuralism and Hermeneutics.* Chicago: University of Chicago Press, 1982.

Duden, Barbara. "Die Frau ohne Unterleib: Zu Judith Butlers Entkörperung—Ein Zeitdokument." *Feministische Studien* 2 (1993): 24–33.

Eaglestone, Robert. *Ethical Criticism: Reading after Levinas.* Edinburgh: Edinburgh University Press, 1997.

Eskin, Michael. "Introduction: The Double 'Turn' to Ethics and Literature?" *Poetics Today* 25 (2004): 557–72.

Felman, Shoshana. *The Juridical Unconscious: Trials and Traumas in the Twentieth Century.* Cambridge, Mass.: Harvard University Press, 2002.

Fletcher, John, and Peter Osborne. "The Other Within: Rethinking Psychoanalysis." Interview with Jean Laplanche. *Radical Philosophy* 10, no. 2 (2000), http://www.radicalphilosophy.com/default.asp?channel_id=2190&editorial_id=10027.

Foucault, Michel. *The Archaeology of Knowledge.* Translated by A. M. Sheridan Smith. New York: Pantheon Books, 1972.

———. *Discipline and Punish: The Birth of the Prison.* Translated by Alan Sheridan. New York: Vintage-Random House, 1977.

———. *Fearless Speech.* Edited by Joseph Pearson. Los Angeles: Semiotext(e), 2001.

———. *The History of Sexuality: An Introduction.* Vol. 1 of *The History of Sexuality.* Translated by Robert Hurley. New York: Vintage–Random House, 1978.

———. "Nietzsche, Genealogy, History." In *The Foucault Reader*, edited by Paul Rabinow, 76–100. New York: Pantheon Books, 1984.

———. *The Order of Things: An Archaeology of the Human Sciences.* Translator unknown. New York: Vintage Books, 1994.

Fraser, Nancy. "False Antitheses: A Response to Seyla Benhabib and Judith Butler." In *Feminist Contentions: A Philosophical Exchange*, by Seyla Benhabib, Judith Butler, Drucilla Cornell, and Nancy Fraser. New York: Routledge, 1995.

———. "Pragmatism, Feminism, and the Linguistic Turn." In *Feminist Contentions: A Philosophical Exchange*, by Seyla Benhabib, Judith Butler, Drucilla Cornell, and Nancy Fraser. New York: Routledge, 1995.

———. "Recognition without Ethics?" *Theory, Culture and Society* 18, nos. 2–3 (2001): 21–42.

———. "Rethinking Recognition." *New Left Review* 3 (2000): 107–20.

Freud, Sigmund. "The Economic Problem of Masochism." In *The Standard Edition of the Complete Psychological Works of Sigmund Freud.* Vol. 19. Translated by James Strachey. London: Hogarth, 1961.

Garber, Marjorie, Beatrice Hanssen, and Rebecca L. Walkowitz, eds. *The Turn to Ethics.* New York: Routledge, 2000.

Gert, Bernard. *Morality: Its Nature and Justification.* New York: Oxford University Press, 1998.

Graf, Friedrich Wilhelm. Review of *Kritik der ethischen Gewalt. Süddeutsche Zeitung* 128 (June 5, 2003), 16, http://www.buecher.de/w1100485sz35185836 11#sz.

Habermas, Jürgen. *Between Facts and Norms: Contributions to a Discourse Theory of Law and Democracy.* Translated by William Rehg. Cambridge, Mass.: MIT Press, 1998.

———. *The Philosophical Discourse of Modernity: Twelve Lectures.* Translated by Frederick G. Lawrence. Cambridge, Mass.: MIT Press, 1987.

———. *Der philosophische Diskurs der Moderne: Zwölf Vorlesungen.* Frankfurt am Main: Suhrkamp, 1985.

———. *The Postnational Constellation: Political Essays.* Translated by Max Pensky. Cambridge, Mass.: MIT Press, 2001.

Haker, Hille. *Ethik der genetischen Frühdiagnostik: Sozialethische Reflexionen zur Verantwortung am Beginn des menschlichen Lebens.* Paderborn: Mentis, 2002.

———. "The Fragility of the Moral Self." *Harvard Theological Review* 97 (2004): 359–81.

Hauskeller, Christine. *Das paradoxe Subjekt: Unterwerfung und Widerstand bei Judith Butler und Michel Foucault.* Tübingen: Edition Diskord, 2000.

Hollywood, Amy. "Performativity, Citationality, Ritualization." *History of Religions* 42 (2002): 95–115.

Honneth, Axel. *Das Andere der Gerechtigkeit: Aufsätze zur praktischen Philosophie.* Frankfurt am Main: Suhrkamp, 2000.

———. *Kampf um Anerkennung: Zur moralischen Grammatik sozialer Konflikte.* Frankfurt am Main: Suhrkamp, 1994.

Honneth, Axel, and Nancy Fraser. *Redistribution or Recognition? A Philosophical Exchange.* Translated by Joel Golb. London: Verso, 2003.

Hume, David. *Enquiry Concerning the Principles of Morals.* Edited by Tom L. Beauchamp. Oxford: Oxford University Press, 1998.

Jankélévitch, Vladimir. *Forgiveness.* Translated by Andrew Kelley. Chicago: University of Chicago Press, 2005.

Jenkins, Fiona. "Plurality, Dialogue and Response: Addressing Vulnerability." *Contretemps* 3 (2002): 85–97.

———. "Toward a Nonviolent Ethics: A Response to Catherine Mills." *differences: A Journal of Feminist Cultural Studies* 18, no. 2 (2007): 157–77.

Kämpf, Heike. "Politische Philosophie as Sprachkritik: Zum Machtdiskurs bei Judith Butler." *Dialektik* 2 (2002): 101–16.

Kant, Immanuel. *Critique of the Power of Judgment.* Translated by Eric Matthews. Edited by Paul Guyer. Cambridge, U.K.: Cambridge University Press, 2000.

———. *Critique of Practical Reason.* Translated and edited by Mary Gregor. Cambridge, U.K.: Cambridge University Press, 1997.

———. *Groundwork of the Metaphysics of Morals.* Translated and edited by Mary Gregor. Cambridge, U.K.: Cambridge University Press, 1998.

Kelly, Michael. "Foucault, Habermas, and the Self-Referentiality of Critique." In *Critique and Power: Recasting the Habermas/Foucault Debate*, edited by Michael Kelly. Cambridge, Mass.: MIT Press, 1994.

———, ed. *Critique and Power: Recasting the Habermas/Foucault Debate.* Cambridge, Mass.: MIT Press, 1994.

Kirby, Vicki. *Judith Butler: Live Theory.* London: Continuum, 2006.

———. "When All That Is Solid Melts into Language: Judith Butler and the Question of Matter." *International Journal of Sexuality and Gender Studies* 7 (2002): 265–80.

Korsgaard, Christine. *Creating the Kingdom of Ends.* Cambridge, U.K.: Cambridge University Press, 1996.

Koselleck, Reinhart. *Vergangene Zukunft: Zur Semantik geschichtlicher Zeiten.* Frankfurt am Main: Suhrkamp, 2000.

LaCapra, Dominick. *History in Transit: Experience, Identity, Critical Theory.* Ithaca, N.Y.: Cornell University Press, 2004.

———. *Writing History, Writing Trauma.* Baltimore, Md.: Johns Hopkins University Press, 2001.

Laclau, Ernesto, and Chantal Mouffe. *Hegemony and Socialist Strategy: Towards a Radical Democratic Politics.* 2nd ed. London: Verso, 2001.

Laplanche, Jean. "Aims of the Psychoanalytic Process." *Journal of European Psychoanalysis* 5 (1997), http://www.psychomedia.it/jep/number5/laplanche.htm.

———. "The Drive and Its Object-Source: Its Fate in the Transference." In *Seduction, Translation, Drives*, translated by Martin Stanton, edited by Martin Stanton and John Fletcher. London: Institute of Contemporary Arts, 1992.

———. "Interpretation between Determinism and Hermeneutics: A Restatement of the Problem." In *Essays on Otherness*, translated by Philip Slotkin. London: Routledge, 1999.

———. "Psychoanalysis, Time and Translation: A Lecture Given at the University of Kent, 30 April 1990." In *Seduction, Translation, Drives*, translated by Martin Stanton, edited by Martin Stanton and John Fletcher. London: Institute of Contemporary Arts, 1992.

———. "Responsabilité et réponse." In *Entre séduction et inspiration: l'homme.* Paris: Quadrige/PUF, 1999.

———. "Time and the Other." In *Essays on Otherness*, translated by Luke Thurston. London: Routledge, 1999.

———. "Transference: Its Provocation by the Analyst." In *Essays on Otherness*, translated by Luke Thurston. London: Routledge, 1999.

———. "The Wall and the Arcade." In *Seduction, Translation, Drives*, translated by Martin Stanton, edited by Martin Stanton and John Fletcher. London: Institute of Contemporary Arts, 1992.

Levenson, Michael. "Speaking to Power: The Performances of Judith Butler." *Lingua Franca* 8, no. 6 (1998): 60–67.

Levinas, Emmanuel. *Difficult Freedom: Essays on Judaism.* Translated by Sean Hand. Baltimore, Md.: Johns Hopkins University Press, 1997.

———. *Entre Nous: On Thinking-of-the-Other.* Translated by Michael B. Smith and Barbara Harshav. New York: Columbia University Press, 1998.

———. "Ethics as First Philosophy." In *The Levinas Reader*, edited by Sean Hand. Cambridge, Mass.: Blackwell, 1989.

———. *God, Death, and Time.* Translated by Bettina Bergo. Stanford, Calif.: Stanford University Press, 2000.

———. *Is It Righteous to Be? Interviews with Emmanuel Levinas.* Edited by Jill Robbins. Stanford, Calif.: Stanford University Press, 2001.

———. *On Escape.* Introduced and annotated by Jacques Rolland. Translated by Bettina Bergo. Stanford, Calif.: Stanford University Press, 2003.

———. *Otherwise Than Being, Or Beyond Essence.* Translated by Alphonso Lingis. Pittsburgh, Pa.: Duquesne University Press, 1998.

———. "Substitution." In *Basic Philosophical Writings*, edited by Adriaan Theodoor Peperzak, Simon Critchley, and Robert Bernasconi. Bloomington: Indiana University Press, 1996.

Leys, Ruth. *Trauma: A Genealogy.* Chicago: University of Chicago Press, 2000.

List, Elisabeth. *Grenzen der Verfügbarkeit: Die Technik, das Subjekt, das Lebendige.* Vienna: Passagen, 2001.

Lloyd, Moya. *Judith Butler: From Norms to Politics.* Cambridge, U.K.: Polity Press, 2006.

———. "Radical Democratic Activism and the Politics of Resignification." *Constellations* 14, no. 1 (2007): 129–46.

Loizidou, Elena. *Judith Butler: Ethics, Law, Politics.* London: Routledge, 2007.

Madison, Gary B., and Marty Fairbairn, eds. *The Ethics of Postmodernity: Current Trends in Continental Thought.* Evanston, Ill.: Northwestern University Press, 1999.

Magnus, Kathy Dow. "The Unaccountable Subject: Judith Butler and the Social Conditions of Intersubjective Agency." *Hypatia* 21 (2006): 81–103.

Mahmood, Saba. *The Politics of Piety: The Islamic Revival and the Feminist Subject.* Princeton, N.J.: Princeton University Press, 2004.

Maihofer, Andrea. *Geschlecht als Existenzweise.* Frankfurt am Main: Suhrkamp, 1995.

Margalit, Avishai. *The Decent Society.* Cambridge, Mass.: Harvard University Press, 1996.

Markell, Patchen. *Bound by Recognition.* Princeton, N.J.: Princeton University Press, 2003.

McNay, Lois. *Gender and Agency: Reconfiguring the Subject in Feminist and Social Theory.* Cambridge, U.K.: Polity Press, 2000.

McRobbie, Angela. "Vulnerability, Violence and (Cosmopolitan) Ethics: Butler's *Precarious Life.*" *British Journal of Sociology* 57 (2006): 69–86.

Miller, J. Hillis. *The Ethics of Reading: Kant, de Man, Eliot, Trollope, James, and Benjamin.* New York: Columbia University Press, 1987.

Mills, Catherine. "Normative Violence, Vulnerability, and Responsibility." *differences: A Journal of Feminist Cultural Studies* 18, no. 2 (2007): 133–56.

Mouffe, Chantal. *The Democratic Paradox.* London: Verso, 2000.

———. *On the Political.* New York: Routledge, 2005.

Mouly, Françoise. "War of Words in France." *The Nation* November 14, 2005 (online edition only), http://www.thenation.com/doc/20051128/mouly.

Murphy, Kara. "France's New Law: Control Immigration Flows, Court the Highly Skilled." *Migration Immigration Source* November 2006, http://www-.migrationinformation.org/Feature/display.cfm?ID=486.

Murray, Stuart J. "Scenes of Address: A Conversation with Judith Butler." *Symposium: Canadian Journal of Continental Philosophy* 11, no. 2 (2007): 415–45.

Nancy, Jean-Luc. "Shattered Love." In *The Inoperative Community*, translated by Peter Connor, Lisa Garbus, Michael Holland, and Simona Sawhney. Minneapolis: University of Minnesota Press, 1991.

Nelson, Lise. "Bodies (and Spaces) Do Matter: The Limits of Performativity." *Gender, Place, and Culture* 6 (1999): 331–53.

Nietzsche, Friedrich. *Jenseits von Gut und Böse* and *Zur Genealogie der Moral.* Edited by Giorgio Colli and Mazzino Montinari. Berlin: Walter de Gruyter, 1988.

———. *On the Genealogy of Morals* and *Ecce Homo.* Translated by Walter Kaufmann and R. J. Hollingdale. Edited by Walter Kaufmann. New York: Vintage–Random House, 1967.

Ophir, Adi. *The Order of Evils: Toward an Ontology of Evils.* Translated by Rela Mazali and Havi Carel. New York: Zone Books, 2005.

Perpich, Diane. "Figurative Language and the 'Face' in Levinas's Philosophy." *Philosophy and Rhetoric* 38, no. 2 (2005): 103–21.

Plato. *The Republic.* Translated by R. E. Allen. New Haven, Conn.: Yale University Press, 2006.

Purtschert, Patricia. "Judith Butler: Macht der Kontingenz—Begriff der Kritik." In *Philosophinnen des 20. Jahrhunderts*, edited by Regine Munz. Darmstadt: Wissenschaftliche Buchgesellschaft, 2004.

Rawls, John. *A Theory of Justice.* Cambridge, Mass.: Belknap Press–Harvard University Press, 1971.

Ricoeur, Paul. *The Course of Recognition.* Translated by David Pellauer. Cambridge, Mass.: Harvard University Press, 2005.

———. *Memory, History, Forgetting.* Translated by Kathleen Blamey and David Pellauer. Chicago: University of Chicago Press, 2004.

———. *Das Rätsel der Vergangenheit: Erinnern—Vergessen—Verzeihen.* Translated by Andris Breitling and Henrik R. Lesaar. Essener Kulturwissenschaftliche Vorträge 2. Göttingen: Wallstein, 1998.

Ronell, Avital. *Finitude's Score: Essays for the End of the Millenium.* Lincoln: University of Nebraska Press, 1994.

Salih, Sara. *Judith Butler.* London: Routledge, 2002.

———. "Judith Butler and the Ethics of 'Difficulty.'" *Critical Quarterly* 45, no. 3 (2003): 42–51.

Schmitt, Carl. *The Concept of the Political.* Translated by George D. Schwab. Chicago: University of Chicago Press, 1996.

Schwartzman, Lisa H. "Hate Speech, Illocution, and Social Context: A Critique of Judith Butler." *Journal of Social Philosophy* 33 (2002): 421–41.

Smith, Adam. *The Theory of Moral Sentiments.* Edited by Knud Haakonssen. Cambridge, U.K.: Cambridge University Press, 2002.

Sontag, Susan. *Regarding the Pain of Others.* New York: Farrar, 2003.

Stanton, Martin. "Interview: Jean Laplanche Talks to Martin Stanton." In *Seduction, Translation, Drives*, translated by Martin Stanton, edited by Martin Stanton and John Fletcher. London: Institute of Contemporary Arts, 1992.

Stegmaier, Werner. *Nietzsches "Genealogie der Moral."* Darmstadt: Wissenschaftliche Buchgesellschaft, 1994.

Taylor, Charles. "The Politics of Recognition." In *Multiculturalism: Examining the Politics of Recognition*, edited by Amy Gutmann. Princeton, N.J.: Princeton University Press, 1994.

Vasterling, Veronica. "Butler's Sophisticated Constructivism: A Critical Assessment." *Hypatia* 14, no. 3 (1999): 17–38.

Villa, Paula-Irene. *Judith Butler.* Frankfurt am Main: Campus, 2003.

Waldenfels, Bernhard. *Schattenrisse der Moral.* Frankfurt am Main: Suhrkamp, 2006.

Wendel, Saskia. *Affektiv und inkarniert: Ansätze Deutscher Mystik als subjekttheoretische Herausforderung*. Regensburg: Pustet, 2002.

Wils, Jean-Pierre. *Sittlichkeit und Subjektivität: Zur Ortsbestimmung der Ethik im Strukturalismus, in der Subjektphilosophie und bei Schleiermacher*. Freiburg: Verlag Herder, 1987.

Wolin, Sheldon S. *Politics and Vision: Continuity and Innovation in Western Political Thought*. Princeton, N.J.: Princeton University Press, 2006.

Wood, David. *The Step Back: Ethics and Politics after Deconstruction*. Albany: State University of New York Press, 2005.

Wyschogrod, Edith, and Gerald P. McKenny, eds. *The Ethical*. Malden, Mass.: Blackwell, 2003.

Young, Iris Marion. *Justice and the Politics of Difference*. Princeton, N.J.: Princeton University Press, 1990.

———. "Unruly Categories: A Critique of Nancy Fraser's Dual Systems Theory." *New Left Review* 222 (1997): 147–60.

Zirelli, Linda. *Feminism and the Abyss of Freedom*. Chicago: University of Chicago Press, 2005.

INDEX